EMERGING PATTERNS OF LITERACY

Sharing books at home is an integral part of the socialisation of young children into literacy. In an original and wide-ranging study, Rhian Jones documents the unique contribution which picturebooks and stories make to the development of the infant mind between the ages of 9 months and 2 years, using video-recorded data to chart children's progress. She then analyses the connections between these very early behaviours and subsequent achievements in literacy.

The work integrates research from a number of disciplines: linguistics, psychology, literary theory, psychoanalysis and anthropology, to draw out the different levels at which book-based interactions may be seen to be 'working'. Issues of general theoretical relevance to early childhood are comprehensively examined for the first time in a reading setting, such as language acquisition, the construction and expression of the infant self, and the relation between affect and achievement.

Written in an accessible and readable style, *Emerging Patterns of Literacy* will be of interest to specialists in developmental psychology, language acquisition, literacy and early childhood education, teachers, speech therapists and child psychotherapists.

Rhian Jones is a member of the Child Language Acquisition and Pathology Research Group at the University of Paris René Descartes.

ROUTLEDGE PROGRESS IN PSYCHOLOGY

1 Emerging Patterns of Literacy: a multidisciplinary perspective
Rhian Jones

EMERGING PATTERNS OF LITERACY

A multidisciplinary perspective

Rhian Jones

LONDON AND NEW YORK

First published 1996
by Routledge
2 Park Square, Milton Park, Abingdon, Oxfordshire OX14 4RN

Simultaneously published in the USA and Canada
by Routledge
711 Third Avenue, New York, NY 10017

First issued in paperback 2015

Routledge is an imprint of the Taylor and Francis Group, an informa business

© 1996 Rhian Jones

Typeset in Garamond by
Datix International Limited, Bungay, Suffolk

All rights reserved. No part of this book may be reprinted or reproduced or utilized in any form or by any electronic, mechanical, or other means, now known or hereafter invented, including photocopying and recording, or in any information storage or retrieval system, without permission in writing from the publishers.

British Library Cataloguing in Publication Data
A catalogue record for this books is available from the British Library

Library of Congress Cataloguing in Publication Data
Jones, Rhian.
Emerging patterns of literacy: a multidisciplinary perspective/Rhian Jones.
(Routledge progress in psychology; 1)
Includes bibliographical references and index.
1. Language acquisition – Parent participation.   2. Reading (Preschool).
3. Reading – Parent participation. 4. Child psychology. 5. Literacy.
I. Title.   II. Series
P118.5.J66   1996
418'.4–dc20   96–594

ISBN 13: 978-1-138-88121-1 (pbk)
ISBN 13: 978-0-415-13049-3 (hbk)

CONTENTS

Acknowledgements   vii
Introduction   1

Part I   Infant–parent interaction   23

1 READING AND THE VERY YOUNG INFANT   25
  1 First contacts with books   25
  2 Processes of socialisation   27
  3 Looking and turntaking   30
  4 Adult linguistic descriptions   38
  5 Discussion: reading gets under way   49
  6 Conclusion   50

2 A SENSE OF SELF: THE INFANT AS INDIVIDUAL   52
  1 Introduction: what is meant by 'self'?   52
  2 The construction of dialogue: the infant's role   53
  3 Patterns of behaviour differentiated   60
  4 First words   78
  5 Discussion: reading and the language acquisition process   84
  6 Conclusion   89

Part II   The semantics of picturebook reading   91

3 PICTUREBOOK READING AND WORD MEANING   93
  1 Introduction: picturebook reading and literacy   93
  2 Theories of meaning   94
  3 Picturebook reading: the adult's purpose   98
  4 Discussion: contributions of picturebook reading   113
  5 Conclusion   116

4 PICTUREBOOK READING AS EVENT INTERPRETATION   117
  1 Introduction: differences of perspective   117

2 Accommodating the infant — 118
3 Modifying infant perspective — 125
4 Turning points: cognitive growth in the 18-month-old child — 130
5 Discussion: the negotiation of meaning — 133
6 Conclusion — 139

Part III The ontogenesis of narrative — 141

5 THE WORLD OF THE STORY — 143
1 Core features of narrative — 143
2 A story with a 14-month-old — 149
3 A story with a 25-month-old — 155
4 Discussion: the central role of the narrator — 159
5 Conclusion — 163

6 STORY GRAMMAR AND TEXT — 164
1 Introduction: structure and style — 164
2 Layers of meaning — 165
3 Reading for meaning at 13–14 months — 168
4 Processes of change: 14–16 months — 181
5 Discussion: paths to literacy — 185
6 Conclusion — 188

Part IV Further aspects of the self — 189

7 MATERNAL SPEECH AND INFANT PSYCHIC DEVELOPMENT — 191
1 Introduction: language and the non-linguistic world — 191
2 The grammar of maternal speech in relation to the two-dimensional world: an example — 195
3 The world view of maternal speech — 197
4 Discussion: maternal speech and the infant psyche — 202
5 The construction of the self: wider implications — 205
6 Conclusion — 207

8 EMERGENT LITERACY: A WINNICOTTIAN VIEW — 208
1 Reading development in the longer term — 208
2 Winnicott's theory of transitional objects and phenomena — 208
3 Transitional objects and the very young infant — 211
4 The object in the period from pre-speech to speech — 218
5 Individual responses to reading — 225
6 Discussion: emerging patterns of literacy — 230
7 Conclusion — 232

CONCLUDING REMARKS — 234

Appendix — 239
Notes — 240
References — 243
Author index — 250
Subject index — 253

ACKNOWLEDGEMENTS

In describing my own children when very young, I cannot help but reflect on some of the most formative influences in my own life. I feel particularly indebted to my parents, and also to the different departments in various institutions where I have, over the years, been privileged to spend time: the Department of French Literature at University College London, and at the University of Geneva; the Department of Linguistics at the Universities of Reading, and Paris René Descartes; and the Institute of Psycho-analysis, and the Squiggle Foundation in London.

To the writing of this book, many have contributed in a more immediate way, not least the authors cited, whose work in many cases has been an inspiration. The Centre National de la Recherche Scientifique in Paris and the University of Paris René Descartes have been responsible for funding this research, while my colleagues at the Laboratoire d'Etude sur l'Acquisition et la Pathologie du Langage chez l'Enfant, led by Christian Hudelot, have always been generously supportive of my endeavours.

Several people have been greatly encouraging with their advice, or by reading parts of the whole, especially: Gillian Brown, George Butterworth, Adam Phillips, Marie-Christine Pouder, Laurence Spurling, and Astrid van der Straten. Vivien Ward, Claire Chandler and their editorial teams at Routledge have been unfailingly helpful in seeing this work through to its completion. I would also like to express my sincere appreciation to Elena Lieven and other (anonymous) reviewers for their very constructive comments on earlier drafts.

But Harold Bourne, Frédéric François, Barry, Rhys and Ceri have brought me more than words can say. It is by way of thanks that I would dedicate this work, collectively, to them.

PERMISSIONS

The author gratefully acknowledges the permission, kindly granted by the following, to quote from the works cited: The Academic Press (*Action, Gesture and Symbol*, A. Lock (ed.), 1978); André Deutsch Children's Books, an imprint of Scholastic Publications (*Alex's Outing*, M. Dickinson, 1984); Basil Blackwell

ACKNOWLEDGEMENTS

(*Wittgenstein on Meaning*, C. McGinn, 1984); Bodley Head (*The Cool Web*, M. Meek, A. Warlow and G. Barton (eds), 1977); Cambridge University Press (*The Domestication of the Savage Mind*, J. Goody, 1977; *Non-verbal Communication*, R. A. Hinde (ed.), 1972; *Concepts and Conceptual Development*, U. Neisser (ed.), 1987; *Sources of the Self*, C. Taylor, 1989; *First Verbs*, M. Tomasello, 1992); Fontana, an imprint of HarperCollins Publishers Ltd (*D. W. Winnicott*, A. Phillips, 1988); Free Association Books Ltd (*Illusion and Spontaneity in Psychoanalysis*, John Klauber and others, 1987; *Human Nature*, D. W. Winnicott, 1988); Harvard University Press (*Actual Minds, Possible Worlds*, J. Bruner, 1968; *The Psychology of Literacy*, S. Scribner and M. Cole, 1981); The Hogarth Press Ltd and Chatto and Windus (*Viewpoints*, C. Rycroft, 1991; *Through Paediatrics to Psychoanalysis*, D. W. Winnicott, 1958); Chatto and Windus, and Peters Fraser and Dunlop agents to the author (*The Innocence of Dreams*, C. Rycroft, 1979); Macmillan Press Ltd (*Psychoanalysis and Psychology*, S. Frosh, 1989); Mark Paterson, on behalf of The Winnicott Trust (D. W. Winnicott: *The Child, the Family and the Outside World*, 1964; *Playing and Reality*, 1974; *Home is Where We Start From*, 1986); Mark Paterson, on behalf of Karnac Books and The Winnicott Trust (*Psycho-analytic Explorations – D. W. Winnicott*, C. Winnicott, R. Shepherd, M. Davis (eds), 1989); M.I.T. Press (*Thought and Language*, L. S. Vygotsky, translated by E. Hanfmann and G. Vakar, 1962; *Language, Thought and Reality: selected writings of Benjamin Lee Whorf*, J. Carroll (ed.), 1956); Oxford University Press (*Papers in Linguistics 1934–1951*, J. R. Firth, 1957; *Pig in a Muddle*, W. Opgenoorth and M. Lobe, 1983); Paul Chapman Publishing Ltd London (*Language and Literacy in the Early Years*, M. R. Whitehead, 1990); Prentice Hall/Harvester Wheatsheaf (*Ape, Primitive Man and Child*, A. R. Luria and L. S. Vygotsky, 1992); Routledge Ltd (*Language Processing in Children and Adults*, M. Harris and M. Coltheart, 1986; *The Family and Individual Development*, D. W. Winnicott, 1989); Springer Verlag (*The Development of Word Meaning*, S. A. Kuczaj and M. D. Barrett (eds), 1986); University of California Press (Edward Sapir: *Selected Writings in Language, Culture, and Personality*, D. G. Mandelbaum (ed.), 1985, © the Regents of the University of California, 1949).

While the author and publishers have made every effort to contact copyright holders of material used in this volume, they would be grateful to hear from any they were unable to contact.

INTRODUCTION

Given the opportunity, infants below the age of two years will sit and contemplate an illustrated book by themselves, but often a parent acts as an intermediary. In this triangular constellation of infant, adult and book, communication of extraordinary subtlety and complexity takes place. What is its nature? What is its function? And what is its value?

The subject of this book is the experience of reading as it occurs at home, in the first two years of life, between parents and their young children. Drawing mainly on research in linguistics, psychology, literary theory and psychoanalysis, and with language as the common denominator between these different disciplines, this enquiry seeks to elucidate some of the many 'layers of meaning' which such an experience contains. Part I is concerned with dialogue, with the rules of conversation appropriate to a reading situation, and with the expression by the infant of an individualised reading personality. Part II looks at the contribution of picturebook reading to the development of the young child's semantic system. Part III focuses upon the ontogenesis of narrative, while the concern of Part IV is with aspects of infant moral, psychosexual and aesthetic development, as manifested in the reading setting.

Any analysis of the contribution, literary, linguistic, or aesthetic, which early reading makes to infant development raises a second issue: the relevance of such activity for the acquisition of literacy at school. What connections are there, if any, between early responses to reading and the reading attitudes of the same children some five years later? Following Vygotsky, development is here considered 'in all its phases and changes' which 'fundamentally means to discover its nature, its essence'. That is to say, the experience of reading is described diachronically, as well as synchronically: as a process in which current behaviours evolve out of earlier ones, and become in turn the starting-point for subsequent developments.

This book is not intended as a set of procedures for teaching children to read. Rather, it resituates reading within the wider context of infant development more generally. Questions of broad theoretical concern are addressed. How, for example, might an analysis of book-based interactions during the transition from pre-speech to speech inform our understanding of early language development? What specific transformations are brought about by a two-dimensional stimulus which can be revisited, reworked, and reflected upon? What part is played by the emotions in learning? What place is given to the construction and expression of the infant 'self'? In what ways does a child remain an individual but yet assimilate parental, and cultural, norms? Infant psychic life as it unfolds within the context of a parent–infant relationship, the association between gender and learning, the primitive origins of a literary response, the interrelationship between 'inner' and 'outer' worlds – these, too, are enduring issues to which this study brings new insights.

Finally, the place of book reading in early caregiving is considered. With all the demands of a busy daily schedule, it is worth making time to share books with very young infants. 'Talking' when looking out of a window, engaging tiny children in 'conversation' about their toys, or watching television are all events in which children are 'exposed' to language, but, it is argued, such activities can but rarely substitute for book reading. The reasons why this should be are discussed, and illustrated, in the chapters which follow.

Relating this study to theories within linguistics, the language of reading is here described, not as an abstract system, but as language in use, in a dialogue setting. A descriptive framework which takes into account the illustrated materials affecting linguistic communication as it occurs between two separate individuals, each with their own personality, provides a frame of reference for the study of acts of meaning in context, and allows us to get a step nearer to understanding what people are effectively 'doing' when they speak. Such an approach to linguistic description clearly falls beyond the scope of the transformational generative model which relies on the notion of an (abstract) speaker–hearer in a homogeneous speech community (Chomsky 1965:3), and to which, it is hoped, this contribution will provide a necessary complement.

The prime concern is thus with meaning: with what people say, and with what they mean by what they say. The descriptions are as comprehensive as possible; discourse, lexis, and grammar, where appropriate, are each examined for their contribution to the meaning of the whole. At each level, the analysis focuses on recurrent patterns, rather than selected exceptions; extracts of the dialogue illustrate aspects of special interest.

Language, then, is here viewed in its relation both to a book's contents present in the speech setting, and to the ongoing circumstances of a child's life which encompass it – the 'real-life' experiences, possessions, significant persons – the 'unuttered context of life' upon which the language of early reading inevitably draws, and to which it always returns. My hope is that readers will be able to recognise something of themselves, or of children whom they know, in the descriptions provided.

INTRODUCTION

1 'READING' IN INFANCY

The achievement of literacy, in its broad sense (i.e. the ability to decipher the written word at a very basic level) and the use which all of us, as individuals, effectively make of this skill, is clearly not contingent upon the introduction of books early in life. Many successful readers might never have encountered a book throughout the whole of their childhood. But some children are introduced early on to books, perhaps, as those in this study, even before they are able to talk. In the Western world, where literacy is a key requirement for life, this practice could be considered as the start of a long road to a culturally specific, highly valued, even indispensable mode of behaviour, the ability to read. Such children could be thought of as readers-in-the-making, as fledgling readers.

However, the fact that printed text follows chronologically upon illustrated books in an individual's history does not entail any connection, theoretical or empirical, between the two types of activity. Indeed, a complete hiatus in developmental terms could even be posited. To what extent, then, might looking at illustrated books with a parent justifiably be termed 'reading'? Are there qualitative links between the early reading of illustrated books, often without text, and the later reading of written text, by the child of school age?

The verb 'to read'

The first indication that reading in infancy may legitimately be considered as somehow equivalent to reading in later childhood is terminological. The lexical structure of the English language makes a formal connection between the early reading of illustrated stories, even without text, and the mapping of written symbols onto the sound and meaning systems of a language, which the act of reading subsequently becomes. People 'read' picturebooks, but they also 'read' novels, or an essay. But in what sense can infants, contemplating books on their parent's knee, and as yet unable to speak, still less decipher written symbols, be legitimately described as 'reading' those books?

The etymology of the verb 'to read' provides some initial clues. The *Concise Oxford Dictionary* gives this definition: 'interpret mentally, declare interpretation or coming development of', and cites, as the complement to this activity, not the written word, but portents, dreams, riddles, the heart. Pictures are interpreted by a young infant, that is, endowed with meaning and significance. Infants read pictures as they might read their mother's face; they are engaged, in part at least, in a search for meaning.

Parents too, with their infant seated on their lap and looking at an illustrated book, might be said to be reading in precisely the dictionary sense; they act as mediator between illustrations and infant, and interpret images, and sometimes (though not necessarily), written symbols. The meaning of book

INTRODUCTION

illustrations also derives from what parents read into them – how they become translated into adult speech.

Acts of interpretation constitute, in many respects, the cornerstone of reading experiences with young infants. Outlined below are some instances of linguistic interpretation by the adult to be discussed in this book:

1 Take a simple illustration of a horse standing by a stretch of water. At a most basic level, both the horse and the water may be named. But it is possible to go further and express, in language, a relationship between these two entities. For the illustration is ambiguous. Is the horse about to drink the water? Walk into it? Or, on the contrary, is the horse reluctant to enter it? Frightened even? Language allows us to relate two separate aspects of a picture, and ascribe motives and intentions to the characters depicted there.[1] Chapter 2 deals particularly with this kind of interpretation.

2 Some illustrations presented to young children are infinitely more complex than the one described above. Imagine a beach scene, extending over a double page, full of visual detail – picnickers and swimmers, sandcastles and sailing boats, buckets and spades, all the paraphernalia of a seaside are displayed. Here the function of language is, perhaps, to integrate a multiplicity of different elements into a unified whole – language here imposing order upon the chaos of non-linguistic reality. But how do children grow to decipher and understand the illustrated material contained in books? These are issues addressed in Chapters 3 and 4.

3 Even more difficult, perhaps, is the explication, not so much of what is depicted 'in' a set of pictures, but of what is effectively absent from them. Pictures which give rise to a storytelling event are never fully explicit; much of what occurs in the story is left to occur, as it were, 'between' the pictures. Consider this example. A first illustration depicts someone taking up a pen to write upon a blank sheet, while a second shows a completed sheet with writing on it. Adult readers deduce that 'in the interval between' a letter has been written. In this instance language assigns an interpretation to what, from the infant reader's standpoint, is nothing other than a blank space. The interpretation of the spaces between forms part of the discussion of Chapter 6.

Toddlers, then, could be said to be fledgling readers because they are embarked on a quest for meaning. But there are other connections to be made between reading in the first two years of life, and the reading which children elect to do for themselves as they reach school age.

The medium itself

What reading in toddlerhood and the reading of print have in common is that both typically involve a book; several features are shared by both. Illustrations in books, and later, text, constitute static, two-dimensional stimuli which appeal predominantly to the eye. Both are associated with a very particular form of

INTRODUCTION

language, and both give rise to a specific form of cognitive activity. Last, reading in infancy, and later, in childhood, is concerned in a fundamental way with use, and what children read for.

1 A static stimulus which allows persistent scrutiny. In his examination of the impact which the introduction of writing has upon cultures across the ages and across the world, Goody ascribes the following characteristics to the written word: 'it can be inspected in much greater detail, in its parts as well as in its whole, backwards as well as forwards, out of context as well as in its setting; in other words, it can be subjected to a quite different type of scrutiny and critique than is possible with purely verbal communication' (Goody 1977:44). Goody's point is that writing does not simply transform the mode of production of language, in that it relies on the hand and eye, instead of the mouth and ear. The introduction of writing totally transforms the nature of the cognitive processes of a literate public.

If 'pictures' are substituted for 'writing' in Goody's account, something of the essence of reading in infancy can be captured. Both the written word, and pictures in a book, constitute a two-dimensional stimulus which is static, not ephemeral. Both represent or 'stand for' aspects of reality. Both print and pictures in books can be revisited, compared, discussed and rediscussed. In other words, the reading situation, as distinct from everyday or real-life situations, allows events within the visual field to recur in a systematic form unlike any other routine activity which might occur in an infant's everyday experience. Images in books, for example, have a permanence which images on a television screen do not; they are constantly and repeatedly available to inspection, just as written symbols one day will be. Indeed, one of the characteristics of reading with infants is that they hear, even demand to hear, the same book read to them over and over again. Part of the purpose of this book is to investigate precisely the evolutionary nature of this repetitive activity and the resulting transformations which occur.

2 An experience which is both visual and tactile. A further similarity between written language and pictures is that both depend on vision. A book has the potential for bringing within the visual experience of the reading infant a whole range of situations, settings, events. Why would this characteristic of books affect the lives of infants in particular? Because research has shown that parents conversing with young infants generally talk about what is available to them in their immediate environment (Snow 1976). Settings which might never normally be encountered on a day-to-day basis: a visit to the beach, to a doughnut factory, a hospital or a zoo, for example, can, potentially, be introduced and explored in the comfort of a front room. The extent to which a parent actually does exploit this opportunity to introduce unfamiliar material is a further dimension in early reading.

Equally important (from a language learning point of view) is that when reading, everything within an infant's visual experience is also available to touch. This tactile dimension to early reading is crucial because in 'real life' referents are often well out of reach — when looking up at a house from a pushchair, for instance. But with a book, by pointing to a set of different referents in turn, an infant, or adult reader is able to distinguish accurately between a roof, a television aeriel or a chimney pot. Such things become possible with a book because of its reduced scale, and its proximity to its reading audience. But again the question may be asked as to what, from the range of items potentially available for discussion on a page, do parents and infants effectively choose to attend, and why.

3 A unique form of language. What, however, of the relationship which obtains between written language and reality? Goody goes on: 'words assume a different relationship to action and to object when they are on paper than when they are spoken. They are no longer bound up directly with "reality"' (Goody 1977:46). If we replace Goody's expression 'words on paper' by 'words spoken to the infant by the adult', we may again come close to the specific nature of reading in the life of an infant. Book presentations often engender a form of language which is densely lexicalised, and, in many cases, broadly comprehensible without the pictures. Reading is of course not alone in giving rise to 'context-independent' language — in the sense defined by Lyons (1972:61). An oral account may retrospectively telescope into a brief description the various stages of a day's event. Alternatively, a visit to a zoo may be lexicalised as it takes place in real time. The reading setting, however, is unique in that it can generate a succint and context-independent description of an event (an outing or a meal, for example) whose essential components, in the telling, are simultaneously present in the form of illustrations, and thus available to visual and tactile inspection.

The purpose for which children read

Literacy is not solely a question of the child's capacity to decipher the written word; it is also concerned with the purpose for which children read. Scholars enquiring into the origins of literacy observe not only that human beings have developed writing systems; they also ask why they might have done so (Gelb 1952; Goody 1977). Children too, read for different purposes, they have preferences for different types of material, they interpret their reading material in different ways. An individual reader's response to books is a possible additional factor which connects early with later reading.

2 EMPIRICAL INVESTIGATIONS INTO READING WITH INFANTS

Reading at all ages is thus characterised by a static stimulus, by the kind of language activity it permits, and by the processes and responses which it engenders. But the argument thus far is theoretical. Some researchers, however, have sought to demonstrate how early and later reading may be connected in practice. Since language is the main concern of this study, the review which follows briefly summarises some of the research which focuses particularly on the linguistic component within early reading. However, neither this, nor any of the reviews in this book, is designed to be comprehensive; the intention is purely to provide an entry point into the subject matter to hand, especially for readers who may be less familiar with the field. More complete discussions of, for instance, language and/or literacy are available elsewhere (e.g. in Gleason 1993; Ingram 1989; Scollon 1985; Teale and Sulzby 1986b; Whitehead 1990).

2.1 Select bibliography

From a sociocultural perspective, Heath, researching in the USA, makes the fundamental point that there is nothing 'natural' in reading; the very act of reading assigns us to, and marks us as members of, a particular cultural group (Heath 1982). From their parents, children receive specific instruction in ways of reading. Reading is context-bound, a reflection of parental values. Those values are passed on — not only in the whether of stories — some children will hear stories, while others do not (McCormick and Mason 1986), but also in the what and why of those stories. Some children will hear Bible stories, others will read fairy tales. But parental values are not reflected only in the nature of the materials chosen. They are also transmitted in the way those materials are exploited. Speakers of Senegalese origin resident in metropolitan France, for example, use picturebooks, not for teaching language but rather to introduce kinship terms and keep alive the memory of relatives absent in West Africa (Rabin-Jamain and Sabeau-Jouannet 1991). Nonetheless, in many cultures, illustrated books are utilised for the precise and express purpose of improving language, with children of varying ages and linguistic ability, and in countries as diverse as the USSR (Luria and Yudovich 1956), Mexico (Valdez-Menchaca and Whitehurst 1992) and the USA (Edwards and Garcia 1994; Whitehurst *et al.* 1988).

A form of acculturation, the activity of reading to children early in life has further been associated with enhanced scholastic and literary achievement when those same children enter mainstream education. Explanations as to why this might be are multiple and very diverse, but parallel linguistic styles between home and school are thought to be a key factor. If the (oral) discourse and literacy events in the home and the school are equivalent, then the child from the 'adapted' home has an automatic advantage (Heath 1982). Other investigations of parents presenting picturebooks to their young children lend support to this view. The segmentation of language into word units, for instance, which then form the object of discussion, provides some infants with a metalinguistic knowledge of their language, of words, sentences, paragraphs, which is of immeasurable benefit when learning to read. Again the home prepares the child for school, since language in a school setting is taught analytically, and broken down into its constituent parts for the purposes of teaching (Olson 1988).

Charting the development of UK children along a variety of measures from infancy to school age, Wells, too, finds enhanced attainment at school to be associated positively with the early reading activities. The routine whereby pupils are asked to 'display' what they know by responding to 'test' questions is a technique which some will have already experienced while picturebook reading (Wells 1985:251). However, Wells finds scholastic achievement to be most strongly associated with listening to stories (1985:253; 1986:51).

In a more sociologically oriented study, Clark (1976) finds that reading fluency in UK children is associated less with parental occupation, and more with a belief of a fluent reader's family in the value of education, and (most significantly for our purposes) with the presence of a consistently available adult to 'read and talk' with the children from an early age. This investigation, however, is conducted retrospectively, by means of questionnaire responses; sadly, by Clark's own admission, no information is given as to what form these dialogues effectively take.

What, however, of studies which have focused exclusively upon reading between mother and infant in the first twenty-four months of life? What can they tell us of the intrinsic contribution of first reading experiences to literary and linguistic growth in the early months, irrespective of any connection with later development? Almost all discussions of early reading (as for example in Olson, or Wells, above) rely, it must be observed, upon a distinction between two 'different' types of reading: storytelling, on the one hand, and picturebook reading, on the other.

Research conducted in the USA into the reading of stories to children of two years of age and above is comprehensively reviewed by Cochran-Smith (1983). This research critique, however, notes a dearth of material documenting the exact details of early reading practices, a view endorsed for the UK by Meek (1991:89). Research into early reading which relies on written diary records is often geared either to assessing the content of the printed materials which children read, and/or documenting the responses of the infant to those materials (but those of the adult less so) (Butler 1979, 1980; Cochran-Smith 1983). A prime concern is the contribution of early literary experiences to learning and enjoyment, rather than the details of the linguistic exchanges which occur in the triangular relationship infant–parent–book.

Picturebook reading, and its contribution to the development of children under two years has, on the other hand, been the subject of detailed investigations which benefit from the use of data recorded live. The focus of the analysis is either the linguistic behaviour of the adult, and/or the active behaviour of the infant. These two features, it is argued, hold the key to what children learn, and will eventually themselves produce. Ninio and Bruner, in a seminal work published in 1978, found picturebook exchanges between a mother and her infant to be characterised by a predominance of utterances of the type: 'That's a dog'; 'It's a goose', an activity which has come to be known as labelling. Early picturebook reading, that is, concerns itself primarily with matching word form and pictorial referent (i.e. with ostensive definition). Picturebook exchanges between mothers (it is invariably mothers) and children under two are further characterised by the existence of a question–answer routine, in which infants are engaged actively in pointing, vocalising, and ultimately producing 'words'. 'Where's the dog?' 'What's that?', or 'What does kitty say?' are typical examples of such parental questioning. These observations accord with the view, almost universally accepted, that picturebook reading is largely, though never exclusively, concerned with the teaching and learning of 'vocabulary', by which is understood 'lexical labels' (Adams and Bullock 1986; DeLoache and DeMendoza 1987; Murphy 1978; Ninio 1980, 1983; Ninio and Bruner 1978; Snow and Goldfield 1983; Snow and Ninio 1986; Wells 1985; Wheeler 1983).

What conclusions, stated or implied, are drawn as to the value (to the infant) of this form of early picturebook activity? The infant's grasp of the association between word form and image is identified as a significant cognitive achievement. However, the activity is observed to be in some sense 'static'; 'little evolution' in labelling procedures occurs between the ages of 9 and 18 months (Ninio and Bruner 1978). For Snow and Ninio, a variety of literacy contracts: joint discussions about a specified topic for example, or the use of decontextualised language, are of obvious benefit to children, although doubts are voiced as to whether the learning of new vocabulary, the acquisition of conversational rules, or even interpretations of pictures are directly relevant to literacy in the longer term (Snow and Ninio 1986:118–122). Other research notes the 'simple' language of very early picturebook reading: 'Apple. Teddy bear. And kitty', based, often, upon somewhat 'simplistic' material (DeLoache and DeMendoza 1987:119). The limited scope of infant language (utterances consisting of a single word) possibly does not allow children much below two years to enter into discussions of complex issues, of motives, consequences, or a character's feelings, for example. Such activity, it is implied, occurs after the onset of two-word utterances, from around two years of age and onwards (Snow and Goldfield 1983:554; Garton and Pratt 1989:53).

2.2 Theoretical starting-points

This section examines some of the assumptions, either descriptive or methodological, which seem to underly many investigations of early reading, particularly those into picturebook reading. The discussion will, at the same time, offer some indication as to the analytical perspectives adopted in the course of this work.

INTRODUCTION

2.2.1 A particular view of language

Descriptive emphasis

No descriptive study of reading, or language, can ever be exhaustive. Often, however, by singling out one dominant issue for consideration, a distorted picture may result. Descriptions may, for instance, focus on certain forms of activity to the relative exclusion of others. A first example (others are given below) is the emphasis which many studies place upon active behaviour or production in the infant.

While it is true that infants are at times actively engaged with the adult when reading, by turning the page, pointing, vocalising, and eventually speaking, one activity indispensable to early reading, listening, has been less intensively studied. Chapter 1 looks at how parents apparently foster in their infants that essential capacity to attend to, and concentrate upon, a book.

Turntaking, and especially the question and answer routine allied to the use of the pointing gesture by the infant, are also observed by many authors to be characteristic of picturebook reading under two years old. Yet the mechanisms for the establishment of what are in effect very complex discourse routines are also little investigated. How children learn to take part actively and appropriately in reading dialogues is considered in Chapters 1 and 2.

Form and function in language

Linguistic theorists are accustomed to analysing language at a variety of different linguistic levels: phonology, grammar, semantics, discourse and pragmatics (for example). However, in much research on early picturebook reading, there is a particular emphasis upon syntactic form, and especially upon one word class: nouns. Indeed, utterances which contain a single word (usually a noun) are, in the literature, invariably described as 'simple'.

But, in the dynamics of the dialogue, utterances which are formally simple may be functionally complex. Or, to put the reverse formulation, it does not necessarily take complex sentences to express complex ideas, intentions, or beliefs. From a theoretical standpoint, short utterances may function, depending on context, in a whole variety of ways. Children may communicate using just a single word, or even non-verbal means, but, from a functional standpoint, what do they 'talk' about? The issue is of especial relevance in the period from age nine months to two years, during which, most infants, including those in this study, move on from the use of gesture to the use of speech.

The multivoicedness of language in use

What is true of a grammatical unit also holds true of lexemes; these, too, can have multiple meanings. Consider as an example: *Psychoanalysis and Psychology:*

INTRODUCTION

minding the gap (Frosh 1989). At one level this title is suggestive of the author's regret, and concern, with the (theoretical) divide between contemporary psychoanalysis and psychology, which, in his view, should be overcome. But some will recognise, in addition, the mischievous allusion to the station announcement issued routinely to passengers travelling on the London Underground to 'mind the gap' as they board their train. The book's title, understood in this light, becomes, in addition, a caveat; the warning about distance is ignored at one's peril. The meaning of this phrase derives, then, from the 'unuttered context' of a reader's life (Voloshinov 1926 [1988:19]). Word meanings in early book-based exchanges are not disembodied, as entries in a lexicon; echoes from the individual infant's everyday experience are of paramount importance.

Vocabulary teaching

Consider now the emphasis given in many studies to labelling activities. The association by the adult of a word form ('dog') with its corresponding representation in iconic form (a picture of a dog), has been interpreted as the teaching of lexical labels (by the adult), or their mastery (by the infant), especially with very young infants. Indeed, picturebook work is almost a by-word for vocabulary learning, some of it unfamiliar to the young reader. However, whether or not infants in their home environment actually do learn 'new' words from their picturebooks will be evaluated by comparing the lexical input (on the part of the adult) with the linguistic knowledge of the infant as he, or she, comes to their reading. But at the same time, some alternative views of 'labelling' activities will be put forward, in Chapters 1 and 3 especially.

Non-verbal communication

Finally, the respective interactional roles of parent and infant must be taken into account. Certainly, adults often take the initiative in reading, but might not infants themselves have a key part to play in guiding and influencing dialogues, even at the age of one year, using gesture, smiles, or direction of gaze? These mutually determining effects must, then, be accounted for, in terms which are dialogical in orientation (cf. Marková and Foppa (eds) 1990).

2.2.2 *The 'experimental' paradigm*

Consider now a second area of theoretical concern: the nature of the descriptive paradigm which underpins much existing research into early reading practice.

INTRODUCTION

The place of affect

Perhaps because of the circumstances in which some reading research is conducted, either in a laboratory or classroom setting, using, sometimes, in the case of infants, a single book imposed, even devised specially, by the investigator, perhaps, too, because of a long-standing view of the infant as an essentially rational being, the impression gained from much research into early reading is that it is primarily a 'cognitive' activity (cf. Frosh 1989:65). Oakhill and Garnham's thorough-going review of research into the development of reading skills, for example, makes almost no mention of an affective response to the materials read (Oakhill and Garnham 1988; cf. Gibson and Levin 1975). The tasks of picturebook reading with infants are described as easy or difficult, familiar or unfamiliar, but rarely as interesting, still less as exciting or enjoyable.

Yet infants do not just think or speak, they also feel, especially when they read. Responses to reading, particularly in young children, are emotional; children read for pleasure (Bettelheim and Zelan 1982). Infants, from nine months, if not younger, are capable both of understanding the feelings of others and of expressing their own (Izard *et al.* 1980; Tomasello 1994). Joy, surprise, interest, sadness and fear are all part of infant experience (Trevarthen 1982:89; Dunn *et al.* 1987:132). More than half a century ago, Vygotsky alerted us to the indissociable connection between affect and intellectual development:

> [The] separation [of affect and intellect] as subjects of study is a major weakness of traditional psychology since it makes the thought process appear as an autonomous flow of 'thoughts thinking themselves,' segregated from the fullness of life, from the personal needs and interests, the inclinations and impulses, of the thinker.
> (Vygotsky 1934 [1962:8])

A central issue for this study is how an affective response, joy and pleasure, functions to promote cognitive and linguistic growth in the reading infant.

An intersystemic view of reading

Cognitive psychology is dedicated in part to understanding how infants learn, and how they learn different and more complicated tasks. This raises an important issue, discussed by, amongst others: Bruner and Haste (1987:2); Bruner (1990); Frosh (1989); Whorf (1927 [1956:40 ff.]), that of the theoretical framework within which much of twentieth-century developmental research is conducted. This theoretical framework often necessitates a quasi-experimental setting in which materials, tasks and procedures are subject to careful control, frequently so as to investigate one or a number of predetermined hypotheses.

Goody and Vygotsky, however, are of the theoretical view, and research has shown empirically (e.g. Donaldson 1978) that what people are asked to look at, think about or discuss must inevitably influence the way in which they talk and

INTRODUCTION

think. Indeed, for Bettelheim and Zelan, what individuals are asked to consider might influence whether they think about it at all; some things are quite simply of no interest. The materials upon which this account is based are therefore those which 'turn up' in the lives of these infants. The role of the child in determining the type of material read to him, or her, and the impact of that material upon the language of both child and adult are issues which are considered. The analysis also elucidates the interrelationship between picturebook reading and narrative, activities which are usually considered as quite separate tasks.

Individual difference

Children are in many ways similar to one another, in reading as in anything else, and research correctly draws attention to their homogeneity. However, an essential part of a reading infant's very identity is constituted, not by similarity but by difference. Each child's perception of the world is unique – aspects of the world which are salient for one (a picture of a tractor, for example) are as if meaningless to another. Individuality is an issue discussed in Chapters 2 and 8 particularly.

Analytic perspective

A final point concerns the attitude of the investigator. Studies of reading often report a single aspect and/or may be analysed so as to verify a particular hypothesis – the use of superordinate terms (Adams and Bullock 1986), the development of pointing (Murphy 1978), the mastery of lexical labels (Ninio and Bruner 1978), the active production in speech of terms previously heard by the infant (Snow and Goldfield 1983). But, at the same time, naturalistic data invite, even require, the observer to listen with free-floating attention for what they might reveal about aspects of the reading process unsuspected or undocumented hitherto (cf. Abrams and Neubauer 1978).

3 ABOUT THIS BOOK

3.1 A multidisciplinary framework

Research into reading has, on the whole, been the concern of the disciplines of psychology and literary theory. On the other hand, an investigation of language (speech) in the adult, and linguistic behaviour (gaze and pointing gestures systematically organised for the express purpose of communicating) in the infant, is, in a fundamental sense, the object of the discipline of linguistics. But again, a concern with the primitive origins of behaviour, with stability and permanence through growth and change, or with individual, as opposed to group concerns, with affect and subjective perception, and with listening to

INTRODUCTION

evidence for what it reveals, owes much to the thinking of psychoanalysis. Analytical perspectives drawn from each of these different disciplines thus become pertinent to an investigation of the language of early reading.

The descriptive framework for the data analysed in the course of this book draws on the work of specialists in each of these fields. In this brief introduction mention is made of just four, from linguistics, psychoanalysis and psychology respectively, in order to give a very general indication of the theoretical perspectives adopted.

Perhaps surprisingly, the British linguist, J. R. Firth, provides the starting-point. While researchers are by no means agreed as to whether or not non-linguistic factors should legitimately form part of conversational analysis (Marková and Foppa 1991:1), Firth's belief is that language should be considered, not as an abstract linguistic system studied independently of the situation in which speech is generated, but rather wholly (or in part) in terms of the connection between it, and the (extra-, or non-linguistic) world of our experience (Firth 1957; cf. Palmer 1976:53 ff.). The context of situation (in which language is produced) becomes a schematic construct to be applied to the analysis of linguistic data, and might incorporate (Firth 1957:182):

- The relevant features of the participants: persons, personalities. The verbal action of the participants; the non-verbal action of the participants.
- The relevant objects.
- The effect of the verbal action.

The relevance of this theory to the current study would include confining statements about linguistic behaviour to a specific context (that of reading), rather than being concerned with language acquisition in general. The identity of the participants, here parent and infant, the infant's age, and non-verbal behaviour (e.g. gestures) must be taken into account. Finally, 'relevant objects' include both the presence of a book in printed form which both participants can see, and touch, and those illustrations which attract attention (as opposed to those which remain undiscussed).

A second aspect of Firth's work is his very particular view of meaning. A text is constituted not by one, but by several layers of meaning, which can be uncovered only gradually, via a series of statements at different levels. A linguist's task is to use a variety of descriptive techniques with which to make partial statements (only) of meaning; such is my purpose throughout this book.

The attention of the reader is drawn, second, to the work of Donald Winnicott who stands out among psychoanalysts by virtue of his belief in the significance to the infant of the actual (not a fantasised) parent–infant relationship. His optimistic belief in the inherent creativity, rather than the potential destructiveness of this relationship, his interest in health (always more difficult to describe than pathology), his view of a baby engaged with a significant other as being mutually rewarding to both parties, rather than primarily satisfying to one, together with the emphasis which he gives to the pre-oedipal phase of development – these are alluring as theoretical starting-points. Of importance, too, is his preoccupation with the infant point of view – with what experiences must feel like to the baby. Finally, with many theorists, Winnicott recognises the drive of the infant toward growth, and the 'environment' as a stimulus to change.

Third, the work of both Bruner and Vygotsky are here much to the fore. For Bruner, language and meaning are central to any approach to understanding the human predicament. Language is endowed with personal meanings, meanings which are private (but yet which can be shared, and thus enter the public domain). But, equally, language is rooted in a wider culture, indeed is the very expression of that culture (Bruner 1990:33). The interrelationship between individual readings (on the one hand) and culturally determined interpretations of pictures (on the other), and how those meanings become jointly constructed over time, and articulated in language – by two people of the same culture but of different generations and levels of competence – are major concerns of this book.

Vygotsky's writings are as a leitmotif for the whole of this work. Four key aspects of his thinking are:

- A belief in the historical approach as the royal route to understanding child development, a belief fundamental, of course, to Donald Winnicott.
- The emphasis given to the practical circumstances of an infant's life as providing opportunities for growth. But equally (as for Winnicott and Bruner), it is the child as individual who develops a relationship with that environment (Vygotsky 1987:32). Joy and pleasure may play a role here, but so, too, may disinclination (Vygotsky 1987:50).
- The belief in the socially distributed nature of the higher mental functions. While contact between child and picture may be direct, it is also the case that it is, frequently, mediated by an attentive adult. For Vygotsky, such mediation constitutes the key to progress; what begins by being on the intermental plane (between adult and child) later becomes intramental (Vygotsky 1987:21).
- Finally, Vygotsky identifies tools, both technical and psychological (linguistic signs), as the defining property of human mental action. Tools transform not only man's environment, but also man himself (cf. Wertsch 1990). What, one may enquire, are the transformations wrought by the use of non-verbal communication (gaze and pointing) and by language (speech), when infant and parent read together?

3.2 Data

Background

This project was initially motivated by observations of a 6-year-old reading aloud from a poetry book. 'Oh! they're the same', she remarked, 'they' being

INTRODUCTION

the final syllables of 'Alice' and 'Palace'. In the orthography of English, homophones are often distinct, as in: 'bough; bow'. Wondering whether understanding of this kind might not form an inherent part of learning to read in English, I speculated, too, as to whether the process of learning to read, just as learning to speak, might not have its own developmental history. It was not until my own children were born that the opportunity arose to try and trace what that history might be.

Subjects

The data for this study are thus derived from exchanges with two monolingual British children – a boy, Rhys [Rees], and his sister, Ceri [Kerry], born one year apart, who were observed reading at home with either their mother or their father, both of whom had continued their education to university level. On a day-to-day basis, both children were mainly looked after through their early childhood by their mother. Attendance at a playgroup was sporadic, totalling some two sessions of three hours each per week, at age four years. Neither child could read passages of print upon entering compulsory schooling (three months before their fifth birthday) though some practice in writing individual letters had been given. The point here is that the experience of reading documented in this enquiry was unexceptional in so far as it precluded the systematic introduction of batteries of materials specifically designed to teach infants to read either letters of the alphabet, or whole words, before they entered mainstream education.

These two children attended the same school (at a one year interval) and were taught to read the written word by the same teacher, using the exact same graded reading scheme materials. Upon entry to school at age 4 years 9 months, each studied the first book of this scheme which teaches individual letter/sound correspondences (i.e. phonics). That is to say, at this age, neither child could make out even the simplest first words of such a scheme. Some two years later, on the Schonell Individual reading test, scores indicated that their reading ability was some two years in advance of their chronological age. The infants studied here, then, did eventually turn out to be readers in the technical sense.

Method

The dialogues upon which this book is based took place as one parent (father or mother) and either Rhys or Ceri sat in an armchair and talked about the book they had in front of them. From infant age 8 months, it was established practice in this family for parent and infant to read a book, or books, together, usually in the early morning. Prior to each reading 'session', a small pile of books would put ready on a table adjacent to the armchair. These were extracted from a larger number of reading materials (kept on a shelf at the end

INTRODUCTION

of the living-room) which were in the process of being read. Videorecordings were made at intervals of four to six weeks for each child respectively, over a period ranging from child age 8 months, to child age 7 years. In this volume, reading exchanges, based on picturebooks and stories, are documented only up until infant age 25–27 months, even if they are reported in the context of literacy events which take place between two, or three and even up to five years later.

The length of each reading encounter was dictated by the participants; each session continued only for as long as both parent and child appeared to enjoy it. Sessions in the first two years lasted for a minimum of seven minutes (at age 9 months) to upwards of twenty-two minutes (from age 18 months onwards). Conversely, the number of books read decreased over the same period, from a maximum of six per session (at age 9 months), to just two, at age 18 months. As the children got older they spent a longer time reading fewer books. It became customary to read each book just once in each age session, but, inevitably, from one age session to the next, some of the same books, the favourites, reappeared. It was not possible, of course, to specify at the outset which books would turn out to be favourites with which child, nor indeed was any particular book imposed on either child for the purposes of this enquiry. The aim was simply to try and obtain a snapshot of an intimate family routine, and so to utilise only those books (whatever they happened to be) which formed the current reading materials for each child.

It is appropriate to comment at this juncture as to why, in this family, reading enjoyed the status of a dedicated activity in a dedicated place. The importance of books in the (professional) lives of both parents was surely one factor. An awareness, albeit unconscious, of the central part played by books in Western children's education was perhaps another. But there were more immediate considerations. The preparation and tidying up required was minimal; had it not been so, reading might well have occurred less often. Book reading not only injected variety into the daily routine of bringing up a toddler at home – a change from the bricks and the bike, or (later) the paint and the puzzles; it also offered a welcome chance to sit down. Relaxing together, in a chair, over a book, was quite simply experienced as pleasurable, physically, mentally and emotionally.

Transcriptions

The videorecorded data for the period under consideration, including speech, vocalisations, and non-vocal behaviour: gestures (especially pointing, turning the page, and other forms of manual contact with the book), smiling, and direction of (infant) gaze in relation to the books' contents, were transcribed into a written protocol. These data were additionally considered in the context of the book pages being read. Which aspects of the book were discussed, how, and why? Observational notes in written form were also incorporated. In the

INTRODUCTION

early months, these related particularly to the vocabulary items which Rhys and Ceri learned exclusively, or chiefly, from their reading. Also documented was the use which these infants made of their reading to interpret the real-world events of life which they encountered.

Materials classification

In the research literature, a picturebook is often defined as a book containing pages organised around a theme, or around a set of alphabet letters. Picturebooks differ greatly; some contain scenes with a strong human element, others are essentially taxonomies grouping a variety of thematically linked referents. In this study, however, the classification of reading materials into 'picturebooks' or 'stories' turns entirely upon the linguistic exploitation of these materials by the parent. Where parents use books (even those which are ostensibly 'story' books) to point out individual items, with no sense of continuity of actor and action from one page to the next, such activity has been categorised as picturebook reading (as in Chapter 3, section 3.1). 'Stories' here are always illustrated books which at the very minimum are presented as including a consistently reappearing character engaged in, at the very least, a sequence of different, but interrelated, actions.

Which components of language are studied? Levels of analysis have been restricted, for each participant, to a consideration of the lexical, syntactic and discourse structures employed, to the relative exclusion of phonological considerations.[2] In addition, those structures which are pervasive and recurrent are distinguished from the unusual or exceptional.

Use of data

The data was subject to different forms of exploitation. In Part I, an 'age-related' approach is adopted, whereby respective age sessions for each child, at child age 9, 14 and 18 months are analysed. These intervals were considered sufficiently far apart for changes of behaviour to be detected, yet close enough for threads of continuity to be discerned. In Parts II and III, a 'materials-related' approach distinguishes picturebook reading and storybook reading, respectively. In Part IV, picturebooks again form the starting-point, but with a change of analytical perspective.

In all cases, key points are illustrated by means of data extracts, from which it will be observed that idiosyncratic, yet similar, uses of language appear in the speech of both these parents; plurals, possessives, prepositions, and auxiliaries, for instance, are sometimes omitted. Although the analysis of this book does not focus on these particular aspects of performance, it must be emphasised that, in this respect, these adults' speech is atypical. It raises the issue of the extent to which two parents living together in one family influence each other's behaviour (as well as influencing, or being influenced by, their offspring).

INTRODUCTION

A final point concerns the recorded data available for each child. While every care was taken not to distort routine practices of reading in this family for the sake of this study by, for example, reading only those books which were currently in vogue when the recordings took place, one observational effect did occur, namely, a concern that the dyad reading should be able to complete their session undisturbed by 'noises off' from the second sibling. Here, it was easier to ensure that the second-born, still very much a baby, stayed calm if her mother attended to her off camera. Thus, although both Rhys and Ceri were read to regularly by both parents, there are more video-recorded examples of Rhys being read to by his father, and of Ceri being read to by her mother.

3.3 The structure of this book

Each of the four parts of this book addresses one aspect of the reading process. Part I is concerned with dialogue; how adult and infant interact one with the other. The development of listening and turntaking attitudes in the very young infant, and the foundations of the ability to point to a two-dimensional image within a question and answer framework, are of especial importance in the initial chapter. The second chapter continues the theme of dialogue, and again focuses on active infant participation, both non-verbal and verbal, between the ages of 14 and 25 months. Rhys and Ceri are, by now, observed to be behaving as individuals (and influencing adult behaviour significantly).

There follows, in Part II, an examination of the lexical content of the adult language of picturebook reading, considered in its relation to infant acquisition at different linguistic levels. Chapter 3 is concerned with product – what it is that adults and infants apparently achieve together, and Chapter 4 with process – how these achievements are negotiated.

Part III is concerned with the ontogenesis of narrative. The attempts of this mother to weave elements of her infant daughter's life into a semi-biographical account, developing thereby a capacity for identification, and imagination, are discussed in Chapter 5. Chapter 6, on the other hand, details some of the processes via which a 1-year-old comprehends the rudiments of narrative structure and written text.

In Part IV issues pertaining to the formation of the infant psyche are considered. Adopting a psychoanalytic (Winnicottian) perspective, Chapter 7 addresses the question of the lexico-syntactic content of adult speech considered in its relation to infant moral development. Chapter 8 investigates the spontaneous reactions of these two infants to book reading, and provides documentary evidence for Winnicott's theory of transitional phenomena as providing a significant link between early responses to books and subsequent aesthetic, that is, literary, development (at age 5 to 7 years).

INTRODUCTION

3.4 Descriptive considerations

There are three areas of descriptive difficulty to which the attention of the reader is drawn. The first is the dual status of the author, as participant in the interaction, and as researcher. Many might see theoretical disadvantages in using one's own children as subjects for research – a possible lack of objectivity, an inability to see one's own situation in perspective, for example. Against this, safeguards have been sought: the findings of this study are, wherever possible, related to other research in the field.

However, in my view, the advantages of research conducted in a family setting are many. The lack of intrusion by an outsider into the intimate situation which is reading allows a spontaneity of response in both adults and children which a laboratory setting might well preclude. The perception which most parents have of (each of) their children as unique beings, different from all others (which cannot but have a profound impact on that infant's development) is available to introspection. The common reservoir of shared experience upon which infant and adults draw, as books become increasingly familiar, a parent's knowledge of their own child's linguistic ability, or, beyond this, the wealth of possessions, experiences and significant persons in the child's life as they accumulate and change over time – all these factors have a bearing on reading and learning, and they can be accessed and articulated where appropriate.

But how should that mother be referred to? Since the children are the author's own, it might have been possible to refer to their mother, when it was the mother, as 'I'. However, this 'mother' and this 'father' are referred to throughout in the third person. The 'experiencing' mother, spontaneous, emotional, and caught up in the ongoing rush of events is often unaware of the processes which, with hindsight, are revealed by restrospective analysis of written data. To use the first person pronoun 'I' would be to confuse these two very different levels of experience. Support for this position comes from ethnomethodological studies, where, it is suggested, a theoretical distinction must obtain between what the observer perceives a mother to be doing, and the experience of that mother as she does it (Super and Harkness 1982). In this book, then, the first person refers to the author-as-researcher, but never to the mother-as-participant.

The second point concerns the limitations of this enquiry. Of necessity, it is restricted – as to its cultural context, these parents' socio-economic and educational background, and the small number of subjects observed. This study cannot, therefore, aim to make statements about early reading in all situations and in all circumstances. Rather, its purpose is to attempt to understand something of the processes involved over a long period of time in this particular circumstance, to document the behaviour of infants as individuals, and to demonstrate something of the subtlety and complexity of human face-to-face interaction, especially between a parent and a young child. Nonetheless it is hoped that the framework evolved, and the insights derived from this approach, will be of interest to all observers of language use in naturalistic situations, and particularly those involving reading.

Third, the adoption of a multidisciplinary perspective is, again, a potential source of difficulty. The terms 'object' and 'language' are often not equivalent in the parlance of a psychologist, a grammarian or a psychoanalyst. 'Object' in this enquiry refers, in the main, to an actual, three-dimensional, real-world, discrete, hard, usually manufactured entity: 'lorry', 'screwdriver'. The exception is in Chapter 8, where, in the discussion on transitional objects and phenomena, the term 'object' is carefully defined, and employed in a very specific, Winnicottian sense. Iconic representations of real-world entities are not 'objects' but 'referents'. Thus, the pictorial equivalents of, say, a farmer, a pet dog, a cork, a bath-hat, beaker, tractor or fork, are 'referents'. For sentence grammar, 'complement', not 'object' is used, as in: subject–verb–complement. With respect to word class usage, the term 'noun' or 'substantive', never 'object label', is employed. The psychoanalytic usage of 'object' to denote a significant person in the infant world (as in 'object-relations' theory) is not a usage adopted here except in one or two cases, again in Chapter 8.

'Language', or 'linguistic behaviour', refers to an organised system of signs or signals, interpretable by the parent, whose realisation may be vocal or non-vocal. Linguistic behaviour may thus take the form either of speech (words) (e.g. 'doggie'), of vocalisations (e.g. the 'eu eu' sound which an infant makes as s/he excitedly recognises a favourite image), or of pointing gestures (with index finger extended, as the infant makes contact with a picture in their book). Pointing gestures may occur either alone or in association with vocalisations or speech. The adjective 'verbal' refers to speech (words). 'Non-verbal', of infants, denotes communication in the form of gesture or vocalisation, alone or in combination; it excludes the use of speech.

'Extra-linguistic' refers to aspects of the physical and material world dissociated from the speaker, for example, three-dimensional, 'real-life' entities in the environment: animals, clothes, toys. The term 'non-linguistic' refers, in the main, to those areas of mental life or psychomotor behaviour of the adult or child which are not language. Crawling in the 8-month-old is qualified as 'non-linguistic' behaviour, while the box in which these children keep their toys is part of the 'extra-linguistic' context in which they live. The terms 'extra-linguistic' and 'non-linguistic' are avoided for book images. These are referred to, as far as possible, as 'two-dimensional' or 'iconic' representations, or 'pictorial' referents.

4 CONCLUSION: THE PURPOSE OF THIS BOOK

Literacy is an integral part of Western culture, and reading, in this book, is considered less in terms of the acquisition of a set of skills upon reaching school age, but more as a matter of individual history; children whose reading experiences are begun in infancy might be said to enjoy a literacy career which extends back into the first two years of life.

This book takes as its point of departure previous research into early reading, while proposing a more dynamic view of first reading experiences, one which takes account of the range of materials used time and again by the same infants between 1 and 2 years old in their own homes. Three main questions are to be addressed.

1 What exactly is 'early reading' and in what terms can it be described?
2 What can book-based interactions tell us about, for example, language acquisition, cognitive growth, the place of the 'unconscious' in parent–infant exchanges?
3 What is the specific relevance of early reading activities for literacy development, whether in the shorter or longer term?

Some answers to these questions have already been suggested; more complete answers are put forward in the remainder of this book.

Part I
INFANT–PARENT INTERACTION

Anyone observing an infant aged 12 months or above in a reading setting is seemingly struck by the degree of apparently effortless, but carefully regulated, and often excited, activity in which the small child is engaged (e.g. Ninio and Bruner 1978). Most obviously through tactile and vocal behaviour, the infant is involved in an active partnership with the adult, either intervening spontaneously, or responding to questions and instructions, sometimes by pointing to pictures in front of them (Meek 1991:90). 'Where's teddy?' the adult asks, and the infant complies by pointing to the image of 'teddy'. Infants, of course, are not active all the time; there are more quiescent moments, as in the following extract, where Ceri listens as mother speaks: 'Oh and they're buying their shopping now Wezzy! Getting sausages and carrots and icecream, yes, like Wezzy has, and marmalade!' This alternation between active intervention and receptive listening may be referred to with a useful shorthand as the dialogic competence of the infant.

At the outset, however, the two infants of this study are far from achieving regulated behaviour on this scale; reading situations, for them, are a totally new experience. Part I of this book is thus concerned with the emergence of dialogic competence between the ages of 9 months and 2 years. Chapter 1 looks at the behaviours, both active and receptive, which these two infants are encouraged to adopt at the time of their first contacts with books. Chapter 2 considers the ways in which newly acquired dialogic skills are actively exploited by Rhys and Ceri respectively. Thus, what is at issue is not the existence of reading appropriate behaviours; it is already well documented that infants listen attentively, take turns and show interest in what they read. The concern instead is with the processes via which such behaviours are established in the first instance.

1
READING AND THE VERY YOUNG INFANT

1 FIRST CONTACTS WITH BOOKS

The earliest reading exchanges recorded in this study take place at infant age 8 to 9 months. At this age, and during all the reading sessions considered in this book, Rhys and Ceri were read to on their own.[1] Although the books used with each infant in the early months are not identical, there are three features which all share: their (small) size (23cm x 19cm is the largest used), their theme (there is a preoccupation with animals and the country or with a baby's life events), and, in some, their complexity. Both children have occasion to look at pages comprising not just a single referent but also complete scenes in which a measure of discrimination among different items is required.

How Rhys and Ceri experience illustrations in books cannot be known exactly, but their behaviour, and that of their parents, provides some clues. This section provides a very general insight into the conduct of these children in the early sessions, as background to the discussion for the remainder of this chapter.

A first feature is an atmosphere of movement and activity, particularly in Rhys. Looking at a book for the first time, Rhys and Ceri explore this three-dimensional object as they would any other, through all the senses, by mouthing it, touching it, dropping it. They observe its peculiar characteristics, discovering to their delight that it has pages which can be turned, both forwards, and backwards. Turning the pages is often of greater fascination than looking at the pictures contained there. The following extracts give an indication of how these adults attempt to divert infant attention away from exploring a book as a three-dimensional object, and encourage them to look at it in a different light – as containing two-dimensional images which are to be contemplated. Typical of the early sessions, these key examples will be used to exemplify a number of salient points throughout this first chapter:

Father	Mother
(Looking at front cover of picturebook)	*(Looking at front cover of picturebook)*
Look! Here's book! Here's book!	Shall we do some books darling?

Father	**Mother**
(*pointing to picture of a teddy*) Here's teddy. Here's teddy. Here's teddy.	Come on then, who shall we do? Shall we do bunny? Where's bunny!
Rhys tries to turn page.	Kezzy see the bunny eating the cabbage, can't you darling? Wezzy see bunny.
(*moving book just out of infant's reach as turns page*) Look! Got to find teddy!	(*as turns page*) And who over the page Wezwez?
(*points to right of first double page*) Look! Here's baba. Baba wake up in morning in cot.	(*points to left of first double page*) Look! Mr foxey. There's Mr foxey. And there's hooty owl.
Rhys moves to turn page.	
(*sidesteps this movement*) What baba say Rhysie? Baaa (*crying noise*) Baba say, euh?	
(*Pointing to left-hand side of double page*) Teddy here! Hmm? Right, let's move over	

At the beginning, then, Rhys and Ceri display little realisation that reading involves them in sustained looking and listening: a maximum of three to four utterances per image, and two or three images per page, is, at the outset, all the adult talk that is realistically possible. The adult, however, is selective: even though, in the example, four different toys are depicted alongside the baby, only the latter is mentioned. Monitoring their child's direction of gaze, these parents often time their interventions to coincide with whatever it is that Rhys or Ceri happens to be looking at (cf. Schaffer *et al.* 1983:354). But gradually these infants learn to listen to what their parents want to discuss. In other words, there has to be give as well as take. But how is the give (on the part of the infant) established?

Reading then, will come to include sitting still, looking and listening. And eventually, too, it will include a two- or three-part question–response (–feedback) structure which involves pointing. But not yet. For all that the activity of these infants in the early weeks is tactile (turning the pages and smacking them accounts for more than two-thirds of total active infant contributions at 9 months, with vocalisations and smiling accounting for fewer than one-third), pointing to images with the index finger extended is not, for these children, part of this involvement. But, efforts are made by the adult to develop within the infant an appreciation of the discourse structure in which pointing gestures eventually may be used – that very capacity which is to be fully established in Rhys and Ceri by around 14 months.

Experimental evidence confirms that, from around age 9 months, children can recognise and re-recognise images in two-dimensional form as representations of reality (Roberts and Horowitz 1986), although it is far from clear that Rhys and Ceri necessarily experience all these representations as lifeless images (see Chapter 8). These infant readers are, moreover, discriminating; some pictures they look at briefly, others they dwell upon for longer. How these parents foster this natural curiosity, and how infant enjoyment is canalised for adult ends conclude the analysis for this chapter.

2 PROCESSES OF SOCIALISATION

Though often discussed in terms of their usefulness for teaching vocabulary, picturebooks play a significant role in preparing the infant for all aspects of reading: understanding how a book is read, knowing what the different parts of a book are called, and concentrating attentively. But, how are these different components of reading put into place?

Reading from start to finish

Contact between these two children and their book is frequently by means of touch. The mouth or the whole body may be involved, as Rhys and Ceri lean forward excitedly as if to bring their entire selves into closer touch with their book. These adults' response is not so much to prevent these spontaneous movements, but rather to anticipate them and canalise them for their own purposes. Even if, early on in a session, an attempt to grasp the book is frustrated by the adult moving it slightly out of reach (see the key example), Rhys eventually gets hold of it and turns the pages forwards and backwards. Parents here are in something of a dilemma. How can they steer Rhys and Ceri toward book-appropriate behaviours (i.e. to a realisation that they must turn the pages forward and in sequence), but yet retain their interest in the book, by allowing them to explore it as they wish?

The answer is to mark linguistically those moments when the parent (and also occasionally the infant) turns the pages forwards, with: 'Let's move over!', 'Who's coming now?', or 'Who over the page?'. Such questions presumably propel Rhys' and Ceri's attention onwards in the direction in which the pages of a book are (conventionally) turned. Conversely, occasions when the pages are turned backwards are left unmarked (even though the infants themselves are left free to turn the pages if they want to). It is a technique used time and again: less desirable behaviours, though rarely explicitly rejected, are simply the subject of minimal comment, whereas attitudes which are to be encouraged are associated simultaneously, or sequentially, with sometimes quite extensive adult talk.

Encouragement to read through from start to finish is a further feature of the early sessions. The beginning of a book is marked explicitly: 'Let's do book! Where's book! Here's book!', while, at a non-linguistic level, the book is invariably opened at, or as near to, the front cover as the infant is prepared to accept. In time, if, as happens at 14 months for example, Ceri wants to get to an inside page with great urgency, her mother moderates her enthusiasm, encouraging her to start at the beginning: 'Wait for Mummy! We'll do that page in a minute.' Endings are rarely emphasised to the same degree, perhaps for the very reason that these adults wish, at this early stage, to avoid drawing attention to stopping. Seeking continuity, both these parents, having finished one book, reach promptly for a second. But as Rhys and Ceri come to accept that more than one book will be read, endings of books read first in the session are spelled out clearly: 'Finished teddy, that's finished that one! Let's have another book shall we?' (Ceri, 14 months).

If chronological order and sequencing are to become increasingly important in presentation, so, too is completeness. During the reading of each book, these adults refer verbally, if possible, to at least one item upon every page. That is to say, they try not to miss any of the pages out. If their infant is not prepared to see the book through to its final page, then often their parents can be observed to turn the pages through singly, one by one, without making any comment before finally shutting it, as if to signal, with non-linguistic means, that a book can only be said to be appropriately finished when all the pages have been considered, and the last one reached. Such presentations are perhaps the non-linguistic precursors of what eventually will become a more complete linguistic reading; eventually, none of the pages (of a story) will be missed out at all.

Acquiring the appropriate terminology

In common with many others, Rhys and Ceri are also introduced very early on to the terminology appropriate to books. The words 'book' and 'page' are among the substantives which occur with the highest degree of frequency in adult speech at the 9-month sessions (see examples). These children hear too, that books have both a particular form – they have a 'front' and a 'back': 'Who's on the back? Doggy!', and a particular manner of exploitation. They can be 'opened': 'Open up' father says, as he turns to the first inside page, and they can be 'read': 'Rhysie read him.'

From the earliest sessions, too, picturebooks are referred to in a manner which anticipates the eventual use of an official title. 'Titles' are, for now, idiosyncratic, an invention of a particular parent–infant dyad. Typically, the form includes a nominator, often a main character, in juxtaposition with the word 'book', as in: 'Noddy book' (Edwards 1978:457). Examples from these dyads are: 'Bunny book', 'Teddy book', 'Puffa book', 'Piggy book'. The actual titles of these books are: *The Happy Bunny*, *Where's Teddy?*, *Puffa on the Farm* and *Piggys Say Oink*, respectively. These inventions may be viewed, perhaps, as precursors to storybook titles; stories, too, are constructed around a central protagonist whose name often features in the title (cf. Rabinowitz 1987:128).

Keeping the session going

Sustained bouts of concentration on the part of the infant are a further goal of the early sessions. When reading, these parents give Rhys and Ceri their undivided attention, but equally, they do their very best to dissuade Rhys or Ceri themselves from breaking off. This is achieved, not by forcing them to read, for they will not be forced, but by talking throughout those moments in the session when infant attention appears to be in danger of waning. When reaching for a second book, Rhys' father, for example, in four successive utterances, repeats these words: 'Rhysie have book', following this with: 'Find another book now!' and, grasping it: 'There's other book! Shall we look at other book?', all this, seemingly, to prevent Rhys from losing concentration and getting down from the chair. At the page turn too, as we have already seen, the momentary disappearance from sight of a referent with which to engage the infant's visual attention is parried with the words: 'Who over the page?' or 'What's coming now!'. Talking both engages and re-engages infant attention; it shortcircuits a possible lapse of concentration and carries the baby over until such time as another image presents itself to engage his or her attention afresh.

Marking the event as special

A final illustration of these parents' attitude to reading is to be found in the clear demarcation in time and space of the reading event itself. Physically, Rhys and Ceri are almost always seated, not at floor level, but high up, on the lap of their parents in an armchair, removed from other distractions. They are not, as in some studies, playing with their toys on the ground, and from time to time breaking off to look at a book. The time of the day chosen is also significant, for book-based activities, in this family, take place, not at bedtime, but early in the morning, when alertness and powers of concentration in an infant are perhaps optimal. With regard to the length of time during which Rhys and Ceri read, sessions last for as long as each is prepared to concentrate, but equally, terminated when they signal that they have had enough.

Young infants are quite capable of communicating that they have had enough – here, by arching their back, closing the book, climbing down from the chair. These non-linguistic cues are interpreted as an indication that it is time to stop. The linguistic boundaries to the whole event are equally explicit: 'Shall we do some books? Come on then! Who shall we do?' and at the end: 'Finished now, bye bye books.' Rhys and Ceri come to sense, perhaps, that reading is an event quite unlike climbing on a plastic trike, which (in this family) is allowed to start, or stop, almost at will; rather, it is an activity that has clear boundaries, which, ideally, is not to be interrupted, and which generally lasts for some time. Such procedures have clear parallels with research conducted in the USA into the attitudes of middle-class parents to reading (Heath 1982; Panofsky 1994). There, as here, in the schedule of both adult and child, reading is assigned priority, both in terms of the time allotted to it, and the importance which it assumes relative to other forms of activity which may be to hand.

3 LOOKING AND TURNTAKING

3.1 Looking as an achievement

With sighted infants, looking is central to all reading tasks; books, as earlier discussed, appeal to the eye. But looking at a picturebook is not a simple process which can be assumed to occur as if almost naturally in the infant, while the 'real work' in reading takes place at other levels, acquiring 'labels' for 'things' (for example). Learning to look at a book, just as learning to speak, for the young infant, requires carefully timed, and carefully chosen, adult help.

Looking, like speaking, is not a uni-dimensional activity; it has many facets to it. But there are complications with trying to understand how different acts of looking are established. Looking, unlike pointing or vocalising, is continuous, not discrete; its onset and cessation are not easily identifiable. Nor does the English language provide lexemes which allow us readily to discriminate between different dimensions of looking. Phrases may be used: 'start to look', 'keep on looking', but these are, in many ways, inadequate. However, despite these difficulties, consider some aspects of looking in early picturebook reading, and how these are fostered by the adult.

Starting to look

In their surroundings, Rhys and Ceri may well find things which are of more interest to them than looking at their book: a noisy aeroplane in the sky, for example. When reading, then, infant attention must first be disengaged from these alternative sources of interest and diverted to their pictures. A major task is to engage infant attention in the first place, to 'get them to look'. In a bid to attract attention, parents in this family talk, not on a monotone, but with great enthusiasm: 'Look! Here's teddy!' They point to the image of teddy, checking their infant's direction of gaze as they do so. Many instances of this may be found by referring back to the key examples quoted above. Talking excitedly about the book is, of itself, often sufficient to attract the attention and interest of a young infant.

Look, but don't touch

Looking (and simply that) is a matter for the eyes, not the hands, or mouth. However, an object within reach of a 9-month-old is generally ripe for exploration, not contemplation! Infants may not be disposed to merely 'looking' at the pictures in their book. 'Look' at a mobile, yes, because it is beyond their grasp, but simply 'look' at a toy within reach, no! The task facing these parents is thus to discourage manipulation of the three-dimensional object, and to construe that same object primarily in terms of a series of two-dimensional images which must be contemplated. So they seek to divert Rhys' and Ceri's attention away from playing with the pages and towards the pictures on them; they talk about 'teddy'.

Active vocal reactions on the part of Ceri and Rhys that s/he is responding to the picture qua picture (rather than fidgeting with the book qua book) are sometimes richly rewarded. 'Little girl going for a walk', mother says, and, as Ceri looks and spontaneously vocalises at the picture of the little girl, her mother responds equally excitedly with high pitch: 'Yes, yes, that's right, darling.' Any appropriate active response to reading is positively encouraged by these adults, and is peculiarly characteristic of all the dialogues studied here. Rhys and Ceri are not expected to sit and look in silence all the time.

Look and see

Talking thus engages attention, but it also brings the act of looking into focus. If this mother catches sight of Ceri looking at a referent, she will respond to that act of looking, and talk about whatever Ceri appears to be looking at. What she actually says is discussed in section 4.2.2, but invariably she names that referent. Nominalisation (e.g. 'teddy') is associated with looking carefully at an image of teddy. But if on one page there is more than one referent, then the act of perception may also be an act of discrimination. Ceri looks at the teddy (in the cot), and not the crocodile, or the duck (on the floor). Through adult language use, referents acquire a degree of salience as other items temporarily recede into the background; infants' perceptions of their book become structured.

Keep looking

Finally, acts of looking are to be sustained; Rhys and Ceri, where possible, are encouraged to concentrate, not to give up looking, (i.e. break away from their book). There are two aspects here, and for both the parents in this family resort to talking. The first involves continuing to talk in cases where Rhys and Ceri appear interested. The parents either repeat the noun, as with: 'Here's teddy, here's teddy, here's teddy', or they expand upon it, adding new information: 'Look! Here's baba! Baba wake up in morning in cot' (see the key example). Both 'teddy' and 'baba' (or 'bunny' and 'Mr foxey') receive more attention than 'teddy', or 'hooty owl' mentioned only fleetingly at the conclusion of the key examples. A second strategy is for the adult to move on quickly if interest in a particular picture appears to be waning, and introduce another one. This, perhaps, is the bookreading equivalent of offering a new toy to a child seated in a pushchair, when the first has lost its appeal. Both parents switch to a new item and/or turn the page in an effort to engage infant concentration afresh.

In the early stages of bookreading, these two infants' concentration upon a single referent, or topic, be it the 'baby', or the 'teddy', is not long. Certainly the number of referents which can be discussed per page is no more than three or four before it becomes imperative to move on. Thus it is that no fewer than six different books, offering a plethora of referents, are discussed with each of these infants in a single 9-month session. The presentation of a variety of topics, together with a careful pacing of their introduction, are aspects of adult linguistic intervention which seem to sustain the visual attention of these two infants when very young.

Infants, then, when starting out, receive not a little instruction in how to look. But let us pose another question. Why, when reading, should these parents need to encourage 'looking' at all? Rhys and Ceri can, after all, 'see'. The answer to this question lies (partly) in the nature of the referent at which they are being asked to look. Babies' attention is readily engaged by referents which make sounds, or move: leaves fluttering, mobiles turning, images on a televison screen. Humans are biologically programmed to detect movement: it signalled the arrival of predators (Lieberman 1991). Furthermore, movement has a significant impact on language acquisition. Infants readily learn words for objects which are manipulable or movable; 'ball' is learned before 'wall' (Nelson 1973:31).

Images in books, however, are static. How, then, do caregivers attract attention, designate a topic, excite curiosity, sustain infant interest and concentration in a situation where, by definition, grasping the rattle and shaking it (or grabbing the ball and rolling it) are excluded? They do so, of course, by resorting to language. The infant may be addressed directly by name: 'Ooh, Rhysie, look!' The particular topic chosen: 'teddy!', or 'baba!', also has a major part to play (see section 4.3). The adoption of changing tones of voice further arouses infant curiosity: 'Ssh! Baba sleepies!' The task of encouraging infants, through talk, to look at images is thus challenging for a parent, but it is also rewarding. Furthermore, adult intervention is an absolute necessity. It is difficult to imagine that a very young infant would, as a matter of routine, look for seven minutes or more at their books, unless an adult were present and available to talk about them.

3.2 Turntaking

Two essential components of reading have so far been considered: processes of socialisation, and aspects of looking. Turntaking, dependent initially on acts of looking, adds a further dimension to the reading process. How are Rhys and Ceri encouraged to take an active part in the reading setting, and behave appropriately (for this cultural context at least) within an exchange structure?

Acts of perception as turns

Despite these infants' inability, as yet, to point or speak, dialogue structures are developed between these parents and infants in a reading setting, and, within those structures, looking (in the infant), an activity which is frequently continuous, may nonetheless function for the adult as a set of discrete acts of visual perception. Furthermore, depending on the dynamics of the interaction, acts of looking (on the part of these two infants) may function as the non-verbal equivalent of turns in the discourse. Just as, in a classroom, when the teacher has asked a question of the whole class, the act of looking at a particular pupil functions as the non-verbal equivalent of a request to respond, so here do Rhys and Ceri, through acts of looking, communicate with their parents.

What are the discourse functions involved? There are, I believe, two main ones, and in both cases, communicative sequences involving acts of looking on the part of Rhys and Ceri evolve, and transform themselves into a kind of proto-dialogue structure. It begins to seem as if the movement of looking in the infant is interpreted by the adult as a deliberate communicative act.

Consider the sequence 'infant looks–parent talks'. Here, an act of looking on the part of the infant may be construed as an initiative, which elicits a verbal response on the part of the adult interlocutor. The infant looks, and possibly vocalises at a picture of a teddy – and the adult responds: 'Teddy, there's teddy.' Looking in this circumstance functions as the non-verbal equivalent of 'I, the infant, have caught sight of a new referent and I want you, the adult, to talk about it.' It constitutes a turn in the dialogue, whose effect is to introduce a new topic into the discussion.

But adult talk is designed not only to respond to what the infant is looking at, but also to encourage that infant to contemplate an image, not of their own, but of the adult's choosing. Adult interventions have the effect of engaging and then directing infant attention to an iconic referent which they, the adults, choose to point out. As the infant moves to turn through the pages, the parent arrests the movement with: 'Look! There's baba!'; Rhys, or Ceri, stops to look. The adult's move may be glossed as: 'This time I, the adult, am looking and talking about something; I want you, the infant, to notice it.' Looking in the infant in this case is a response to an adult exhortation to look.

Thus we have two distinct acts of infant perception – one the equivalent of a discourse initiative and the other the equivalent of a discourse response. Since these infant acts of perception occupy a position, or place – a space within the dialogue, and since they have a meaning or function which the adult interprets, they function as contributions within a dialogic framework. In both instances, the act of looking by the infant is structured, linguistically, by the adult, as a kind of visual precursor to an act of ostensive monstration. Rhys and Ceri are, in effect, pointing out something with their eyes, understood as a possible bid to get the adult to speak, or as a response to an adult request to look at something. This use of the eyes is somewhat different from listening and looking attentively as the adult talks. They are the junior equivalent of an adult discourse turn. The infant effectively initiates a topic, or responds to the adult by complying with a task set by that adult. As will be seen, pointing with the index finger will step into those dialogue positions previously occupied by acts of infant perception.

A privileged discourse routine

The remainder of this section is concerned with the second of the two sequences, the proto question–answer structure, in which these infants comply with a task. At 14 months, 40 per cent (at least) of these infants' contributions to reading dialogues are responses to adult questions. But how is this routine developed?

When parents read picturebooks with their infants, they frequently rely upon a question–response structure which includes a range of different question words: '*What*'s coming now! Oh! drum!'; '*Who*'s that? Bunny!' That question form, according to some observers, is initially 'rhetorical'. It is the parent who both asks: 'What's this?', 'Who's this?', or 'Who's coming now?', and then goes on to 'answer' their own question, naming the referent as they do so: 'Who's this? Buzzy bee!' The response function will, eventually, be taken over by the child, at the appropriate age, using a word form to respond verbally. Eventually, pointing to a picture of a hammer, adults will say: 'What's this?' and it will be the 2-year-old who will answer: 'Hammer.'

An infant response to 'Who's this?', or 'What's this?', in the view of some, has to wait, until the infant can either speak, or use an onomatopoeic attribute as indicator (as in: 'What's this' – 'woof woof'). However, consider the case of 'Where's the ... ?', – frequently a variation on 'Who's this?', or 'What's this?' The contention here is that reading infants are able to respond to the question '*Where's* teddy?' at a very young age, and well before they are able to speak, vocalise or point. In other words, at this early age, such questions are not rhetorical but actual.

How can Rhys and Ceri, unable as yet either to speak or to point, effectively comply with such a question? They do so, of course, because the response required involves neither identifying teddy by name: 'There's teddy', nor stating where he is: 'Teddy's in the cupboard.' 'All' that is required is 'simply' an indication that the word form 'teddy' has been understood, and matched with the appropriate picture. Infants provide that indication with their eyes; they 'look' on the page at where 'teddy' is to be found.

It follows, then, that the question–answer format prefaced by 'Where's teddy?' or 'Who's this?', and followed by 'There's teddy', or 'It's teddy', is not only directed at teaching the 'name' of something; the infant is also being introduced to the question–answer routine. Indeed, since infants know full well what a teddy is, both what he looks like and what he is called, it could be argued that these adults are primarily concerned with discourse structure, not lexical acquisition.

READING AND THE VERY YOUNG INFANT

In the case of the early sessions, a shift of analytical emphasis away from lexical mastery and towards turntaking routines is, in my opinion, well-founded. The exhortation to 'look for' teddy and to 'show' (somehow) that he has been found, is a priority at this stage. It is a preoccupation manifest in the use, by these adults, of no less than four different strategies, all of them dedicated to the question–answer routine. Graded according to difficulty, these strategies, or phases, consist of a two-part (proto-) question and answer structure. Phases are to be distinguished, however, by two features:

- the syntactic form of the question, or exhortation, to 'look';
- the presence, or absence, in the context of situation of the iconic equivalent of the substantive of the question.

Three of the four phases are found concurrently in the early sessions; let us now examine them in detail.

The first phase involves ascertaining that Rhys and Ceri, who can neither speak nor point to teddy, nonetheless know the meaning of the word 'teddy'. That is, the adult needs to check that they can show by looking that the lexical form 'teddy' matches the picture of the fluffy brown animal, and not the green scaly reptile with the big teeth. This the adult does, as we have already seen, by naming the item in the presence of its two-dimensional representation, nomination here having the additional function of an instruction (to look in the right place). The response takes the form of complying with the instruction. Hearing the word form 'teddy': 'Teddy, here's teddy!', these infants look at the picture of the teddy on the page open in front of them.

Almost without exception Rhys and Ceri do look in the right direction as their father or mother labels an item. As has been shown many times, parents habitually set tasks which are within their infant's grasp. If image and word form are not matched correctly, however, the parent takes steps to adjust the infant response, as may be seen from this exceptional example in which Ceri seemingly gets it wrong. Mother is describing an image, and pointing to it: 'Pussy cat, here's pussy cat.' She sees Ceri looking away to the wrong side of the page. Pointing appropriately, mother says gently: 'No, that's not pussy cat there! That's bunny, that's bunny! Here's pussy cat, down there.' (Ceri, 9 months).

The second phase comes with the inclusion of a question word: 'Teddy, there's teddy' becomes 'Where's teddy?' Although the question word is added, the noun of the instruction is (still) uttered in the presence of its iconic equivalent, a picture of teddy, and again the infant response is an appropriate act of looking. Parents provide help; they describe the task in hand: 'Where's teddy? Got to *find* teddy!' These infants are not asked to hold the word 'teddy' in their mind for very long because the picture of the teddy is right there, in front of them. For an infant to respond to this directive, appropriate direction of gaze is sufficient; the infant's act of looking may here be glossed as 'I, the infant, am looking at something in order to indicate to you, the adult, that I have located what you have asked me to search for.'

The third phase comes when the infant is invited to find 'teddy', but in a situation where teddy himself is out of sight. The instruction: 'Where's teddy? Got to find teddy', has now become more testing, for the image of 'teddy' may be inside the book, not on the front cover which both participants are looking at when the words 'Where's teddy?' are uttered. These infants have now both to understand and remember what they have to look for, and in addition turn to the appropriate page in the book where teddy is to be found. In the first part of phase three, the adult accomplishes the task, initially, on the infant's behalf. As this mother opens a book in which a known favourite is due to appear after some five pages, Ceri vocalises excitedly. This signal of anticipation is responded to by announcing the imminent arrival of teddy: 'Yes! Wezzy *knows* its going to be teddy bear!' In turning the pages towards the image of the teddy, parents' voices build to a crescendo, and finally, in a rush of excitement, announce the arrival of 'teddy' (Ceri) or 'buzzy bee' (Rhys) as the case may be.

The second part of phase three follows closely upon the first. Having been invited to join in as a parent looks for the 'missing' referent, each infant is immediately asked to execute the task on their own. A new level of self-regulation is reached. Each infant is handed the book with a view to locating that same special referent for themselves. 'You want to find teddy, hmm! Kezzy do it then!', comments the parent. As the baby, or the adult for her, turns slowly through the book towards the teddy page, the task to hand is repeated: 'Kezzy going to do it then! You *find* teddy darling! *Where*'s teddy? *Show* Mummy teddy.' The reaction, emotional and linguistic, when teddy (or the bee) are reached after some five pages, takes the form of squeals of laughter, on the part of infant and parent alike: 'There he is, clever girly, That's the girly, Kezzy got him. Kezzy got teddy!' Enjoyment and fun are important elements in this new task.

The picturebook material for this last task does not consist of complex scenes, but of single-item-per-page books, in which reaching a page, stopping and looking at it, is, of itself, sufficient indication that the correct referent has been located. The timing, too, is critical – these routines never take place initially in a session, but only after practice with the adult, on phases one and two, using different types of materials. The discourse framework within which Rhys and Ceri will be invited to point to teddy autonomously has recently been rehearsed and is fresh in their mind.

The three phases, or rather, approaches, to developing an understanding of the question–response format run in parallel; all co-exist in the early sessions, and represent a set of techniques whose ultimate purpose, I believe, is to encourage participation in a question–response structure within reading. Thus, not only do these parents use a variety of images to interest the infant; they also use a variety of means with which to exploit those images. Variety adds spice to the process of letting a parent know where teddy is. Nobody, and especially a very young infant, seemingly, likes doing the same thing in the same way over and over again for the whole session. However, the advance represented by the second part of phase three, that is, the autonomous acquisition of a process already accomplished with the parent, comes close to Vygotsky's view that self-regulating functions are, in the first instance, interpersonal.

In phase four, towards the end of the first year, there arises the expectation that Rhys and Ceri point, rather than look, in response to an adult request to identify a referent using the question form 'where' (cf. Ninio 1980). One of the first examples on these tapes occurs at age 11 months, when Ceri singles out, by means of a pointing gesture, from a multiplicity of images, the referent she had been asked for. Her mother's pleasure when she does so is clearly evident.

Adult	Ceri (11 months)
Oh Wezzy! Where's pussy on this page Wezzy?	
Where's the pussy?	
	Ceri points to cat.
(*excitedly*) There, yes, Wezzy got pussy!	
Good girl, Wezzy!	
She *pointed* to pussy, haven't you darling!	

Thus, between tactile exploration (8 to 9 months) and the development of the capacity to point (11 to 14 months) is evolved a question–answer framework whose evolution within the reading setting for these two subjects is summarised in Table 1.1.

Table 1.1 The establishment of the question–response structure

Infant age	(9 months)*			(11 months)*
Phase	I	II	III	IV
Exhortation	Noun	Question word plus noun	Question word plus noun	Question word plus noun
	Referent present	Referent present	Referent absent	Referent present
Example	Teddy!	Where's teddy?	Where's teddy, Got to find teddy!	Show Mummy with your finger where's teddy!
Infant response	Looks	Looks (vocalises)	Stops at appropriate page. Looks (vocalises)	Points

* Ages given are approximate, and reflect the data of this study only.

Thus, the ability of Rhys and Ceri to point is integrated into a discourse routine whose communicative functions have been established some two months previously. The advantages of pointing over looking as a means of communication, the range of linguistic uses to which it is put, and its significance for language acquisition, are the subject of the next chapter.

In sum then, looking, looking at, looking for and finding referents – these activities dominate the earliest book reading exchanges with Rhys and Ceri. The verb forms of adult speech bear this out; the majority of verb or verb-like structures in adult speech at the early sessions have as their subject, not the characters of the book, as in: 'Baba crying', but rather the infant or adult reader of the book, as in: 'Got to find teddy.' 'Find', 'turn over', 'look', 'see', all these verbs are an indication of the importance which the adults attach to shaping their infants' relationship with the book and the images contained there. As these attitudes become established, verb forms in parental speech become increasingly concerned, not with what Rhys and Ceri can or might do with their book, but with what the characters depicted accomplish. At the beginning, however, the children's relationship with the book, and their interactive relationship with the reading adult are apparently fostered as a priority.

4 ADULT LINGUISTIC DESCRIPTIONS

4.1 Labelling in theory

Having focused thus far on infant behaviour, how Rhys and Ceri are encouraged to look at their book and take part in a structured exchange with the adult, attention is now turned to what they are invited to listen to. The adult language of early picturebook reading has often been evaluated in terms of its capacity to promote lexical acquisition in the infant. By pointing to and labelling the pictures, or so it is argued, the parent teaches the infant names for things (see key examples). On the one hand, the connection between the adult's pointing gesture and its target is optimally grasped, for both pointing gesture and target are within the visual field of the infant (Butterworth and Jarrett 1991). On the other hand, by providing a linguistic label, that is, a linguistic (acoustic) form 'dog' in the presence of an iconic representation or picture of a dog, the infant is able more easily to fuse word form and referent – the signifier, and the signified – within a single sign, or word (Saussure 1916 [1972:99]).

The process via which infants eventually come to acquire the signs or words is said to arise directly out of infant smiling, pointing gestures, and vocalisations, interpreted by the adult as a request for a lexical form, which infants then go on to take over and produce for themselves. Theoretically the argument runs as follows:

- Active indications on the part of the infant – smiling, reaching out, pointing – are interpreted by the adult as a request to label.
- The infant, as it were, takes the lead, for it is his/her active responses which prompt the adult to label. Infant vocalisations are shaped, and in this way

children are said to learn words from picturebooks (Ninio and Bruner 1978; Snow and Ninio 1986).

However, before the details of adult language use are presented, two points have emerged which have a particular bearing on the argument. The first point to note is the multifunctional nature of adult speech. Speech act theory suggests, perhaps, that utterances have but a single main function. This chapter has clearly shown, however, that utterances often serve more than one purpose. The question: 'Who's coming now?' at the page turn, for instance, acts both to inform the infant of the existence of a picture on the next page, but at the same time sustains a possible loss of concentration at the moment where illustrations disappear from view. Talking in the reading adult often has a regulatory effect, intended, not only to communicate information, but also to influence behaviour.

The second point to mention is, once again, the inherent danger of all linguistic descriptions: descriptive emphasis. The attention placed upon language, and especially that of the adult in shaping attitudes to reading, must not obscure the very important place of non-linguistic features of infant behaviour. Adults begin by starting where the infant is. They exploit aspects of infant behaviour which are not specific to reading (looking, for example), and then seek to develop and encourage their use within a reading situation to foster reading appropriate attributes − much in the way, perhaps, that a general ability to strike a ball might be fostered in the interests of a particular sport. Four additional characteristics upon which these particular adults build especially are: interest, pleasure, anticipation, and a fascination with loss and rediscovery.

1 A greater or lesser degree of interest in different aspects of the environment is correlated with systematic variations in the direction and duration of infant gaze (Langsdorf *et al.* 1983). If Ceri or Rhys looks at a pictorial referent for a relatively longer period of time, their parents interpret this as a sign of enhanced interest in that referent.
2 The affective responses of infants were discussed briefly in the Introduction. In this particular reading situation, spontaneous recognition and enjoyment of some pictorial referents by Rhys and Ceri, expressed by smiling, vocalisation or other active reactions, kicking the legs excitedly, or leaning down towards a picture, for instance, are interpreted by these parents as a manifestation of pleasure.
3 As early as 6 months old, babies develop an ability to predict a future event from a current one. Hearing their mother approach, and her voice in the distance, a baby ceases crying, in anticipation, presumably of the attention they are about to receive (van der Straten 1991). This capacity to anticipate is certainly exploited by both these parents to encourage the infant to look forward to an item which is to come later in the book, but the capacity itself is, of course, not necessarily contingent upon language.

4 From around 6 to 8 months, all babies play games involving losing something and finding it again. Peekaboo, the game where an adult hides their face and then suddenly reappears, is an activity known to engage all children, and of which hide-and-seek and hunt-the-thimble are more sophisticated variations (Bruner 1983:47). As will be observed, versions of the same game also occur in reading.

The point I wish to make from these observations is that adults are sometimes described as 'taking the lead' in picturebook sessions; they 'assume responsibility' for the interaction. Indeed, it might well appear from the key examples furnished in section 1 that, since only the adult speaks, it is he, or she, who chooses what to talk about, when, and for how long. However, linguistic activity is mutually determined by both adult and infant; the utterances of adult speech are tacitly guided by the reactions of the infant reader. Part of this guidance takes the form of interest, enjoyment, anticipation, and a fascination with loss and rediscovery. The child acts as an invisible speaker, animating and breathing life into adult linguistic descriptions. The children convey by their actions, looking, smiling and so on, what engages them most, and the adults respond.

4.2 Labelling in practice

With these preliminary remarks in mind, let us turn to the adults' linguistic descriptions as they occur in practice. Any picturebook contains all kinds of items; the farmyard book, for instance, contains a plethora of detail, both inanimate: buildings, tractors, rabbit hutches, as well as animate: the farmer's wife, rabbits, cows, goats, dogs, geese. Neither parent describes all these features. So let us examine how these parents are guided by their infant as to what is discussed, and consider which topics are effectively talked about, and what it is that is (apparently) being achieved.

4.2.1 Infant predisposition

According to this argument, the linguistic presentations of these parents are inspired, in part, by the infant reader. But how exactly does adult behaviour become affected by the individual infant reader? Consider first the place of infant interest and affect, and, second, the role of loss and the anticipation of rediscovery, as active determinants of adult lexical choice.

Interest and affect

In both infants, interest, or for that matter, extreme pleasure, as opposed to disinterest in, or lack of enjoyment of, picturebook items is signalled by contrasting behaviours. What form those behaviours effectively take is, however, an individual matter. With Ceri, vocalisation, and smiling signal interest, whereas simply looking, briefly and without enthusiasm, are taken by the adult as an indication that referents are less than preoccupying. For Rhys, smiling, laughter and, sometimes, sustained looking are signs of especial interest; they generally contrast with movement (turning the pages over), restlessness, and looking away. In other words, Ceri expresses herself positively by smiling and vocalising (contrasted with silence), while with Rhys, enthusiasm and attentiveness are contrasted with restless movement. But whatever means an infant chooses to express their interest and delight (or lack of it), the effect of infant emotions on the interaction cannot be underestimated. Perception (in the infant), repetition (in the adult), and communication (between adult and infant) are very largely a consequence of a reaction of interest and/or pleasure in the infant.

Affect orients infant perception. Manifest joy and pleasure on the part of the child at the sight of a particular pictorial referent confer upon that image a special degree of salience. Consider this description of a farmyard scene from *The Happy Bunny*. In the picture, various animals (e.g. a pig, a donkey and a cow) are stabled, a rabbit devours a turnip, cockerels and ducks cross the farmyard, children are to be seen running. But Ceri's attention is captured particularly by the cat. The 'cat' is of greater emotional significance to her than almost anything else in this scene, and this the adult notices.

Mother	**Ceri (9 months)**
(*Moving finger around page*)	
Donkey, yes! Donkey	
And pussy!	
	Vocalises enthusiastically.
	[e: e]
Yes, she running away Kezwez.	
	[e]
	Reaches out to touch book.
Yes, pussy running away, pussy is.	
There! (*turns page*)	

Affect is an incentive to the adult to communicate. As may be seen from the above example, and in the following one, what the infant appears to be interested in, the adult will talk about.

Father	**Ceri (8 months)**
Teddy bear!	
Is that Kezwez's teddy bear?	
	[e]
Lovely teddy bear! Teddy bear	

Over time, descriptions of images in which these infants appear interested lengthen. The adult may reiterate the noun and its accompanying description, or introduce further information, and hence also use other verbs and prepositions.

Affect as the basis of a shared bond. Picturebook reading not only causes pleasure within the infant; it also gives rise to affects shared by adult and infant. Often an expression of pleasure in the infant will be matched by the adult with an expression of their own joy. Again the adult is drawn into reiterating the appropriate label, but the phonological component of parental utterances is adjusted in addition. Using a very wide range of pitch, falling from high to low, mother repeats the label. Only favourite items generate such extremes of pitch range in the adult: 'Teddy! There's teddy.' How wonderful! mother implies, with a kind of excitement that would greet a long lost friend who had returned unexpectedly after years of absence.

Thus do the emotions bind an infant with his/her parent. But emotions also surround a particular image or word form. Joy and pleasure are the emotions most frequently contained in these parents' tone of voice, but they are not the only ones. A variety of affects may be conveyed, ranging from appropriately low and gentle tones to suggest care and concern when a referent appears vulnerable, as when this father describes to Ceri a picture of a baby asleep, to a certain sharpness or mock wariness in the presence of more dangerous creatures. Drawing his breath in sharply, Daddy says: 'Oooh! bee!' as much as to say 'Watch out!' in the presence of a referent which is potentially threatening. Parents evoke a mood or atmosphere for an image; they too may behave as if images are 'real'. This aspect of early reading is further discussed in Chapters 4, 5 and 8.

Affect leads participants to repeat an experience. Adult and infant enjoy their reading. If they have experienced pleasure in contemplating a particular picture, they endeavour to re-experience that pleasure. They actively seek out further, identical, sources of pleasure, albeit at the expense of looking at other items. Parent and infant together return to that preferred item, if it recurs on a different page in the same book, or even in a different book. From the infant's standpoint, the referent has been lost from sight and then rediscovered. Ceri and Rhys delight in returning to the same referent over and over again.

A fascination with loss and rediscovery

With very young infants, then, the emotions play a significant role in orienting both perception and presentation of picturebook material. Consider now in slightly more detail the infant's fascination with loss and rediscovery, and the use which the parents make of this preoccupation for book reading purposes. As already described, the infant's ability to anticipate the arrival of a referent is purposefully exploited by both adults. Having discussed a (favourite) item, they engineer its disappearance by shutting the book and asking Rhys or Ceri to open the pages and rediscover for themselves the same missing referent.

There are many variations on the loss and recovery theme to be observed in early reading. This father covers up the picture of the rabbit with his thumb and then asks Rhys to 'find' him. Adult and child enjoy the joke as bunny is unearthed from its hiding place; both burst out laughing. Another variation is the use of books which have flaps to lift up; they rely on exactly the principle of uncovering a concealed referent and then hiding it again. These aspects of reading encourage practice in responding to 'Where's teddy?', or 'Where's teddy gone?'

But there is a further version of this game which is peculiarly appropriate for reading. Some books are constructed so that a given referent (a tiny duck or a mouse) recurs from one page to the next. In Rhys' session, for example, the infant can be observed to be gazing intently at the cat. The adult interprets: 'Who can we see here? Miaou, miaou, pussy cat! Pussy cat miaou.' The description ends affectionately: 'Aaah, pussy cat!' Rhys then turns to another page of the book on which the cat again appears, and the adult singles it out for particular attention: 'Where's pussy cat gone? Find pussy cat. Here he is. Pussy cat!', while Rhys looks on. From Rhys' and Ceri's point of view, as the page is turned, the referent disappears from sight, only to reappear on a subsequent page. Labelled on its first occurence, it is relabelled on its return. This phenomenon I shall refer to as the phenomenon of cyclical return. It remains a permanent feature of reading with these two children right up until 2 years old, and is of singular importance in these dialogues in both picturebook work and storytelling.

To summarise, the referents chosen by the adult when reading are, to a significant extent, a function of the infant reader's age and predisposition. Let us now turn to a second issue. What is it that parents and infants talk about together?

4.2.2 The lexical content of adult speech

Nouns, in frequency terms, are a dominant word class in adult speech, whether by token or by type (see Appendix). They are also a useful indicator of the topics chosen for discussion. The use of nouns thus provides key insights as to how these adults approach the early stages of picturebook description.

Frequency and distribution of nouns

The pattern of noun usage in adult speech exhibits the same tendency in each parent, namely that they are drawn to talk repeatedly about a very small number of items, while other referents receive but scant mention. Table 1.2 gives the detail of the distribution of nouns within adult speech at the 9-month session, for Rhys and Ceri respectively.

Table 1.2 The nouns of adult speech at child age 9 months

	Rhys' session with father				Ceri's session with mother			
	Different nouns		Mentions		Different nouns		Mentions	
	N	%	N	%	N	%	N	%
Group 1 Six or more mentions per noun (e.g. teddy, pussy cat, moocow, page)	7	21	78	63	14	23	189	65
Group 2 Between two and five mentions per noun (e.g. tortoise, butterfly)	14	42	34	27	27	43	83	28
Group 3 One mention only (e.g. cot, mirror, pocket, wheel)	12	36	12	10	21	34	21	7
Total	33	(100)	124	100	62	100	293	100

The disparity in the distribution of nouns in adult speech is striking. From Table 1.2 it may be seen that, of the total linguistically available in adult speech, there is a first group (totalling just over 20 per cent of the different substantives employed overall) which receives a minimum of six mentions each throughout the session. In stark contrast to this frequently recurring, but numerically small, group of nouns, there is, for each child, a (numerically) larger group of nouns (some 35 per cent of the different nouns occurring in adult speech) which receive but a single mention throughout the session. Indeed, it may be seen that this latter group, in terms of the whole, scarcely features at all (10 per cent and 7 per cent of total mentions in adult speech for Rhys and Ceri respectively). The energies of both parents are apparently devoted to describing and redescribing a proportionately small set of nouns (which by itself accounts for almost two-thirds of the noun mentions in adult speech), while referring more briefly, sometimes just once only, to the remainder.

In other words, there is a tension between cyclical return – a desire to seek out and return to the same referent, and variety, born of the necessity to introduce new referents as interest in the familiar ones wanes. The nouns which these parents cite most often are: (for Rhys) 'teddy', 'baba', 'ickly prickly' (hedgehog), 'pussy cat', and 'moo cow'; (for Ceri) 'teddy', 'pussy cat', 'bunny', 'moo cow' and 'birdy'. (Two other nouns, 'page' and 'book', also appear with a high degree of frequency but for reasons of teaching appropriate terminology.)

The phenomenon of cyclical return

If we examine those items to which these parents return within the same book (as opposed to those they mention most), it may be observed that such items are, most significantly, those for which the infant shows a special preference, irrespective of whether the items are, from the adult viewpoint, mere details within a picture. For example, in Rhys' 9-month session, based in part on the book *The Happy Bunny*, the rabbit, the hero of the book as written, appears on each one of eight pages, but he receives a mention on just one of his eight separate appearances. The 'hedgehog', the 'cow' and the 'dog', on the other hand, are returned to several times in adult speech. The prominence given to those aspects of the book to which Rhys and Ceri are spontaneously drawn is an indication of these parents' concern to pay attention, for the moment, to whatever the infant (not the parent, nor even the book's author, or illustrator) identifies as salient. They apparently wish to ensure that reading reflects, above all, the preoccupations of their infant reader.

But at the same time, these adults have perhaps a second, covert, intention: in drawing attention to the same or similar item on different pages, they underline by means of language that characteristic which is so fundamental to storytelling, namely, that referents return in similar if not identical form from one page to the next. In a transformed version this may easily constitute the basis of the notion of a hero, who links together a whole sequence of pages. In fostering this literary response, these adults exploit not just any recurring item but a young reader's 'favourite'.

The recourse to recurring items is also important for language development. Not only are parents afforded a fresh opportunity to associate a word form with a referent – to teach for a second time what a caterpillar looks like for example. It must also be noted that the pictorial representations of some animals, the cow for example, differ. The cow on page one of the 'bunny book' is brown; that on page four is black and white. Both however are tokens of a general 'cow' type. The word form 'cow' thus designates not just a particular cow in a particular instance, but also the whole category or class 'cow'. In semantic parlance, the exercise is one of both reference, and denotation. It is a universal characteristic of language which all infants must grasp (Lyons 1977:206).

Adopting a multifunctional view of language behaviour, there is some justification, perhaps, for advancing the view that the formal features of lexical usage in adult speech in the early sessions may be explained by two factors. On the one hand there is the infant's existing predisposition, and on the other, the adult's awareness of the infant's impending need to listen to, and understand stories, and to accede to language. The adult builds towards the latter on the foundations provided by the former. There is a degree of synchrony between these children's (current) spontaneous interests, and these adults' sense of their child's (future) needs.

Known versus unknown nouns

How do the oft-repeated nouns relate to these infants' pre-existing linguistic knowledge? Could it be for instance that nouns repeatedly labelled are those which the infant does not know? Again, the converse is true. If the nouns which occur in adult speech are compared with each infant's existing linguistic knowledge, of the top three most favoured nouns (those receiving the highest number of mentions in each session) two, 'teddy' and 'baba' (for Rhys), 'teddy' and 'cat' (for Ceri), are familiar from everyday life. But, in contrast to the observations of some scholars, the findings of this study are that not all the items presented are familiar. The everyday items, those which are known and can be recognised from first-hand experience, account for two-thirds of the different noun types presented to each child, while those which are introduced exclusively through the book (here, 'hamster', 'goldfish', 'turnip') account for one-third of the different nouns. This balance obtains in the speech of each parent at child age 9 months.

Animate versus inanimate

Also to be noted is the tendency to focus on living things, in preference to lifeless objects. A clear majority of adult mentions of nouns refers to animate nouns, either human ('baba', the 'Mummy') or animal ('bunny', 'cat', 'ickly prickly'), while inanimate nouns ('mirror', 'drawers', 'cot') in the case of both children, are in the minority, totalling just one-third of noun mentions in adult speech, in each of these two parents. One can only speculate as to why adult and child are drawn to describing animate nouns in preference to inanimate ones. Possibly it has to do with the fact that these infants are not as yet differentiated with regard to 'object' choice (which in turn possibly has to do with gender identity (see Chapter 8)). But maybe too it has to do with preparing for the introduction of humans and animals as characters in stories. In support of this latter argument we note the existence of a certain degree of anthropomorphism of non-human animate nouns when verbs are used. The lexical content of the verbs which describe animals effectively equates them with humans: 'What does doggy say?' or 'There's bunny, running away!', the beginning, perhaps, of a narrative process in which animals frequently feature as the equivalent of humans in the role of protagonist.

What these findings indicate, however, is the systematicity and similarity of behaviour in both these children at a very young age with regard to object choice. By object choice I refer to the tendency to discuss animate nouns in preference to inanimate ones, and familiar ones in preference to unfamiliar ones. For the time being at least, reading patterns, for these criteria, are similar in both children; more individual patterns of response which are later to differentiate them on precisely these measures have not yet emerged.

Utterances typology

The use of noun phrases is, of itself, an extensive and preoccupying activity in the early sessions. The word forms employed, however, are often not those found in the lexicon: alliterations, diminutives and other idiosyncratic inventions are used: 'buzzy bee', 'ickly prickly' (hedgehog), 'sammy snail', 'mickey mouse', 'dicky birds', 'Mr foxey', 'gooseygander' are all non-standard forms used within a particular parent–infant dyad.

Much of the time the use of a single noun is sufficient; no further description is offered. 'Where's doggie? There's doggie!' are typical of adult utterances in the early sessions. Sometimes, however, substantives are expanded, and adults go on to offer a more extended description. Adjectives are relatively little used for this purpose; at the first sessions, phrases of the type: 'Naughty bunny' are exceptional. Instead, descriptions take the form of a noun and prepositional phrase: 'Doggy in the water'; 'baba in cot'. Or alternatively the noun becomes the subject of a main verb, or verblike construction: 'There's bunny, running away'; 'baba crying'; 'baba sleepies'. However, as stated earlier, the use of verbs to describe the activities of the characters in the book (e.g. 'baba crying') is far less frequent than is the use of verbs to describe what Rhys and Ceri themselves do with their book (e.g. 'Rhysie find teddy!').

What is of interest, however, is that already parental descriptions, although formally incomplete, have a structure resembling a sentence; they are, in fact, proto-sentences: 'Baba crying' or 'baba in cot'. Second, from the point of view of their content, descriptions most frequently indicate either action (what baby does), or location (where baby is). (Onomatopoiec references are considered separately below.) Why, on the occasions when adults do go on to describe referents in more detail, should they concentrate on specifying what baby does or where s/he is? There are after all many other aspects of baby which could be described, what baby wears, for example. One can again but speculate as to reasons, but it may well be that action and location are essential facets of narrative (see Chapter 6).

Further aspects of linguistic description

Two further aspects of linguistic description are to be developed extensively in the coming months. The first is onomatopoeia: the association of a word form (bee) with a specific attribute: its particular sound (bzz). Why onomatopoeia should be so widely used in adult–infant interaction (but perhaps especially in reading) has been noted frequently by researchers and will be discussed more fully in Chapters 3 and 4; suffice to observe that it is, in these dialogues, one of the earliest forms of expansion ever to be introduced. Second, and again in common with other authors, the phenomenon of bridging is to be observed. Already in these early sessions the contents of the book and the baby's own life experiences are explicitly linked: 'Baba put socks on – like Rhysie'; 'All drawers

– like Mummy's' (a reference to the chest-of-drawers in these parents' bedroom). The purpose of such connections is discussed later, in Chapter 4, with reference to picturebook reading, and in Chapter 5, with reference to infant responses to stories.

4.3 The purpose of 'labelling'

That labelling of referents in picturebooks occurs with very young infants is indisputable. But, from a developmental perspective, what is it that is being achieved?

For the time being, and for many months to come, the sighted infant is invited to associate spoken word form and iconic referent in the presence of that referent. Eventually of course Rhys and Ceri will leave pictures behind and grasp meaning by relying solely on word forms alone. But here each is required, in a reading situation, to focus jointly with an adult, on an iconic referent, and to associate it with its corresponding word form, or vice versa. To this extent picturebook reading may in part be concerned with the acquisition of word meaning through a process of ostensive monstration.

However, the emphasis on using well-known words and highly favoured items raises the possibility that what these parents are in fact seeking is not so much the acquisition of a word form (i.e. that Rhys and Ceri learn language as such) for, as has been shown, they already know the two words used most frequently: 'teddy' and 'cat'. Possibly, these parents' interest lies in fostering and reflecting their infant's pleasure in books. The language of early reading is, perhaps, much more concerned with promoting interest and enjoyment than with the teaching of lexical forms.

Interest and pleasure in what is being discussed leads directly to that indispensable facet of infant development as it relates to book reading: prolonged acts of sustained visual attention, during which time the infant looks at a referent, and listens to what a parent has to say about it. One of the prime ways of sustaining attention is, it seems, for adults to speak. They speak, not about just any picture which comes into view, but about those which Rhys and Ceri manifestly enjoy. And if Rhys and Ceri are observed to be looking (i.e. staring) at an image, these adults go on speaking about it, seeking thereby to prolong infant looking time as much as they can. This suggests that a main purpose of all this description is not so much to teach the word form for a referent, but to encourage the infant first to locate, and then look at, a referent, and to do so for as long as possible. Sustained acts of visual and auditory attention in the infant are at the heart of all early reading activity, but such skills are not innate. They are achieved, and they are achieved via a judiciously managed process of adult intervention.

5 DISCUSSION: READING GETS UNDER WAY

I return now to the issue with which this book began. What is it that changes if an adult reads with, or alongside, a very young infant, as opposed to the latter looking at a book for themselves? Or, how do these adults use language when reading?

5.1 Linguistic and literary foundations of reading

A main argument of this chapter has been that sustained visual attention, listening, turntaking, and even interest and enjoyment, so often considered as a starting-point in reading, are in fact, an endpoint, the outcome of a process. These are fostered by the adult through carefully orchestrated intervention in which coercion, it seems, plays little part. Adopting a longer term view, adult descriptions, at a very early stage, have both a linguistic and a literary purpose. The direct association of word form and referent is an inherent part of picturebook reading. But at the same time, the return to the self-same recurring, and usually animate, item, the emphasis on what protagonists say or do, or on location, or on mood: these are all features which are relevant to narrative. Rhys and Ceri are far, as yet, from hearing stories, but the rudiments of narrative structure are perhaps already being put into place.

5.2 Reading specific behaviours in the infant

In the first year of life, infants get to know (real-world) people by interacting with them, and (real-world) objects, by banging, manipulating, shaking, throwing or stacking them. Looking, just looking, at something (i.e. without touching it very much) for the purposes of constructing a dialogue, in which Rhys and Ceri look, not at the adult, but at a referent, and where they allow time for the adult to speak without interruption, before being granted, or taking a turn to speak themselves – this is an unusual, possibly unique form of early exchange which is fostered here. An essential component of early book-based activities, one can only ponder the implications for classroom life, where schoolchildren are sometimes required to listen to extensive commentaries by a mediating adult when contemplating referents which are available only in static, two-dimensional form: maps, diagrams, or written text.

5.3 Affect in relation to achievement

Given these achievements, it is essential to observe, too, the absolutely indispensable place accorded to the emotions. Perhaps one of the most important lessons to be learned from this study of very young infants is that parents and infants together reach out in books for that which affords pleasure and enjoyment. Affect is central in that it orients both perception (what infants observe as salient), communication (what adults and infants talk about), and interpersonal relationships (infant and adult share a pleasurable experience of a most intimate kind).

But it does more than this. New and more challenging tasks are centred around items which are of especial emotional significance to the individual infant. When searching through a book for the first time to 'find' an item, the referent selected is not random; it is one of Rhys' and Ceri's favourites. In seeking to sustain infant attention, topics discussed for longest are the highly cathected ones. The items which form the link from one page to the next, the forerunners perhaps, of a hero or heroine, these, again, are ones these children prefer. When starting to point in response to an adult directive, the pictorial referent selected by the adult for the task is, again, special. These examples are, in my view, ample exemplification of Vygotsky's assertion that intellect and emotions are not to be dissociated. Affective responses in the infant act as a spur to further cognitive development.

But what might be the implications for language acquisition of this association between affect and development? Could it be that the basis of acquisition in reading is not that infants learn the nouns, any noun, which a parent happens to provide, but rather that a parent responds to what their infant reader apparently wants to hear about, and that it is the emotional involvement with what is being discussed which, often, triggers the infant into producing words? Chapter 2 looks more closely at this hypothesis.

5.4 Becoming a reader

An important aspect of the development of each of these children, also to be studied in detail in the next chapter, is the use which each makes of his/her newly acquired dialogic skills. Often these lead to an expression of individuality within the reading setting. However, such differences as eventually emerge are not readily apparent in Rhys and Ceri when they are very young. On the contrary, what is so striking in the early sessions is the marked similarity of behaviour between two different adults, and between two different children, respectively, and this despite the use of different sets of material presented at an interval of one year. These adults' efforts at socialisation, these infants' capacity for dialogue, the content of adult speech, both lexical and syntactic, all these very important facets of the linguistic behaviour of two different adults and two different infants are almost identical in the first sessions analysed in detail here. At a very early age, procedures which develop reading appropriate behaviours appear to be central.

6 CONCLUSION

This chapter has documented how essential aspects of reading: looking, listening, turntaking, or infant interest and enjoyment, are carefully nurtured in the first stages of picturebook activity. Other conventions, more literary in kind, are simultaneously established. The argument has been that the reading setting has its own rules which infants acquire with adult help. In other words, if Rhys or Ceri is to become a recognisably individual reader, each must first become, in some very basic sense, a reader.

2
A SENSE OF SELF
The infant as individual

1 INTRODUCTION: WHAT IS MEANT BY 'SELF'?

Human activity is often analysed as a set of behaviours which are in part universal, and in part culturally dependent. Eating, or grieving, are two examples (Super and Harkness 1982); language is another. With regard to language, structural linguists in particular have emphasised universal features, while others have been concerned with norms of development for a particular cultural group. There has in consequence been a preoccupation with how parents transmit patterns of behaviour to their children, and with how infants assimilate those norms. The weight of the evidence finds that infants indeed become like their parents in some sense: 'Children move from a modest skill level in some domain to full adult competence (i.e. they converge)' (Adams and Bullock 1986:157).

There is, however, a further dimension to human behaviour which I believe it is essential to consider if the processes of reading are to be adequately understood. It is the fact that, in their reading, as in other areas of life, children behave as individuals. Scholars from a range of traditions have drawn attention to the theoretical importance of the individual, even as that individual remains a member of a social group (Emde 1992; Hinde 1992; Mead 1936; Taylor 1989). One of the main tasks of the family group is to confer upon each of its members an identity which is unique (de Singly 1994). The expression of that identity may hinge upon linguistic behaviour: 'In spite of the fact that language acts as a socializing and uniformizing force, it is at the same time the most potent single known factor for the growth of individuality' (Sapir 1933 [1985:17]; and cf. Stern 1985:28).

The thesis of this chapter is that, in the reading situation, itself crucially dependent on language, the behaviour of these infants testifies to the emergence of an individual self, that is, of a personal response to reading. But what is the 'self'? A definition proposed by Rycroft forms a useful starting-point. A first quality is continuity through time. 'This self that one is or has, ... continues throughout life; despite growth, experience and the accumulation of memories, the self remains the same self'. The second attribute is consistency.

Synchronically too, despite those variations in behaviour which inevitably result from changes of situation: at school, on vacation, at work, people somehow remain the 'same' person. A third characteristic is uniqueness; people consider themselves, and others consider them, to be unique, unlike anybody else. Last, the self often resists compliance with externally composed constraints: 'What is at stake is the maintenance of a consistent, continuous, unique pattern of growth in a changing world' (Rycroft 1991b:149 ff.).

This chapter argues that, within the general conversational framework established between parents and infants when reading, children develop and display what to their parents are individual patterns of active behaviour which are systematic, and stable, across time. It is not so much in the nature of the code (for both the infants of this study use gesture and speech) but in its use that children are to be differentiated. When reading as infants, Rhys and Ceri use gesture in different ways; later on, in speech, they speak about certain topics in preference to others. As readers both of illustrated books and ultimately of the printed word, they exhibit a preference for certain types of material as opposed to others. These different facets of development are, moreover, interconnected; as infants exploit gestures, so they behave in speech. They develop, in effect, an individual linguistic profile, a means of 'going on being' which renders them unique in the eyes of their parents. The levels at which these differences appear in reading, and the processes which lead to the establishment of a personal reading style are among the main issues to be considered in this chapter.

This chapter begins, and ends, then, with what in linguistic terms are universal phenomena, the ability to point, and the ability to speak. Individual behaviour, however, implies the existence of cultural norms; an individual can only be an individual with respect to a social process. Outlined first, therefore, is the general structure of adult–infant reading dialogues from the age of 13 months which forms the backdrop to the analysis of these infants' capacity for self-expression using non-verbal means. The final section maps out the route which each child reader takes on the long road to the development of speech. The aim is to highlight the extent to which the reading experience is shaped, and profoundly so, by the individualised responses of a young reader.

2 THE CONSTRUCTION OF DIALOGUE: THE INFANT'S ROLE

The first weeks of reading activity were concerned with the development of reading appropriate behaviours. A proto-dialogue was constructed in which the infant took up an interactional position using gaze, or, occasionally, vocalisation and smiling (Chapter 1). Over a period of months, however, these infants gradually take a more explicitly active part in the exchange, first through the use of pointing gestures, and/or vocalisations, and, ultimately, through speech. The following is an uncomplicated extract of dialogue from a session early in the second year, by way of a simple illustration.

Father
Where's Mr Owl?

There he is!

Rhys (14 months)

Points to the picture of the owl.

Thus, between the ages of 9 and 14 months, the infants of this study, in common with others, have developed the ability to point and with it an enhanced capacity to communicate. The period spanning 12 to 18 months of age is known to be the age at which pointing gestures are most used by children (Cox 1986:19), while book reading has been identified as the setting in which infants point frequently, in comparison with other situations (Murphy 1978), and mother as the interlocutor with whom they point most characteristically (Blurton-Jones and Leach 1972). Pointing in a reading situation is cited by the UK Government Health Department as a criterion of 'normal' development in young children (Sheridan 1960). Thus, on grounds of both child age and speech setting, infant pointing gestures can be considered as typifying reading dialogues in much of the second year of life.

The two infants in this study are no exception. Active involvement in the dialogue, and extensive use of the pointing gesture are both features. At the 14- and 18-month sessions, for example, child contributions, in the form of gesture, vocalisations or speech, number 466, with child contributions at each session totalling not less than 100. At each session also, pointing gestures are present in at least 50 per cent of their contributions; they are used either alone, or in combination with vocalisations, or speech. Pointing is thus both an indication of the 'normality' of these infants, while its high incidence of occurrence in the reading situation offers the opportunity to study its functional role, both synchronically, in the construction of dialogue at any given session, and diachronically, as each child moves from the use of pointing gestures to the acquisition of speech.

2.1 Theoretical importance of pointing

In the child's progression from the earliest forms of communication (crying or smiling, for example) towards the ultimate goal, the ability to produce words, pointing represents a milestone in linguistic development. Consider some of the linguistic features of pointing, which, in non-reading situations, make it such an important step for a young infant.

First, while crying is an expression of a baby's physical or emotional state (hunger, thirst, anxiety), pointing directs attention away from the self, outwards, towards people, or objects in the environment. Seated at the table, an infant points spontaneously, for example, to a bowl containing lumps of sugar.

Pointing is interactionally directed. Unlike crying, which occurs in both the presence and the absence of an interlocutor, pointing, in association with gaze orientation and vocalisation, almost invariably engages the attention of an interlocutor present in the speech situation. The infant points to the sugar lump in order that mother might notice.

Compared with gaze, pointing is relatively specific with regard to topic; it ensures that the attention of both participants within the interaction is accurately and jointly focused. For instance, mother and infant both look at the sugar lump (and not the cup and saucer).

Pointing has illocutionary force – the gesture has meaning in context. In identifying the sugar lump using a pointing gesture, the baby is not, in this particular case, seeking to have the referent labelled: 'That is a sugar lump' but is effectively asking for it: 'I would like that sugar lump.'

Pointing has perlocutionary force – something happens in the hearer as a result of an infant's pointing gesture. The mother passes the sugar lump as the baby had asked, or she might resist or decline, or offer an apple instead.

Within the reading situation, the ability to point enhances immeasurably the interactional status of the infant. Because of the close proximity of the pictures, infants can communicate clearly, forcefully and unambiguously. They are able to indicate, usually quite specifically, what they see on the page by pointing to a particular image. Pointing gestures, furthermore, are not so easily ignored (Clark 1978). Where an adult might pass over, misinterpret, or possibly not even notice an act of looking in the infant, it is almost impossible for an attentive adult not to observe a pointing gesture. While a parent might well hand over the sugar lump but say nothing, when reading a verbal, lexicalised interpretation is almost invariably forthcoming (see Appendix) which again in contrast to many situations is immediate, not deferred (cf. Golinkoff 1986). Pointing gestures have manifest illocutionary and perlocutionary force (Austin 1962).

2.2 General uses of non-verbal behaviour by the infant

Infant contributions to the exchanges described here fall into two broad interactional categories. 'Responses', by Rhys and by Ceri, to questions or directives put to them by the adult are one category. Spontaneous contributions, or 'initiatives', those infant contributions which are not immediately preceded by a parental directive to participate, are the second. In the two age sessions discussed in detail in this chapter, initiatives never fall below 32 per cent of total child contributions (Rhys, 14 months); they may even reach 70 per cent of active child contributions (Ceri, 18 months). Active infant contributions of both categories are almost invariably heeded by the adult reader, with the vast majority of explicit feedback moves on the part of that adult being positive.

Within this general interactional framework, the pointing gesture has a variety of applications, equivalent in some sense to discrete discourse moves. Consider first some of the ways in which spontaneous non-verbal behaviours, on the part of Rhys and Ceri, affect the course of the dialogue.

Parents often respond to infant pointing gestures by naming the referent designated, and/or by extending discussion of it. In other words, when used spontaneously by Rhys or Ceri, such a gesture may cause the parent to talk about just those aspects of the illustration which they themselves would like to hear discussed. In the following example, the use of a quick and rapid gesture allows Ceri to introduce into the dialogue topics of her own choosing. The topics selected (here, 'cat' and 'teddy') may be unrelated to the one being discussed by the previous (adult) speaker, in which case pointing has the effect of bringing about a change of topic.

Mother	Ceri (14 months)
(*Adult is identifying the main (human) protagonists in the story*)	
Oh Wezzy, who comes in?	
	Points to book character.
There's Roy, good girl.	
	Points to cat.
	[pussy]
There's pussy.	
	Points to teddy.
And teddy, yes, good girly	
(*continues the storyline*)	
And there's Renee, standing at the door.	

Occasionally, pointing gestures fulfil the reverse function, and serve as an unsolicited act of confirmation that the infant participant is in fact engaged by the same topic as that being discussed by the adult. An infant cannot say: 'I'm listening carefully and following exactly what you're saying', but she can gesture to this effect, as in the following example:

Mother	Ceri (14 months)
(*Turning to new page*)	
Now then, who's here?	
There's Wendy!	
	Points (spontaneously) to Wendy.

In the above two instances, pointing gestures are indicative of the focus of cognitive attention between adult and child; Ceri's attention is concentrated upon a different, or upon the same, referent as that of the adult. But pointing gestures allow these infants to communicate not just their perception of a page, but along with it their degree of interest in one aspect or another of that page. In the next example, Rhys' gestures, associated with a series of high-pitched vocalisations, signal a pressing preoccupation. Seemingly unable to contain his excitement, Rhys insists that his topic be taken up. Effectively he is trying to say: 'What I really want to hear about is . . .'

Father	**Rhys (14 months)**
(*Picture of farmyard scene*)	
	Points to book.
	[eu, eu]
What you see? Which animal are you pointing to?	
	Points to book.
	[eu]
The bunny, or the foxey?	
	Points to book.
	[eu]
There are the foxies, yes, the foxies!	

Especial interest may also be signalled by reintroducing an item already discussed, when that referent recurs in similar or identical form on another page or pages, in the same or a different book. The phenomenon of cyclical return to a preferred referent (effected at 9 months through gaze, or leaning towards the book, vocalisation, or a combination of these) can now be enacted through pointing (with or without vocalisation). Such items come to be clearly established as a child's favourite topics.

Spontaneous pointing gestures in Rhys and Ceri do not, however, serve merely to alter the topic under discussion, or to indicate their degree of enthusiasm for a picture. They are also a means via which infants may, directly or indirectly, extend the discussion of a topic already in hand. The length of the adult description in the following reference to 'Alex' may be contrasted with the brevity of the description following the equally spontaneous infant pointing gestures which introduced 'cat' and 'teddy' in the example quoted earlier:

Mother	**Ceri (14 months)**
	Ceri points to Alex (hero of story).
And look, there's Alex, hiding behind the door!	
	Keeps finger on Alex.
He's cross isn't he!	
	Still keeps finger on Alex.
He doesn't want to come and play with Roy! No!	

A gesture's duration cues the adult as to how long he or she should speak for, and about which topic. Succinct finger movements generally elicit short responses on the part of the adult, while more prolonged contact between index finger and image acts as a request to the adult to develop the theme. Ceri is not able to say with words 'I want you to tell me more about Alex', but the effect of her gesture is the same. What is important is that the adult begins to note which topics meet with requests for more extensive discussion, in other words, which aspects of an adult's presentation are most likely to engage an infant's attention.

By pointing spontaneously to their book, then, Rhys and Ceri may initiate, reintroduce, extend, or instigate changes in the topic of discussion. Their active control over the dynamics of the exchange is therefore considerable. These parents, in turn, can both ascertain unambiguously what Rhys and Ceri perceive in their book, and gauge clearly how interested s/he is in a variety of different topics. These responses are registered, perhaps unconsciously, by these adults, for they are reflected increasingly in the discussions which will take place in the ensuing months.

Consider now parental questioning techniques. The integration of pointing gestures into an 'adult question–child response–(optional) adult feedback' format whereby infants are asked to identify a particular iconic referent by means of a pointing gesture is well documented in the literature.[1] A 'closed' question: 'Where's the pussy cat?' may be accompanied by a follow-up question, also requiring a specific response: 'What does pussy cat say?' The issue to address is therefore not the existence, but the role and purpose of such questioning techniques.

Two dominant uses for a question–answer structure in which Ceri and Rhys are required to point things out in their book are to be identified. The first concerns the exploitation of infant pointing gestures following immediately upon the presentation of a referent by the adult. The adult points to a picture, naming the referent as they do so, and then straightaway invites the infant to identify that same referent with their finger, using, as an instruction: 'Where's the ...', or 'Show Daddy the ...'. Such a structure was already found at 9 months but at that time the response slot was filled by the infant's gaze and/or by adult speech.

Picturebook presentations particularly include this type of questioning. But why do adults pose questions of this kind, and why is it important that the infant comply with this kind of directive? A Western cultural tendency to encourage active participation when reading may be one factor (Panofsky 1994:225). Activity, rather than passivity, is arguably conducive to learning (Greenfield 1984:28). But the adult reader's need for explicit reassurance that the attention of both participants is, indeed, jointly focused must play some part, especially with infants able, as yet, to speak only very little or not at all.

For, from the age of 14 months, and even before, the pages of the material presented in this study contain, not one, but several referents – up to fifteen or eighteen per page. Such books contrast with those containing a very limited number of items per page; perhaps for this reason the issue of why adults invite infants to answer specific questions has not been fully addressed. With detailed illustrations, gaze of itself cannot confirm to a parent that their infant is in fact looking at the appropriate referent as they speak about it. But if a child does not match word form and referent accurately, and focuses, for instance, on the picture of the bucket (and not the spade) as mother says 'bucket', the naming relationship, or the correspondence between signifier and signified, is misunderstood.

The fact that babies and their mothers tend to look in the same direction is crucial for . . . learning, because it is only when mother and child are attending to the same thing that a mother's comments about the actions and objects involved in their interaction can be interpreted [by the infant].
(Harris and Coltheart 1986:39)

One way of checking that both participants have indeed been attending to the 'same thing' is for the adult to name an item, and then ask the infant straightaway to point to it: 'She [the mother] becomes confident that the child is aware of the naming relation when the child can *point to the named object*, or can *give the appropriate sound when an object is pointed to*' (Clark 1978:257). The acquisition process necessarily involves parents not only speaking to their infant about word form–referent relationships, but also seeking some indication from the infant that he or she has grasped the connection correctly. Pointing, a very public manifestation of infant comprehension, has replaced looking as a key means of monitoring infant understanding of the link between linguistic form and two-dimensional image.

The second use of the question and answer format represents an entirely new development. Adult questioning monitors not merely comprehension, but recall. At home, opening a book at the start of a new day, a parent can pick out items presented at a previous session and find out, by putting questions, whether Rhys or Ceri remembers anything of what they have already heard. In such instances, these adults do not, on that page, or even in that session, point to an item first, and then ask Rhys or Ceri to do the same. Instead, they have to identify it, without being reminded. Although most questions of this type are well within their capacity to remember, occasionally mismatched responses occur:

Father	Rhys (14 months)
Where's the turkey?	
	Points to duck.
(*kindly*) That's not the turkey! Where's the turkey?	

Such routines assume especial importance when monitoring an infant's receptive knowledge of items which have been learned only through picturebooks. An effective means of finding out whether children recollect what a lion, zebra or giraffe looks like is to ask them to point them out in their book. Questions testing the infant's memory in this way not only invite the infant to 'display' to an adult what s/he knows, reading adults may gain important insights into the state of their infant's ongoing linguistic knowledge – how much of their reading they understand and retain. The changing state of each child's linguistic knowledge is an ever-present preoccupation for these adults; their own speech is profoundly affected in turn (see Chapter 3).

To summarise, the emphasis of certain authors upon the extent to which infants are led by the adult when reading has possibly obscured the capacity which a child, using non-verbal means, has for influencing the course of the dialogues in which s/he participates actively. As unambiguous turntakers in the exchange, Rhys and Ceri are now able to exert considerable control over the topics to be discussed, the length of the discussion, and the direction it might take. The capacity to point also allows these infants to respond to questions designed to monitor their attentiveness to pictorial referents. Equally, adults are now able to check infant recall of linguistic terms previously presented.

From a linguistic standpoint, an equitable balance between infants providing information, and responding to adult directives, has been shown by research into adult–child dialogues in non-book situations, to be associated, in Western cultures at least, with enhanced development of speech (Harris and Coltheart 1986:48 ff.). However, adopting a longer term view, active interchange with the adult when sharing books may represent the start of a culturally determined attitude, enshrined in much academic teaching at university level in the UK, whereby readers are expected not so much to commit a written text unquestioningly to memory, but instead actively to interrogate it (cf. Kuhlman 1992).

3 PATTERNS OF BEHAVIOUR DIFFERENTIATED

When analysed in the dynamics of these exchanges, pointing fulfils a variety of communicative functions; the interactional opportunities now opened up are potentially very great. In practice however, Rhys and Ceri do not show the same sensitivity to all these possibilities; they use the options available to them in different ways. Initially, any incipient differences between brother and sister were subsumed by more general considerations about book reading (Chapter 1), but early in the second year the variations between Rhys and Ceri are so marked that it is impossible not to take account of them.

The approaches used in the description of this phenomenon were, first, the adoption of a self-report method, whereby each parent wrote down, without conferring, when Ceri was aged 14 and 18 months, his or her own experience of each child when reading. Second, an analysis was conducted of the relative frequency of occurrence of different uses of pointing by each child respectively.

Both approaches revealed differences at three levels: interactionally, in the question–answer routine; at the level of topic, that is, those pictorial aspects of a scene which each infant perceives to be of especial interest; and in the sequenced contributions, the type of additional information which Rhys or Ceri either contributes, or seeks to obtain, with regard to a selected topic. The variations in active infant participation at these levels and their consequent impact upon adult behaviour are analysed for each subject at age 14 and 18 months via an examination of the totality of each child's contributions at each of these two age sessions.

A SENSE OF SELF

3.1 Individual non-verbal behaviour at age 14 months

Pointing in response to closed questions of the type: 'Show me the ...', or 'Where's the ... ?' falls well within the capacity of both Rhys and Ceri by the age of 14 months. But parental questioning of this kind encounters mixed reactions. Rhys' responses may be characterised as enthusiastic, prompt, accurate and appropriate, while Ceri's are sometimes reluctant, and even, at times, totally at variance with the focus of parental directives.

Evidence to justify this statement concerns, first, the nature of the response which each child gives. Specific questions: 'Where's the moocow?' or 'What does moocow say?' meet with a swift reaction in Rhys. A smooth flowing question–answer routine is established, typified in this next extract:

Father	**Rhys (14 months)**
Who's that!	
	[hum hum] (*his sound for a dog barking*).
Woof woof! Doggie!	
Where's the dicky birds?	
	Points to birds.
	[eu]
There they are!	
What do they say?	
	[high pitched squeal] (*his sound for birdsong*).

Rhys' responses are brisk and to the point, requiring minimal adult encouragement; they are in addition, for the most part, accurate. Ceri, on the other hand, although capable of responding to such questions, does so not only with an apparent very great reluctance, but also (perhaps not without a degree of ingenuity on her part) with a clear ability to direct attention away from aspects of the picture or story of the adult's choosing, towards topics which possibly interest her more. These parents are, in effect, frequently frustrated in their attempts at putting questions to her, as the following extracts demonstrate:

Mother	**Ceri (14 months)**
Where's the bus?	
Show Mummy the bus!	
	Points to the fox.
That's Mr foxey!	

Where's the potatoes?	
	Points to Alex's Mummy.
That's Alex's Mummy!	
Now! Where's the potatoes!	

The mismatch between adult question and child response involves not only a switch at the grammatical level (from the inanimate noun of the question to the animate referent of the response), but also a complete shift of lexical field, to an area quite unconnected with the adult's question. At age 14 months there are no fewer than seven occurrences of this kind, to which may be added a further seven occasions upon which Ceri evades the adult's question, for example by seeking distractions in the extra-linguistic context of situation – something in the room. These mismatched reactions account for fourteen in a total of forty-nine responses in all – 29 per cent. Doubts become raised in the parents' mind as to the value of seeking to involve Ceri in this way, particularly so when 'bus' and 'potatoes' are items whose comprehension can be monitored in everyday life.

The effort required on the part of both parents in order to evoke a response to their question is a further indication of Ceri's lack of enthusiasm for closed questions. The next extract illustrates just how much prompting is sometimes required before she replies:

Mother	Ceri (14 months)
Show Mummy car!	
Where's the car Wezzy?	
Do it, come on!	
Show Mummy car!	
Where's the car?	
	Points to the car.
Good girl! The man going to drive it, isn't he.	

If the question–answer routine is looked upon as a kind of language game, in which parents provide a framework within which infants are invited to participate, there can be no mistaking the fact that this type of game holds little or no interest for Ceri (further examples are provided subsequently). The impact on the adult of these differing responses is very marked; even at 14 months, interactional patterns begin to assume an individual quality. The form and content of parental questions are adapted to suit their particular child's preferences, in an attempt, presumably, to arrive at a type of exchange which runs easily and effortlessly; no one wants a dialogue which is experienced as heavy going.

In Rhys' case, these parents ask specific questions about referents which they themselves freely select; at 14 months, for example, he is asked to identify different animals in series and produce the relevant sound (see Chapter 3). In Ceri's case, the form of adult questioning is adjusted. 'Open' questions, which allow her wider scope for a response: 'What can you see on this page?' replace or supplement closed questions of the type: 'Show me the . . ', for these latter place her under an obligation not merely to contribute, but to do so by identifying an iconic referent of the adult's choosing. Also modified is the content of adult questioning. The density and complexity of the material presented to Ceri offer ample opportunity to question her about all manner of items, from utensils in the kitchen, to toys and furniture in the living room, to items more usually found in the bathroom. That is, not only the illustrated material itself,

A SENSE OF SELF

but the adult's description of it, contains a vast range of referents, any one of which might potentially form the focus of an adult question or spontaneous child intervention. In practice, however, only a small subset of these items generates a spontaneous contribution on Ceri's part. Registering this, perhaps unconsciously, and in a bid to encourage her to respond to questions (as her elder brother had done), this mother endeavours to match the topic area of her questions with the perceived interests of her infant as revealed through spontaneous intervention. Table 2.1 identifies the topics introduced through Ceri's

Table 2.1 Referential content of adult questions and child initiatives, Ceri 14 months

	Adult questions	Child initiatives
Animate		
Human	Roy	Alex**
	Policeman	Granny
	Little boy on slide	Wendy
		Miss Piggy
		Baby
Non-human	Pussy**	Pussy***
	Dog*	
	Moocow	
	Birdies	
	Elephant	
	Lion	
Inanimate		
Soft toys	Teddy**	Teddy***
Toys/	Car (actual)	Car (pedal)*
(mechanical) equipment	Train (toy)	Train (actual)
	Seesaw (equipment in playground)	Seesaw
	Bike (child's tricycle)	Bicycle (adult)
	Aeroplane (actual)	
	Ball*	
	Balloons	
	Buggy (i.e. child's pushchair)	
	Bus (i.e. forty-passenger vehicle)	
	Slide (equipment in playground)	
Food/drink	Juice	Juice
	Bread	
	Potatoes	
Parts of body	Tongue	Hair*
		Head
Personal items	Hat*	Shoes
	Glasses (spectacles)	

* Denotes item returned to on second (*) or subsequent (**) occasion in the same session
Base: All referents which form the focus of closed adult questions and child initiatives (gesture, vocalisation, speech). Four books presented, three stories, one picturebook. Child responses to open adult questions, and mismatched child responses, excluded

own initiative, compared with those to which her attention is directed through adult questioning.

As may be seen, adult questions and infant areas of interest are matched fairly closely. 'Teddy' and 'pussy', for instance, are topics which generate almost as many adult questions as spontaneous child contributions in this single 14-month session. The two topic areas over which there is a degree of discrepancy between the participants are pictures of humans, for which Ceri signals a clear preference, while inanimate referents (aeroplane or bus) occupy her mother's attention. This discrepancy is destined to become the object of further adjustments in the ensuing months.

Turning now to spontaneous uses of gesture by these infants, consider the type of parental comment induced by infant initiatives. As was observed in the example quoted earlier (section 2.2), Ceri's sustained gesture induced a description about a character's emotional state. Adult speech in consequence contains a number of verbs of volition: 'Alex', or 'the little boy' doesn't 'want' to play. But while Ceri is disposed to hearing about feelings and the internal world, Rhys points rapidly and in turn to different images. Apparently content to expand his repertoire of knowledge about real-world entities, he elicits labels from the reading adult.

At 14 months, however, in an entirely new discourse development, Rhys and Ceri both use spontaneous gesture and/or vocalisation to extend the discussion. They participate in a sequence of interrelated turns on a single topic, in which they contribute new (and relevant) information. An expression of each child's individuality, these conversations are, however, different for each.

Rhys' spontaneous associations are essentially of two kinds. Either he specifies an attribute of a referent by reproducing its characteristic sound onomatopoeically. Or, faced with a referent which interests him on the page, he points away from the text, either to himself, or to a place elsewhere in the room, to the adjacent room, or to some unspecified location out of the window. His purpose is to refer to a second and similar item (sometimes out of sight), of which he himself has had first-hand experience. Consider these examples, taken from sessions with his mother and his father respectively:

Mother	Rhys (13 months)	Father	Rhys (14 months)
(*Points to a picture of a girl*) Look! Little girl. Little girl got hat on, hasn't she?		(*Points to picture of ladybird sitting on leaf*) Who's this! Ladybird!	
	Points to his own head.		Points to room to large plastic ladybird.
Yes, you have a hat on sometimes. Hmm. You do!		You've got ladybird over there, in your toy box, yes!	

Comparable examples devolve from adult mentions of 'the mushrooms in the field' and 'carrots' (in the book), both of which prompt him to point to the kitchen, and to what he knows is habitually stored there. It may be observed that conversational sequences are, here, brief; their purpose is apparently to indicate a second token of a type, and then specify its location. Taking the book as a reference point, Rhys seems to say: 'I know where (in real life) another one of these is to be found, which matches this one (almost exactly).' Rhys' associations to pictorial referents are almost exclusively of this kind, and while they do appear in Ceri's exchanges (pointing to herself as if to say: 'I have hair, or a bath-hat too'), they are by no means, for her, the dominant form of topic development.

Ceri's associations, in contrast, develop in linear form an in-depth description of a selected image. Unlike Rhys, whose additions at 14 months rarely extend beyond a total of three adult and child turns, Ceri, at an equivalent age, comes across as a great conversationalist; sequences around a topic are lengthy. The example which follows contains a total seven adult and child turns in all, though sequences of up to nine turns in length may be found, even at age 14 months:

Mother	Ceri (14 months)
Then they go to see Granny.	
	Points to picture of Granny.
There's Granny, yes.	
	Points to shoes.
Granny's shoes, yes.	
And can you see Granny's hat?	
	Points to hat.
Good girly, yes.	
That's right.	

Rhys, here, might well have extended the discussion of Granny by pointing out of the window as if to say: 'I, too, have a Granny, and she lives in London.' What he might have done, that is, is to indicate further members of a particular category type; his sister, in contrast, seeks not to categorise, but rather to develop a sequenced discussion based around a designated topic.

In sum, these two infants 'use' pointing gestures in different ways. Rhys' pattern consists of a quickfire question–answer routine covering a range of (non-human) referents, many of them introduced by the adult, with categorisation as the dominant association. Ceri's dialogues by contrast are oriented increasingly towards topics which she determines; there is a clear indication, too, that human beings and feelings are of especial interest.

3.2 Individual non-verbal behaviour at age 18 months

The evolution in infant behaviour is described by considering in detail what occurs at infant age 18 months. Each child reads two picturebooks each at this age session: *It's Fun Finding Out About People and Places* (Purnell Books, 1980) and *Shapes* (Hamlyn, 1981) for Rhys; *Lucy and Tom's ABC* (Gollancz, 1984) and *My Day* (Ladybird Books, 1983) for Ceri. Different hypotheses are possible with respect to developments in this four-month period. A parent might use the book, for example, to encourage each infant to move in the direction which was least in evidence at 14 months. But in fact what occurs in this family is the converse. The qualitative differences in gesture use alter little; rather they are perpetuated, even intensified. In simple terms, aspects of the routines with which the 14-month-old had appeared comfortable, or had particularly enjoyed are retained, while others, seemingly less successful, come to feature less prominently.

The analysis for this section focuses on those infant contributions which contain gestures, or vocalisations, but excludes, as far as possible, those using words alone. The emphasis placed upon individual patterns of behaviour is not designed simply to distinguish these two children one from the other. The intention is to highlight, in addition, the degree of continuity which obtains in a number of aspects of individual development (despite the significant changes over time at other linguistic levels which are discussed in Chapters 3 to 6).

Rhys' behaviour is described first. The alacrity and relative degree of accuracy with which he points out pictorial referents in response to a specific parental directive encourages the adult in this mode of interaction. But, what is the impact on the dialogue? The effect is most noticeable at the level of breadth of substantival coverage. In terms of number, Rhys himself points out no fewer than fifty-four different referents in a single twenty-two minute session at age 18 months, invariably evoking, from the adult, a naming and/or defining response:

Father	Rhys (18 months)
What else do we see? Helicopter?	
	Points to helicopter.
There. Balloon? Where's the balloon, the hot air balloon?	
	Points to hot air balloon.
That's right. Hot air balloon. It goes up in the sky. You have a balloon don't you, it's the same thing.	

Father
Where's the puffa train?

There's the puffa train.
Where's the glider?

There's the glider. It's a plane with no engine, isn't it.

Rhys (18 months)

Points to train.

Points to glider.

In terms of content, the analysis of the substantives of adult speech in this same session confirms dominant topic areas, or themes, to be as follows: mechanised transport; adult (male) professions; manufacturing and crop production, with their associated locations; geometric forms (see Table 2.2).

To be noted, then, is not merely the range of noun types cited in adult speech, but also their grammatical features. There is a particular emphasis on the selection of inanimate (including abstract) nouns as topics. From amongst these are selected Rhys' recurrent favourites – those items which he chooses to identify not once but several times over in a session. With regard to their content, the Red Indian is a persistent favourite, but so too are mechanised objects. The lorry is an item to which Rhys returns of his own accord on no less than four different occasions in the session, the helicopter, almost as popular, three times, and the crane and cars twice.

What of the sequences in which this child becomes engaged? At one-and-a-half years, identifying by means of a pointing gesture real-life exemplars of a particular book type remains Rhys' favourite form of conversation. Most often, the real-life equivalents are neither present, nor visible in the speech situation. Examples are the totem pole, located a mile from his house, in a playground, to which he refers spontaneously when a totem pole in his book is being discussed, his football (which cannot be seen and which he plays with in the garden), and a crane (actually some two miles away from home on a building site).

Adult questioning begins, in turn, to exploit the propensity of this little boy for locating tokens of a type; he is asked to find, on a given page within his book, a second exemplar of a particular noun:

Father
Church! Where's the church?

Another church?

Post box?

Another post box?

Rhys (18 months)

Points to a church.

Points out a second church.

Points to a post box.

Points to a second post box.

The 'game' of finding a second example of a noun is soon extended to finding not one, but several other examples. The adult counts, as Rhys, unable as yet to

Table 2.2 Principal themes and topics of adult speech, Rhys, 18 months

	Different nouns (N)
Mechanised transport (e.g. rickshaw, rocket, air balloon)	25
Adult (male) occupations (e.g. gaucho, lumberjack, mountie, farmer, soldier, waiter)	23
Manufacturing/crop production (e.g. bananas, rubber, wheat, pineapples, wine)	23
Locations (e.g. factory, hospital, building site, circus, harbour)	16
Animals (e.g. llama, donkey)	11
Sports (e.g. sailing, boxing)	7
Geometric shapes (e.g. triangle, square)	5

Base: 110 of the 235 different substantives in adult speech addressed to Rhys at age 18 months; two picturebooks presented

speak, identifies up to five, and eventually (at age 21 months) up to ten examples of the same referent: 'all the lorries' or 'all the apples', on a single or double page. The naming game becomes, in effect, a counting game. Arithmetical activity of this kind, though included spasmodically in Ceri's sessions, never dominates picturebook presentations for her as it does in some instances for her brother.

Consider now the case of Ceri. The expectations of these parents that their second-born child would enjoy naming games as Rhys had done remain unfulfilled. Yet, mindful, possibly, of how well the question–answer routine had worked for Ceri's elder brother, these adults persist, perhaps mistakenly, in their bid to encourage their infant daughter to point things out. But to little avail. The following extract from Ceri's 16-month session illustrates the near impossibility, when reading, of obliging a small child to engage in a type of interaction which apparently offers so little sense of enjoyment:

Mother	**Ceri (16 months)**
(*Refers to double-page illustration in which two protagonists, pig and cat, are pictured seated together; the page had been read by now over a period of three months. Having mentioned pig and cat by name, the adult continues*)	ɩ

Mother	**Ceri (16 months)**
Can you see them Wez?	
Where are they? (*pause*)	
Where are they in this picture?	
Can you show me? (*pause*)	
Where are they darling?	
	Points to her book.
There they are, good girl.	
Yes.	
Wezzy see them!	

So great is the degree of encouragement required to evoke a response that the pace of the dialogue slows dramatically. Gradually it dawns that this form of direct questioning is just not worth it. Ceri's responses to closed adult questions represent a mere 19 per cent of her total contributions at 18 months, as against 41 per cent for her brother at an equivalent age.

From the point of view of the dialogue, three consequences are to be noted. First, despite persistent adult efforts, Ceri remains true to herself; she resists not only changes of time and circumstance, but also pressure to conform to what her parents wish for her (cf. Rycroft 1991b). Second, the interaction tends to depend on spontaneous contributions; these, rather than answers to specific adult questions, offer the necessary reassurance that Ceri is indeed focusing correctly on the items featured in adult speech. Third, the ineffectiveness of direct questions as a means of checking specific vocabulary knowledge leads to profound modifications with regard to the presentation of unfamiliar lexemes (see section 3.3).

The topics selected for discussion also remain largely unaltered. Animate, especially human, referents generate maximal spontaneous response from Ceri overall. Both reactive initiatives (those spontaneous gestures which confirm to the adult that the infant is following) and isolated spontaneous contributions (where the infant herself singles out items which the adult then discusses) are engendered almost exclusively by illustrations of animate members of the family group (Mummy, Daddy, baby, boy and girl). Inanimate referents indicated in this way total just three isolated examples (kite, moon and the baby's buggy); other inanimate referents which Ceri identifies form a sub-part of descriptions relating to people or animals. Unlike her brother, then, Ceri does not, on the whole, go round the page pointing out items for their own sake, in order to master the labels. Multiple references to the same recurrent favourites, are, in terms of their content, in marked contrast to Rhys; soft toys and pets (teddy, dolly, dog and cat), not hard objects, are the topics which attract her most.

Sequences for Ceri also continue as they appeared at 14 months; they are not one child turn interventions but lengthy conversations on a single topic, involving two, and often more, active child contributions. In terms of topic, again, animate nouns are the aspects of the pictures which generate most interest. Animals certainly feature: the giraffe and his long neck, and the squirrel running in the park are the subjects of separate sequences of between five and nine adult/child turns respectively. But, as at 14 months, it is topics of human interest which are most engaging. No fewer than seven separate sequences, each comprising up to nine adult/child turns, are centred on the 'little boy' or the 'little girl'. In topic terms, the trigger for Ceri's interest is a person; in discourse terms, she is inclined to extend discussions on a single topic, rather than, as her brother, moving speedily from one item to the next in quick succession.

In a further difference with her brother, the emotions, especially distress, play an increasingly significant part. The strategy already employed with success at 14 months, that is, the insistent use of a pointing gesture which obliges the adult interlocutor to talk for longer on a given theme is again exploited. Here, the theme is one of an infant in crisis. The adult reader offers suggestions as to how a character's feelings might be interpreted from the evidence given.

Mother	Ceri (18 months)
	Points to book.
	[Oh look!]
Oh look! Little boy cross, isn't he!	
Doesn't want his supper.	
Hmm, doesn't want his supper Wez.	
	Points again to same image and keeps her finger in place.
That boy's very cross!	
Look, he got red face.	
He's shouting, isn't he!	
'No, don't want my supper!'	
Very cross, Wezzy.	

Physical appearance (how a character looks, or what they are doing), in conjunction with direct speech (what they might say in context) and descriptions of internal states, or underlying causes (how a character is feeling) – all these often contribute to the construction of a picture's interpretation in Ceri's sessions.

In sum, active non-verbal behaviours at age 18 months, whether spontaneous, or in response to questions, differ for Rhys and Ceri at the levels of both topic and discourse (see Table 2.3).

These interactive styles, based on the analysis of active infant contributions, are characteristic of the exchanges within each parent–infant dyad at this age. Lengthier, more speculative, conversational exchanges centred upon human beings and their emotions, contrast with extensive coverage of a range of inanimate referents, which are little discussed. Such contrasts are necessarily associated with differences of organisation within adult speech. To these 'internal' differences of adult linguistic input let us now turn.

3.3 The impact of infant behaviour upon adult speech

At the same time as the behaviour of each infant continues to be both internally consistent, and increasingly divergent with that of the sibling, adult behaviour is significantly affected. It is not simply the infant who has a systematic way of behaving; adults, too, develop recognisable patterns of behaviour, adopted as a function of each individual child. The result for each adult–infant dyad is a particular genre, or characteristic way of working. These individual patterns of adult and child behaviour become mutually reinforcing; in effect, a modus operandi or relatively set and unshifting form of active verbal exploitation of pictures is evolved for Ceri and Rhys respectively.

Adjustments in questioning techniques have already been noted. The influence of individual child behaviour upon adult speech is manifest at three further levels: lexical choice, utterance typology, and material selection. An analysis of the entire lexical and syntactic content of adult speech at the 18 months' session allows aspects of these issues to be addressed in turn.

Lexis

The level at which these parents are most consciously aware of the impact of infant behaviour is lexical choice. Lexical mastery is now of much greater concern than in the first weeks. Is the adult to introduce, and include, a range of terms which are not familiar to the infant from everyday experience? The answer lies in the readiness with which Rhys and Ceri respond to adult questions. Systematic monitoring of Ceri's understanding of the referential content

Table 2.3 Active non-verbal behaviours at child age eighteen months

Rhys	Ceri
Topic	
Contributions directed mainly towards	
Inanimate referents	Animate referents: family group members
Recurrent favourites	
Forms of mechanised transport	Cuddly toys and pets
Discourse	
Interaction	
Responses to closed adult questions comparatively high; enthusiasm	Responses to closed adult questions relatively low; reluctance
Topic sequences	
Maximum of four adult and child turns per topic sequence	Topic sequences of between five and up to nine adult and child turns
Epistemological status of adult descriptions	
Lack of ambiguity: referents perceptible; descriptions objectively verifiable	Some discussions of internal states; some interpretations putative

of new lexemes via direct questioning is, by and large, not an option. A diary entry early in the second year expresses this sentiment clearly:

> Ceri seems to resist/have trouble/doesn't want to answer questions accurately – I ask for 'ball', she points to 'juice'. Too inaccurate/ uninterested to learn 'new' words via the book. I try at least to get her to point out things she knows, or describe to her things she knows, then I know she can follow. The direction is from reality to the book. In this way, there is no need to check comprehension. I know she can understand. But it means I don't involve her so much (i.e. by direct questioning). It doesn't work!

In consequence, the content of adult speech, certainly when picturebook reading, is largely restricted to lexical terms already familiar from everyday life. The substantives contained in adult speech to Ceri at age 18 months, when analysed fully, confirm this general orientation. Table 2.4 lists the main themes (mealtimes, clothing, etc.) and topics (e.g. 'dog', 'cat' and 'teddy') contained in the speech of this mother when reading picturebooks to Ceri at this age. Themes common to the 14- and 18-month sessions are noted by means of an

Table 2.4 Themes and topics of adult speech, Ceri, 18 months

	Noun mentions (N)
Referents familiar from first-hand experience	
Animate	
Human	
*Mummy, Daddy, girl, boy, baby, granny (only)	50
All other humans	17
Non-human	
(e.g. *doggy, *pussy, duck, fox)	48
Inanimate	
*Soft toys (e.g. teddy, dolly)	35
*Children's play activities (e.g. crayons, painting, paintbrushes)	45
*Meals, eating and drinking (e.g. marmalade, cornflakes)	28
*Parts of body (e.g. mouth, head, eyes, arm)	23
*Household (e.g. cupboard, floor, window)	20
*Locations (e.g. supermarket, park, shops)	15
*Baby items (e.g. nappy, cot, buggy)	8
*Clothing (e.g. trousers, hat, shoes)	6
Other 'everyday' inanimate items	17
Referents not familiar from first-hand experience	
Miscellaneous (acrobat, tightrope, palace)	17
Total noun mentions	329

* Denotes theme which also features at 14-month session
Base: All substantives in adult speech addressed to Ceri at age 18 months; two picturebooks presented

asterisk (*). As may be seen, with one or two exceptions, unfamiliar lexical units are rarely the focus of explicit teaching and testing.

Rhys' routines are a complete contrast. The possibility of monitoring his comprehension of lexical terms leads to the introduction of picturebook material which allows for the pointing out and naming of referents. The contents of his picturebooks vary with age: at 14 to 16 months the focus is on animals, both wild and domestic. Between 18 and 27 months there is a veritable explosion of themes presented. The office, the hospital, the factory, people in far-off places (e.g. Africa or America), exotic animals, modes of transport around the world, the building site, car showrooms, geometric shapes – all these are encountered, often for the first time in Rhys' life. At 18 months alone, 235 different nouns, which, when repeated, total altogether nearly 700 noun mentions, are quoted in adult speech in a little over 20 minutes (see Appendix), with much of the vocabulary unfamiliar from everyday experience (see Table 2.2).

What may be concluded from these observations? A main point must be the (potential) depth of lexical knowledge of this non-verbal infant. The emphasis in much published research upon speech production has perhaps obscured just how much children can be capable of absorbing. Reading permits this little boy, as yet a non-speaker, to accumulate, through his picturebook activities, a vast receptive vocabulary.

Utterance typology

The different emphasis in presentations to Rhys and to Ceri also has repercussions at the syntactic level. How is it that syntax and lexis become so intertwined? The answer lies in an implicit 'rule' which seems to characterise almost all these adults' presentations of unfamiliar substantives in the reading setting. When reading, lexical units (nouns) are almost never used in combination within a sentential structure, with its appropriate phonological shape, unless, or until, the adult is reasonably sure that both the word form and its referential content are quite familiar to the child. In simple terms, if an adult reader uses a long utterance, unbroken by pauses, it is almost certain that the listening infant knows the meaning of each of the constituent substantives of that utterance.

Consider two examples. In the first, the unfamiliar referent/lexeme is 'waiter'. The illustration shows two people seated at a table in a restaurant being served by a waiter dressed in black and white. Pointing to the picture of the waiter, this father says: 'There's the waiter', and then goes on: 'He's the man that serves the food.' Three features characterise this presentation. First, in the adult discourse, the new item is isolated within a separate tone group, or utterance, of its own: 'There's the waiter.' Second, through the use of a pointing gesture, the adult draws explicit attention to the picture of the waiter. He slows the pace as he does so, in order to ensure that Rhys has time to locate the image in question from among all the others on the page. The word form 'waiter' is unambiguously associated with its corresponding iconic representation. Third, paraphrase is used to expand on the meaning of 'waiter'. Familiar lexemes ('man', 'serve' and 'food') are combined to form a complete sentence enunciated at normal speed: 'He's the man that serves the food.'

In the second example: 'There's the little boy carrying his candyfloss', this mother interrupts her presentation, points precisely to the picture of the candyfloss, and says: 'See the candyfloss there?' Here she uses the unknown lexeme 'candyfloss' in combination with other words, but then pauses immediately in order to indicate, using a gesture of ostensive monstration, what 'candyfloss' is.

This approach characterises the presentation of a whole range of unfamiliar referents (e.g. llama, astronaut), especially to Rhys. Little known lexical items generally command an utterance of their own, to allow for ostensive monstration, while individual units which are fully comprehensible to the infant interlocutor are combined to form much lengthier sentences. In consequence, picturebook sessions with Rhys, up until 18 months, are often word based: 'Oil rig? Where's the oil rig?', while in Ceri's picturebook sessions, adult speech is, from a syntactic point of view, more extensive and complex: 'He doesn't seem to want his supper, does he?' Thus the state of an infant's lexical knowledge conditions the syntactic choices in the speech of the adult.

The belief that picturebook material invariably teaches new words to young infants is thus not confirmed unreservedly by the findings of this enquiry. It is the infant who, seemingly, has a major say in whether or not the adult exploits this dimension of picturebook reading. In this study, new words connect with a willingness to point when requested to do so. Every effort had been made to encourage Ceri to point referents out in response to a parental directive, but this was not a 'game' which she enjoyed. The consequence is a restriction, in picturebook reading, in the use of unfamiliar lexemes as the focus of disembedded teaching. This leads to the third level of impact upon behaviour: the selection of picturebook materials themselves.

Material selection

Interactional behaviour further influences choice of material. At age 18 months, picturebooks full of detail are chosen for Rhys, who enjoys pointing out and learning words. In addition to *It's Fun Finding Out About People and Places* and *Shapes* (discussed in section 3.2), Rhys' picturebooks up to the age of 27 months include *What We Do* (Galley Press, 1984), which depicts a variety of items and equipment used in work activities: housebuilding or a car show room, and *On Holiday* (Galley Press, 1984), which details possible activities for children out of school hours: beach scene, circus, camping. Conversely, those selected for Ceri depict, most usually, scenes with a strong human element, and drawn from everyday life: getting up, getting dressed, caring for baby, eating and so on. Materials vary in their appeal.

Inevitably, then, interactional behaviour and material selection become intertwined. Let it not be concluded however, that picturebook reading is of little value to Ceri on the grounds that few 'new words' are introduced through this medium. Lexical items as they occur, not in isolation, but in relation one to the other have yet to be considered, for both children (Chapter 3). Furthermore, to consider picturebook reading independently of storybooks is to disregard the reality of how reading activities effectively function in these children's lives. This section is therefore concluded with an analysis of areas of common ground between Ceri and Rhys in matters of material selection.

The following observations, it must be emphasised, are speculative, but I hope interesting nonetheless. Despite many differences, Rhys and Ceri are in two respects similar with regard to the materials read under the age of two years. I have in mind, first, the importance of picturebook work in the first year and a half of life, and the role it has in directing an adult's subsequent choice of narrative fictional material for children too young to choose it for themselves. Second, despite the specific orientation of picturebooks just described, there exists, even so, a balance within reading as a whole, for each child, between different 'worlds': the familiar, and the exotic.

Topic continuity

With the hindsight afforded by this research, and only then, it emerges that the recurrent (favourite) topics identified during the first and second years of picturebook reading might give invaluable guidance when choosing stories to suit each infant as an individual. Consider these examples. Among Ceri's favourite themes in picturebook activities at age 18 months were family group members, teddy, the cat, food and emotional distress. Months later, these re-emerge in combination to form the basis of two stories:

> *Maisie Middleton* (25 months): a little girl and her teddy get up from bed in advance of Mummy and Daddy to prepare for themselves, and other animals, in secret, a feast for their breakfast.
> *Mog and the Baby* (25 months): a disruptive baby's distress at being left with a strange Mummy can only be alleviated by contact with the family's pet cat.

Similarly, among Rhys' areas of interest were: adult male professions (what people can be when they grow up); hard mechanical objects (lorry, helicopter); exotic animals; unfamiliar locations. Fictional narrative up to the age of 27 months includes:

> *Why Can't a Hippotamus be a . . .?*: a humorous exposition of the reasons why a hippo would be unsuitable for a variety of (adult male) professions (e.g. a piano player).
> *The Truck Stuck on the Track*: the story of a lorry whose breakdown on the railway track causes catastrophe when the train arrives.
> *Mr Ginger's Potato*: a gardener's prize potato is airlifted by helicopter to the horticultural show, causing a serious fire in the village on the way.

Bringing the Rains to the African Plains: the story of an African herdsman and his efforts to bring the rains in order that his animals may feed.

These examples indicate that, in terms of topic, links exist between earlier (picturebook) reading, and later (narrative) texts. In both cases, it is not a single topic – 'cat', 'man' or 'steam engine', which, on its own, contributes to the success of the stories. Each topic is effectively merged with a selection from among the range of themes which engage each infant individually. At child age 2 then, it seems that these parents are inspired by earlier experiences of picturebook reading as to the kinds of topics are likely to appeal when reading stories.

A balance between two worlds

In this chapter, reading materials have been considered as a possible resource for the disembedded teaching of vocabulary items. The more exotic contents of Rhys' picturebooks have been contrasted with the more homely scenes presented to Ceri, in almost all of her picturebook work, and some narrative as well. But it is far from the case that these two children are respectively presented only with materials which reflect these differences of setting. When the whole range of materials is considered, a very different picture emerges of the tension between exotic and familiar.

In the reading experience of both Rhys and Ceri, picturebooks and stories complement one another. The often unfamiliar content of Rhys' picturebook work, in which he participates actively, is offset by a choice of settings in narrative which frequently (though by no means exclusively) is domestic in tone. Among his favourite stories to which he listens with a relative degree of passivity are: *Teddy Bears Go Shopping* (for everyday items in a supermarket), *New Boots for Tom*, the story of a little boy with new wellington boots, and *Alfie Gets In First*, a small child returning from a shopping trip with his mother and sister. Unlike his picturebook work, all of these stories contain situations of life which replicate his own: a visit to the supermarket where members of the teddy group split up and search for different items on the shopping list; getting dressed in boots to go into the garden; accidentally locking his mother and sister out of the house and being momentarily separated from them. These are stories in which Rhys might recognise himself, situations of which he has, to an extent, first-hand experience. In some there is an element of drama. Both *Teddy Bears Go Shopping* and *Alfie* for example, depend for their intrigue on a separation from, and an eventual safe reunion with, loved ones, a perhaps not inappropriate topic for a 16- to 20-month-old whose growing autonomy and emerging capacity to separate physically from his parents are increasing almost daily.

Likewise, mutatis mutandi, for Ceri. The cosy and intimate setting of much of the narrative and picturebook work in which she actively participates is contrasted with the settings of stories to which she listens but, relatively speaking, takes little active part. By and large the dominant themes are: (a) imprisonment and escape, often leading to the exploration of (b) unlikely and exotic locations, followed by (c) a safe passage home. Examples are:

Jacko (22 months): a monkey in captivity escapes during an encounter with a pirate ship and is safely reunited on a desert island with his family (themes a,b,c).
A Story (24 months): the African skygod challenges Ananse, the spiderman, to capture three dangerous creatures, and bring them back to his kingdom in order that children might have the gift of storytelling (b,c).
Pig in a Muddle (13 months, 14 months and 16 months): having escaped from her owner, Miss Piggy is involved in a series of scrapes, including a flight in an aeroplane, before landing finally in a wood and founding a family of her own (a,b,c)
The Ballooning Adventures of Paddy Pork (25 months): an adventurous pig in a hot air balloon rescues a fellow pig imprisoned by gorillas on a desert island, only to become involved in a dramatic escape from polar bears, before returning home safely (a,b,c).
Hairy McClary (22 months): out walking with his friends, a small dog is terrified by the experience of meeting a vicious cat, from whom all escape and return to the safety of home (a,b,c).

Without analysing the content of these children's books from a psychoanalytic point of view, it may be noted that each of the subjects in this study, before the age of two, seeks out different but complementary forms of experience from their reading. A need to escape into settings which take them right away from the familiarity of their own lives is apparently balanced in both by a need to find themselves again in more familiar surroundings, which resemble more closely life as they experience it day to day. The critical distinction between them, and what defines them as an individual, hinges upon what it is that each explores actively.

Summary

In the reading setting, a parent tentatively explores how to exploit a book linguistically. Rhys and Ceri clearly signal preferences of their own. Either by entering into or rejecting the options available, each infant, together with their parent, establishes patterns of communication which are self-perpetuating and mutually reinforcing. For each adult–child dyad, patterns remain, in certain fundamental respects, little altered. It would be surprising if, in these circumstances, the nature of the speech actively produced by Rhys and Ceri at the one-word stage bore no relation to such activity. Consider now these and related aspects of Rhys and Ceri's behaviour.

4 FIRST WORDS

Children vary as to the age at which first words are produced (e.g. Bates *et al.* 1994); Ceri and Rhys are no exception. In everyday life, Ceri produces some words recognisable to her parents at age 11 months, much earlier than Rhys, who, at 18 months, has a productive vocabulary of just five words. Not until some seven months following the emergence of first words in non-book situations, in each case, does the majority of infant contributions to a single reading session include words. The reading session at age 18 months for Ceri, and at age 25 months for Rhys, are taken here as exemplars of the one-word stage.

These two sessions form the basis for this discussion of the transition from gesture to speech; the enquiry is based on an analysis of the total speech production of each infant at each respective one-word session. Both situations, it must be noted, contain instances of the use of pointing (see section 3.2); as with adults, this gesture may be used alone, or accompanied by words. Of course, these sessions do not contain the very first child words produced. Earlier reading sessions will have contained mention by each infant of at least some words. But these will either have been very repetitive ('bibis' (baby) for Ceri; 'man' for Rhys), and/or in a minority. The 'first words' of the sessions analysed here are (a) varied in lexical content, (b) appear (singly) in a majority of child contributions for that session, (c) also feature (in some instances, and in both children) in utterances of more than one word.

Consider Rhys first. The three books analysed are a story, read by his mother: *Goldilocks and the Three Bears*, and two picturebooks, read by his father: *What We Do* and *On Holiday*. Table 2.5 provides details of Rhys' active contributions as he participates in the 25-month session. Lexemes which form part of his active repertoire (i.e. those which are produced in speech), are distinguished from referents identified with a pointing gesture. It may be seen that Rhys now uses speech in preference to pointing. Table 2.5 also distinguishes those words learned exclusively from books (e.g. 'parachute', 'pirate') from those which are rehearsed in real-life situations ('telephone', 'light', 'spanner'). Rhys clearly both retains and produces words which he encounters only in his reading.

Three observations are appropriate. First, irrespective of the adult reader and of the material presented, whether picturebook or story, the dominant characteristic of Rhys' speech production is the provision, in context, of a lexical form. He contributes precisely the item required just as, non-verbally, he had been ready to respond appropriately with a pointing gesture to: 'Where's the dog?' That is, objectively, in a context requiring a specific lexeme (or lexemes), Rhys not only produces it, but does so accurately. Compare this extract from *Goldilocks*:

Mother	Rhys (25 months)
First she climbed on the . . .	
	[gate big chair]
chair, and that was too . . .	
	[ard]
hard	
And then she tried the medium-sized chair	
But that was too . . .	
	[oft]
soft (etc.)	

with this non-fictional example of how doughnuts are manufactured:

Father	Rhys (25 months)
(*Illustration of doughnuts being made in a factory*)	
And what's this coming out here?	
	[dough]
Dough, that's right	
And it goes up the . . .	
	[coveyelt]
Conveyor belt. Conveyor belt	
Down through the machine and . . .	
poutscher poutscher . . . stamps out the doughnuts!	

Across time, and across situations, Rhys' capacity to respond appropriately in a closed context remains unchanged. But whereas previously (at age 18 months) lexemes, when unfamiliar, were the focus of a separate utterance, here, each forms part of a lengthy description. Recalling the earlier rule, word forms, once known, are eligible for incorporation into an extended utterance. Even the language of picturebook reading tends increasingly to bear the hallmarks of extended discourse.

The range of topics contained in Rhys' active speech contributions is also of note. Not only is there a broad coverage of different topic areas, as there was in non-verbal behaviour at 18 months, but there remains, still a preponderance of inanimate referents (Table 2.5). The third observation concerns the use of picturebooks as a resource for teaching unfamiliar vocabulary. Words which have been learned exclusively through reading make up a substantial proportion of the different lexeme types produced in speech by this infant in this session. This is testimony to the potential which picturebooks have for extending a linguistic repertoire in cases where the infant himself is predisposed towards absorbing and reproducing objective knowledge in this way. ('Objective' is used here in the sense that his answers may be categorised as true or false. Either the picture is of a screwdriver, or it is not.)

Early speech production by Ceri is in stark contrast. Only rarely did she identify referents upon request so that they might be named; her active speech production in picturebook situations contain few new words learned from her reading. Her interest was in hearing descriptions of people and animals, of motives, feelings and intentions rather than in learning names for things. And it is the case that utterances which at a formal level are composed of just one word, even if they are nouns, function in the dialogue not as a designator of a

Table 2.5 Active child contributions, Rhys, 25 months

Derived exclusively from books			Learned also from other sources	
Medium	*(in speech)*	*(via gesture)*	*(in speech)*	*(via gesture)*
		Two picturebooks		
Nouns				
Animate				
Human	Soldier	Electrician	Man	Doctor
	Pirate	Painter		Little boy
	Teacher	Plumber		on bicycle
	Sawman (i.e. carpenter)			
Non-human	Tiger/lion/giraffe Camel/elephant/seal		Mouse/dog	
Inanimate				
Equipment	Tongs/frier	Rods	Telephone/car	Dustpan
	Clock/rubber	Calculator	Bath (i.e. bathtub)	and brush
	(i.e. eraser)	Helicopter	Hammer/spanner	Crane
	Typewriter		Ladder/cleaner	
	Conveyor belt		Screwdriver/door	
	Forklift truck		Ironing board	
	Pipe (of plumber)		Light/boxes/string	
	Parachute		Pens/(news)paper	
Locations	Factory	Lighthouse	Shop/house	
Food/drink	Dough		Cup coffee/cup tea Sandwich/icecream	
Parts of body			Thumb	
Verbs				
	That's torned (of book page) Stamps out/stirs		Touch it	
Adjectives			Hot	
Other	Arf arf (seal sound) Pssh (stirring sound) Ssss (frying sound) Trunk out (of elephant)		Out In there Bang bang (hammer sound) No	

Table 2.5 continued

Medium	Derived exclusively from books		Learned also from other sources	
	(in speech)	*(via gesture)*	*(in speech)*	*(via gesture)*
	One story – *Goldilocks and the Three Bears*			
Nouns				
Animate			Daddy (bear)	Daddy bear
			Baby	Mummy bear
				Baby bear
Inanimate	Taste		Great big chair	
			Daddy chair	
			Walk/house	
Verbs	Tipt in de (tiptoed in)			
Adjectives	Hard/soft/right		Hot/cold	
Other	Crack!		Upstairs	

Base: Contributions (speech/onomatopoeic sounds/gesture) by Rhys at 25-month session. Repetitions/recurrences and vocalisations (e.g. euh euh) excluded

referent in its location, but as an indication of purpose – why characters, human or animal, behave as they do. In the following extract, it may be seen that 'mouf' (mouth), in the infant's discourse, is not proffered as a label for the duck's beak, but is understood as an expression of the duck's intention with respect to a piece of bread:

Mother	**Ceri (18 months)**
(*Points to children holding out their hands to ducks, evidently for the purposes of feeding them*)	
Here, they're feeding bread to the ducks, look Wez!	
	Points to duck approaching [mouf]
Hmm.	
	Points again [mouf]
He's got his mouth open hasn't he!	
They're going to get the bread as well, yes!	
They're going to gobble it all up.	

In the next extract we may observe that 'and' (sand) in Ceri's discourse is intended not so much to identify sand as 'sand' ('there's the sand'), but rather is voiced as a cause, or explanation, of the little boy's tears: 'It is because of the sand (in his eyes) that this little boy is crying':

Mother	Ceri (18 months)
	Points to book
	[oh look]
Little boy crying, isn't he?	
	[and]
You think the sand got in his eyes, do you Wez?	
	[es]
Yes, I think it did.	
Or maybe he's lost his Mummy.	
Maybe he doesn't know where his Mummy is.	
	[euh?]
We don't know. Yes I think he probably got sand in his eyes, darling, and it's hurting him. He's crying.	
'Yes', he's saying, 'that little girl threw sand at me.'	
He's pointing at her, isn't he?	

Both in terms of topic, and in terms of the nature of the extended sequences developed around a theme, Ceri's active speech production resembles the gesture patterns observed earlier. Certainly, at a formal level, one-word utterances here contain names for referents. But functionally, in the dynamics of the discourse, they are an expression of motive and purpose. (From the point of view of the adult reader, of course, they constitute a subjective interpretation which cannot be empirically verified; issues of truth, or falsehood, are not relevant here.) The point to emphasise, perhaps, is how much can be achieved in early reading even by utterances containing just a single word.

Differences between Rhys and Ceri when they learn to speak may, then, be found at various levels. The scope and content of their lexical knowledge, and the meaning or illocutionary force of their one-word utterances reflect closely the values of earlier times. A final difference in speech production concerns the nature of the construction which each places on the pictures in their book. While Rhys, still, is more prepared to internalise factual descriptions of events and objects, and reproduce these in answers to closed questions, Ceri remains concerned with matters of personal interpretation. The following extract illustrates how she sometimes creates a reading of a picturebook scene which is hers alone; nothing in the illustration suggests that the bath water to which she refers is in fact 'hot':

A SENSE OF SELF

Mother	Ceri (18 months)
(*Picture of female adult preparing to lift infant into a tub of water*)	
Oh Wezzy! Going to have bath now darling.	
	[is hot]
It's hot, is it darling?	
	[es]
Oh! What going to do?	
	[ap]
Put cold in shall we? Put cold water in?	
	[es]
ssss (*onomatopoeic sound of water running in*)	

Continuity may thus be observed in the move from pre-linguistic to linguistic communication (Bruner 1983:126). The principal features of the interactional modus operandi established between parent and each individual infant in active

Table 2.6 Active child reading behaviours

Rhys	Ceri
\multicolumn{2}{c}{*Mode of intervention*}
Enthusiasm/persistence in answering closed questions	Sequences; apparent reluctance/hesitation in responding to closed adult questions
\multicolumn{2}{c}{*Setting*}
The unfamiliar; the exotic world of far-off lands; situations never experienced at first hand (e.g. factory, docks, office)	The everyday; routine experiences of daily life predominate (e.g. supermarket, home, playground)
\multicolumn{2}{c}{*Type of linguistic construction provided by adult*}
Names/definitions of iconic referents. Frequent labelling of inanimate referents	Interpretations of behaviour can be in terms of emotions/objectives/motives. Animate (human) emphasis (e.g. the family group)
\multicolumn{2}{c}{*Focus*}
The visible world, shared by others	(At times) the internal world, not directly observable
\multicolumn{2}{c}{*Epistemological status of adult descriptions*}
Unambiguous – can be verified on a true/false basis, and/or corroborated/invalidated by a third party	A degree of doubt and ambiguity present: 'perhaps this, or maybe that'. Issues of truth/falsehood less relevant
\multicolumn{2}{c}{*Nature of interpretation proffered by child*}
Identification in context of vast repertoire of linguistic terms; many acquired exclusively through reading. Contributions objectively verifiable	Creativity and originality of some interpretations are to be noted. Some subjectively constructed contributions

picturebook exchanges, at the pre-verbal and first words stage, are summarised in Table 2.6. In both cases, dimensions of pleasure/displeasure, as well as activity/passivity are considered (Emde 1992). It must be emphasised, however, that the differences between the two profiles are not absolute. Ceri, for instance, does produce some 'new' words, but few compared with Rhys. On the other hand, the emotions are an area which is almost always, though never entirely, hers.

Summary

Using reports written by each parent and data recorded on videotape, certain active behavioural characteristics of Rhys and Ceri as readers have been described.[2] Systematic for each child, these features remain stable irrespective of the material presented (different types of book, for example) or of the adult interlocutor (mother or father) who reads. Moreover, despite (in some cases) encouragement to alter, these patterns of behaviour remain constant between the ages of 1 and 2 years; in some sense, these children remain resolutely and recognisably themselves. Consistency and continuity through time are, for Rycroft (1991b), the hallmarks of the development of the self. With respect to the reading setting, one may perhaps legitimately speak, in the case of each child, of a characteristic style, the expression of an individual reading self.

5 DISCUSSION: READING AND THE LANGUAGE ACQUISITION PROCESS

How might the language acquisition process be informed by this longitudinal study of reading behaviour?

5.1 Pointing gestures as antecedents of speech

The origins of infant language development are necessarily and inevitably sought by studying the relation between the speech of the child and the speech of the parent (e.g. Goldfield 1993). But to what extent should non-verbal dimensions of behaviour on the infant's part be taken into account? This study suggests that, in the reading setting, pointing gestures, allied sometimes, but not necessarily, with vocalisations, are endowed with many of the properties of human verbal language. These include discreteness, illocutionary force, and even displacement: the capacity to refer to things remote in time and space (Thorpe 1972:28). The deictic function, which identifies for the interlocutor the object about which one is making a predication is, theoretically, the 'ontogenetic source of reference' (Lyons 1972:74). It is, of course, the adult who, initially, for and on behalf of the young child, interprets the deictic gesture, identifies in language the image:referent, and then enunciates the predication: 'Teddy – he's got a vest on, hasn't he?', but with time, the infant takes over many of these functions (see Table 2.6).

The introduction of a topic, its maintenance, extension, or change, the contribution of parallel examples, and requests for further information – these, too, are characteristic of verbal dialogue, and have been observed here in infants using pointing gestures. Thus, while babbling and vocalisation have always been considered, and correctly so, as the antecedents of speech, it may be noted that pointing gestures are themselves precursors. In the reading setting at least, the use which children make of gesture often directly prefigures the use which, in the beginning, they make of speech.

5.2 Early reading dialogues as partly child-driven

Rhys and Ceri have been observed to differ, to an extent, in the use each makes of the gesture/speech code. This study is not the first, of course, to note differences between children from the same culture taking divergent routes into the language system. It has already been suggested with reference to the reading situation that different children might well follow different paths to language acquisition (Ninio and Bruner 1978). In non-book situations, Lieven finds that individual children oblige different adults to adopt similar patterns of speech behaviour, thus supporting the hypothesis that exchanges with children are strongly child-driven (Lieven 1978). Nelson, too, in her 1973 study of the first fifty words produced in everyday life situations by a group of eighteen children aged between one and two-and-a-half years old, distinguishes between a 'referential' group and an 'expressive' group, but the direction of the influence (whether the child is influenced by the parent, or conversely), remains an open question (Nelson 1973, 1981; Furrow and Nelson 1984).

With respect to book-based interactions, this investigation offers support for the view that certain aspects (only) of early reading exchanges are subject to considerable influence on the part of the child. This is particularly the case with interactional and thematic features (though not at the level of lexical relations or of process; see Chapters 3 and 4). In this study neither parent, for instance, is able to establish a free-flowing question–response routine with Ceri, whereas exchanges with Rhys remain with both parents, heavily dependent on this form of interaction. As regards topic selection, these reading adults are again observed to be strongly influenced by their individual child. This finding is corroborated by a longitudinal study of a slightly older child (boy) undertaken by Snow and Goldfield (1983). There too the pictures selected for discussion were strongly under the control of the child reader, regarded by these authors as significant.

If, as it appears, there arises, in the reading setting, a kind of linguistic modus operandi within which Rhys and Ceri learn to talk, and if what is in the domain of the inter-personal becomes intra-personal, could it be that much of what enters that domain, and indeed what is excluded from it, is determined to an extent by the child? In other words, if Rhys and Ceri actively produce language in a reading setting, it is not only because adult speech is densely lexicalised, and highly repetitive (see Appendix). Nor is it simply because Rhys and Ceri can indicate what it is they are prepared to listen to (which surely must have a bearing upon their motivation to then adopt the linguistic terms used *in situ* by the adult). There is also the fact that there exists, a priori, on the part of these two children, a considerable degree of emotional investment in the linguistic behaviour of their parents at a variety of levels, not only as regards topic, but also mode of intervention, and the materials presented to them. It is, of course, the task of the available adult to notice, respond to, and develop, on an individual basis, what sparks a young infant most (Nelson 1973:103). Herein lies a major difference between reading with an adult, and that same infant listening to predetermined input: story cassettes or television programmes. Responsiveness to the infant's signals, by the adult speaker, is paramount. The significance for development of adult engagement with the infant's point of view is further discussed in Chapter 4.

5.3 Non-linguistic origins of individual difference

Children thus vary, but to assert that Rhys and Ceri are different at a very early stage does not constitute an explanation of the origin of those differences. Why, between the ages of 14 and 25 months, in a reading situation, should one child be so actively concerned with inanimate referents and the other with feelings, for example? Certainly these behavioural differences are multi-faceted, and a small study such as this is ill-equipped to determine what the reasons might be. But using diary notes, and with some recourse to the existing literature, three hypotheses as to possible origins of individual variation may be entertained, based on differences of sex, of pre-linguistic orientation, and of birth order.

Sex differences

Studies conducted at pre-school age into children's social awareness have shown that boys are, relatively speaking, less vocal, more active, and task oriented in their interactions, while girls are said to be more socially oriented, inclined to interpret others' actions, attaching importance to getting to know one another directly (Golombok and Fivush 1994:126). Conversations about feeling states are also said to be relatively more encouraged in girls than boys (Dunn *et al.* 1987). As regards topic, males allegedly exhibit an early preference for hard objects while girls incline towards dolls and soft toys (Golombok and Fivush 1994:119; Hudson and Jacot 1991:50; Nelson 1973:58). Issues of sexual identification are deferred until Chapter 8, but if the supposition that a father's linguistic repertoire is both more directive, and involves a more extensive use of vocabulary than does that of the mother, then it may be, if identification with a parent of the same sex is a factor, that an eagerness to comply with the role prescribed for him could be a significant influence on the linguistic career of young Rhys (Barton and Tomasello 1994). Two points must be emphasised here. First, if, and in so far as, individual variations are due to differences of sex, such variations as have been noted are never absolute (feelings may be discussed by boys, just as girls learn labels for things). Second, while many of the attributes described are not reading specific (they may be observed in other situations), they are, even so, transposed onto the reading setting and can be seen there, possibly in more intense form. Our purpose must then become to analyse their impact in that setting.

Pre-linguistic orientation

Variations in linguistic behaviour, both verbal, and non-verbal, might further be explained with reference to an individual infant's pre-linguistic orientation with regard to the world as a baby. Personal observations of Rhys and Ceri in their own home reveal differences, even at a very early age, in their respective attitudes to the world around. From birth, Rhys appeared already to be looking at inanimate referents in the real world; both parents responded by talking to him about them. Gaze prefigured gestured behaviour; from the age of about 10 weeks, reaching for, and grasping objects was a constant preoccupation. Ceri at 3 months was not attracted by real-world objects on anything like the scale her elder brother had been one year earlier. A relative lack of psychomotor activity of this kind entails, possibly, relatively fewer instances of labelling; conversely, in Rhys' case, his parents had ample opportunity to name whatever it was that he looked at, held or manipulated.

Evidence from the research literature supports the view that infants not only display differences of pre-conceptual organisation – which in turn affect cognitive and linguistic processes in important ways (Nelson 1973:101). It also appears that a greater or lesser degree of object orientation may be a key factor. It was observed in one study that babies as young as 2 or 3 months can be readily classified as object oriented or human oriented. Primary figures in the infant's milieu tend to respond selectively, thereby reinforcing existing predispositions (Abrams and Neubauer 1978).[3] It seems likely that language development will reflect such differences of (non-linguistic) personal orientation in the infant, and also the inevitable differences of adult linguistic input which occur as parents selectively adapt to them.

Birth order

The impact on language of a child's position within the family group has been studied in non-book situations. First-born children of academic parents are inclined to be referentially oriented (Nelson 1973:60-61); second-borns, it is said, tend to be 'expressive' in orientation (Nelson 1981:173; and cf. Bates *et al.* 1994). In addition, second-born infants (at age 19 months and upwards) display enhanced conversational abilities when compared with a first-born sibling (Barton and Tomasello 1994; and cf. Dunn and Shatz 1989; Pine 1995). These findings are possibly of relevance before speech dominates, which may in part explain Ceri's early preference for extended conversational sequences. But why, for instance, is she apparently so disinclined to learn words for things?

The author's personal observations are that, in everyday life, the naming function, from very early on, formed a proportionately much smaller part of the linguistic interchanges between Ceri and her mother than it had with Rhys. This lower incidence of labelling can only in part be explained by the reduction in parental time available to a second sibling, or Rhys' fascination with extra-linguistic realia which, I suggested, becomes transposed onto the reading situation. Ceri also handled toys, for example, but when opportunities for labelling did arise, fewer were taken up.

Why? Because again, in part, nurture builds on nature. Language, or rather, naming practices, instead of strengthening the bond which Ceri enjoyed with an object in the real world, actually appeared to disrupt it. She would even stop playing with her toys if they were forthcoming, a situation which this mother sought to avoid. But environmental factors (here, birth order) also played their part. Any parental reference to what Ceri was playing with immediately brought Rhys toddling over with the intention of taking from her the very item which had excited attention. In consequence, Ceri was often left to play alone, undisturbed, and in silence, with whatever came to hand.

In sum, this study suggests that language development takes place within a culturally bound, but also individualised, interactive matrix. While infant language development is of course shaped by those adults and children with whom a baby comes into contact, many non-linguistic postures of that infant towards the world are, at the same time, and from the beginning, recognised, respected, and enjoyed. Reading behaviours before two years are thus in part an imprint of an individual infant's (earlier) non-linguistic orientation, or mode of being. The implication is that recipes for sharing books can neither be prescribed, nor imposed; the process is inevitably shaped by the likes and preferences of the individual child reader – by what he, or she, is not only able, but willing to make of the opportunities provided (Marcelli 1983:30).

5.4 Picturebooks as a linguistic resource

Although picturebooks do have a role in the disembedded teaching of isolated words, quantitative measures (the number of new words taught and learned) cannot be the sole criterion of a book's value. If it were, none of us would read novels. Picturebook reading has an altogether more fundamental contribution to make, because it opens the door to aspects of life which small children cannot, in the normal way, 'see'. Through his picturebooks, Rhys travels in space to a different setting, even a different country, and there encounters unfamiliar 'things', for which he learns unfamiliar 'words'. Or, familiar word forms, combined into relatively lengthy utterances, allows Ceri to 'read into' the pictures motives, intentions and feelings, more frequently and in greater depth, than might occur in everyday exchanges. In the one case, language is a tool for greater objective knowledge, in the other, a means to a deeper understanding of what underlies human behaviour. Through their reading, these children are taken to a world which, in the normal course of life, remains to a large extent, if not totally, hidden from view.

To what extent, then, might television usefully substitute for picturebook material as a medium through which vocabulary, in particular, might be taught (Lemish and Rice 1986)? The care and effort which these parents put into monitoring a young infant's level of comprehension, and the scale and extent of description practised, effectively disqualify television as a replacement for the printed page. Given the ephemeral nature of the television image, it is difficult to see how a toddler can point out anything; pictures vanish even before he or she can reach the set. Lastly, book reading is about interpretations which are jointly constructed by two partners in common. With television viewing, however, two auditory stimuli compete and no one, certainly not a small child, can be expected to attend to both the television and the parent at the same time.

If the language of picturebook work contrasts with television, how does it compare with the language of everyday routines? Adults, on a day-to-day basis, are not always concerned with precise levels of comprehension, because, with young infants, everyday life activities (eating, washing) can often continue apace regardless of what a parent actually says. Passing references to 'sterile water' or 'ballistic toothbrushes' do not impede the process of washing a young baby (cf. Snow 1976). But, in the reading setting, language, in conjunction with (static) pictures, is the sole means of retaining the attention of an infant reader. The degree of linguistic adaptation required of the adult and the level of linguistic understanding exacted of the child are probably, in the reading circumstance, unique.

6 CONCLUSION

The adults in this study do not simply 'read out' a book to small infants; instead, a varied set of illustrated materials serves as a starting-point for a type of exchange which is jointly constructed and in which the young infant, due in no small measure to a capacity to vocalise and point, enjoys unparalleled opportunities for linguistic self-expression. Over time, certain facets of infant participation come across as characteristic; they form a continuum from pre-speech to speech and are apparently little susceptible of parental modification. In the eyes of these parents, this constitutes the expression of their individual child's reading personality.

Parents, in their turn, adapt their strategies as a function of child preferences, leading to the establishment of a relatively fixed interactional configuration between adult and child. As a result, in the reading setting, routes to speech development which are in theory open to each and every child become, in the initial stages of acquisition at least, effectively closed. The implication is that children, as well as being apprentices when learning language in the reading setting, in certain respects act as architects of that self-same process.

But it also comes about that Rhys and Ceri, at other levels, adopt many of the (cultural and personal) norms and conventions of their parents' descriptions. What aspects of semantic and narrative understanding are acquired by these particular infants when reading jointly with an adult? And how is this achieved below the age of two years? This is to be the subject of the next four chapters.

Part II
THE SEMANTICS OF PICTUREBOOK READING

Part I of this book has documented the appropriation and exploitation of a set of reading specific behaviours. The next four chapters differentiate between picturebook reading and storytelling. Part II is dedicated to the semantics of picturebook reading. The perspective of Chapter 3 is predominantly intra-linguistic; the lexical content of adult speech is construed as a self-contained system governed by a specifiable set of meaning relations. The contribution of picturebook reading to the development of the infant semantic system and the relevance of this type of activity for literacy development are the main concerns. Chapter 4 describes the dynamics of the interaction over time – how meanings in picturebook reading are negotiated.

3

PICTUREBOOK READING AND WORD MEANING

1 INTRODUCTION: PICTUREBOOK READING AND LITERACY

Sharing books with very young children is associated with enhanced progress in literacy when those children reach school age. Central to the process is language, and the role of books in developing a child's linguistic knowledge. The intention in this chapter is therefore to evaluate the linguistic component of picturebook reading and particularly to examine the contribution of such reading to these children's understanding of word meaning. The lexemes of adult speech are considered both as isolated units and as interrelated within an organised system, governed by a set of specifiable relationships which together form part of the semantic structure of English. Word meaning, I shall suggest, arises from the network of meaning relations which a given lexeme contracts with other forms in the language.

But what is the connection with literacy? Literacy, by definition, cannot avoid considerations of semantics; the reading of a text involves mapping graphic forms not only on to the sound system of a language, but on to its semantic system as well (Garman 1990:26). Young children learning their native language might 'read' a word in the phonological sense (as an English speaker might 'read' French), yet have no idea what that word means. Moreover, the capacity to read words via the mapping of the letter structure of a word on to the meaning system of a language is of particular relevance when reading English, the orthography of which is often not isomorphic with the sound system. The grapheme–phoneme mappings of 'because' become apparent only after the word has been identified, not before (cf. Garman 1990:38). The value of picturebook reading to the fledgling reader, I shall argue, is at the semantic level; the same relations govern both the spoken and written forms of language.

The theoretical background to this discussion of lexical development is restricted to a presentation of just two approaches, derived from very different starting-points, though implications for other approaches to semantic acquisition, for example, lexical constraints theory (Golinkoff *et al.* 1994) may be inferred from the empirical evidence presented. The first approach is allied historically to theories of structural linguistics in which language is viewed as an abstract system of signs. The second is more empirically based, founded on observations of infants as they endeavour to learn word meanings in their native language, English.

2 THEORIES OF MEANING

2.1 Meaning relations

Consider a question of major theoretical concern to many linguists. How do native speakers know that certain lexemes are more closely related than are certain others? How do people understand, for example, that 'cat' and 'dog' are more closely connected than, say, 'cat' and 'seabed'. Consider a second question. What types of relationship govern different sets of words? What is the relationship between, say, 'tulip, daffodil : flower', on the one hand, and how is this similar to, or different from that governing, for example, 'dog, cat : pet'? Consider a third question. If the meaning of an isolated linguistic term is derived, in part, from the relations which it contracts with others in the system (part of the meaning of the word 'daffodil' is that it is a 'flower'), what procedures should be used to establish these meaning relations in the first instance?

Relations between words, some would argue, must be established entirely (Cruse 1986:1), or in part (Lyons 1968:427), on formal grounds, that is, with reference to the linguistic system. Contextual approaches to meaning in particular specify that information about a word's meaning must be derived from its 'actual and potential linguistic contexts' (Cruse 1986:1). That is to say, 'ducks', 'swans' and 'geese' cannot be described as related (and more related to one another than for example, 'ducks' are to 'pencils') because they are, say, juxtaposed in an extra-linguistic context (on the pond). Nor is perceptual similarity a sufficient reason for grouping 'duck' with 'swan'. That a duck 'looks' more like a swan than a pencil is not of itself relevant (though of course such differences may be reflected in the language system). Nor is it sufficient for the linguist to appeal to intuition (i.e. to 'think' that 'fork' and 'knife' are close, while 'cow' and 'seabed' are not).

Instead, linguists may note, for example, that individual words appear in an infinite number of (linguistic) contexts of occurrence: 'the cat sits on the mat'; 'a cat drinks milk'; 'the cat is called Lucy'; 'this cat is black'; 'that cat is a tabby'. These are but five possible environments for 'cat'. Individual words of course share contexts of occurrence with other words; by virtue of the linguistic contexts which nouns share linearly, or syntagmatically, they become related paradigmatically. In the following examples, the syntagmatic linguistic contexts common to 'cat' and 'dog' are italicised. Cats stand in paradigmatic relationship with dogs here; both are four-legged domestic pets.

> A dog/cat *is a domestic pet.*
> A dog /cat *is a four-legged animal.*

The latter context may also be shared with tigers and lions:

> A tiger/lion is a four-legged animal.

but the former may not:

> The lion is a domestic pet.

While 'dog' and 'cat' share many contexts, and it could be said that, by virtue of the syntagmatic contexts which they have in common, 'dog' and 'cat' are linguistically closely related (much more so than say 'dogs' and 'lions', because they have a higher number of contexts of occurrence in common), 'dog' and 'cat' must also be distinguished. There are linguistic contexts which these two lexemes cannot and do not share. For example, 'dogs miaouing' or 'cats barking' would be at the least surprising, if not poetic.

Because the word 'cat' shares the context of the word 'miaou', we can say that the meaning of 'cat' is constituted in part by the meaning of the word 'miaou'. 'Miaou', in other words, is a semantic trait or feature of 'cat'. Cruse (1986) distinguishes different levels of necessity of traits or features. Those whose absence is regarded as a defect can be called 'canonical'. To ascertain which features are canonical, as opposed to merely incidental, the terms 'typical' or 'defective' can be usefully employed in a formal test of the following type (cf. Cruse 1986:19):

> The typical cat has four legs.
> A cat which does not have four legs is defective.
> A typical cat miaous.

Contrast these features with other ways of describing a cat:

> A typical cat sleeps in an armchair?

Sleeping in an armchair is not a canonical trait of 'cat'. Returning to the need to distinguish 'cat' from 'dog', we could say that some traits or features (a furry animal, for example) may be associated with or characterise both, while others, (especially) 'miaouing', are uniquely specific to 'cat'. Put more simply, the statement: 'I know a cat is a cat because it is black' cannot apply, because so are dogs (and rabbits or cows) sometimes. But, in contrast, when we hear: 'miaou', we generally think: 'cat!'.

The significance of traits of this kind should not escape our attention; 'labels', by themselves, specify little of what a word actually means. Pointing to a packet of cigarettes and labelling them is sufficient only to indicate that the speaker wishes to refer to that item (as opposed to any other). Two fingers placed at the lips in replication of a smoking gesture, however, conveys something of what that label means (Trân Duc Thao 1973:63). So, perhaps, with the specific qualities of the unfamiliar substantives presented in early childhood; spelling out essential properties is an inherent part of understanding meaning (Palmer 1976:23).

What is important to retain from this discussion is that word meaning cannot be confined solely to ostensive definition, however predominant this aspect of semantic development may be in many picturebook activities (cf. Lyons 1977:228; Palmer 1976:22). Children must also learn that the word form 'cat' denotes the category or class 'cat' (Lyons 1977:206 ff.; Palmer 1976:18). Further, they must acquire a knowledge of the network of contextual and sense relations internal to a language, and into which a particular word form may enter.

Some sense relations, at an abstract level, are sufficiently systematic, and sufficiently generalisable (i.e. characterise a variety of sets of words, and are found in all languages, not just English) as to be worthy of especial note. Examples are the relation of antonymy, or relational opposites: tall:short; complementarity, or relational converseness: parent:child; buy:sell; part:whole relations: door:house; and, most importantly, hyponymy, or the relation of inclusion. 'Cat' and 'dog' for example are both hyponyms of a superordinate term 'animal'. The inclusion of lexical terms in other terms is a universal feature of natural languages and is instrumental in helping people to grasp meaning. Native speakers may well have an idea that 'turbot' is a 'kind of' fish even if they cannot define exactly what differentiates turbot from other varieties of fish (Lyons 1977:293).

Thus, hyponyms work at two levels. They must in one sense be recognised as similar one to another (it is the animalness of elephants and giraffes which allows them to be classed as co-hyponyms of 'animal'), yet at another level 'elephant' and 'giraffe' must be distinguished. One has a trunk, the other a long neck. The janus-like quality of lexemes which may in one sense be related one to the other (because they are co-hyponyms of a superordinate term, for example), yet in another sense are different from the other members of the paradigm to which they belong, is a further aspect of early picturebook reading.

2.2 Views from psychology

Barrett's theory of word meaning is based on the behaviour of his infant son aged 12 to 18 months learning to speak in a home environment (Barrett 1986; cf. Harris *et al.* 1988; Barrett *et al.* 1991). For Barrett, as for many psychologists interested in how infants learn to categorise entities in the real world, the infant elaborates and then constantly reworks a hypothesis with regard to a word's meaning. Evidence comes from the 'errors' which young children make when first learning to speak.

Two types of deviation from adult usage are said to be significant: underextension, whereby an infant overrestricts the use of a word to a particular context – for example, the infant says 'car' only when looking out of the window to the street, but never when riding in the car, and overextension, extending a word's use inappropriately (e.g. using the word 'duck' to refer to all the birds on the lake, until the infant adds 'swans' and 'geese' to its vocabulary). These are taken as evidence that a child constantly redefines what may be appropriately subsumed by the use of a particular word and what may not. At least four types of information are necessary to the establishment of the meaning of an 'object name' (i.e. noun) as follows:

- a representation of the prototypical referent of the word [e.g. duck]
- a specification of some of the principal perceptual and/or functional features which characterize the prototype [e.g. floats, webbed feet]
- a specification of the semantic field to which the word has been assigned [e.g. waterfowl?]
- a specification of the contrastive features which differentiate the prototype of the word from the prototypes of the other words which have been assigned to the same semantic field [e.g. swans and geese have long necks, ducks do not]

(Barrett 1986:54; [examples added by way of clarification])

The acquisition of word meaning may thus be studied via the growth of individual words in a child's lexicon. However, a child's understanding can also be approached via the notion of thematic scripts for everyday activities. 'A script is defined as a spatially–temporally organized body of knowledge that defines the actors, actions, and objects likely to be present in a given situation' (Fivush 1987:236). Scripts allow infants to anticipate and predict what happens when they take part in various events. It is within the context of events: a mealtime, or getting dressed, that categories come to be established. Meat, or yoghurt, are classified as something to eat. As part of a washing event, an infant will clean their teeth, using a brush, paste and soap. As a result, brush, paste, and soap may become more closely related non-linguistically for such an infant than, for example, brush (tooth) and brush (as in dustpan and brush) (Fivush 1987:252).

I shall not enter here into a discussion which is more properly the province of psychologists as to whether language and word meanings are learned from the word unit outwards via a word-based, prototype method, or from a larger unit downwards (i.e. deriving the sense of an individual word within the context of an event-based script). Retained for the purposes of this study, however, is the notion of a higher order experience for children known as an event extending beyond the confines of a word-based approach to meaning. But with this difference. When reading, infants experience an event of the real world in two-dimensional form; from 12 months, and even before, pages contain not a single image, but a scene, for example, of a picnic, a zoo trip, or a circus. In consequence, the various aspects of the overall event are simultaneously (not sequentially) present. And infants experience such events, not just visually (non-linguistically), by looking at pictures, but also linguistically, by hearing the adult's description of those pictures. It is the nature of the association between the strongly lexicalised (adult) description and (pictured) event which makes reading such a powerful medium for enhancing an infant's grasp of the semantic relations of their language. It is via a theory of semantic relations that word level and event level descriptions, which psychologists have distinguished, may be interrelated, and the contribution of parental linguistic input to the construction of a word's meaning (partly) assessed.

3 PICTUREBOOK READING: THE ADULT'S PURPOSE

Given these theoretical starting-points, the contribution of picturebook reading to the development of word meaning in children aged 11 to 27 months is now investigated. Adult speech, and its internal organisation at the lexical level, are considered from the dual perspective which follows:

- as it relates to the semantic theories outlined above. Which features are to be found typically in adult picturebook descriptions?
- as it relates to the illustrated material contained on each of the pages presented to the infant. Which aspects of the illustrated material do these adults elect to describe, and how? And what do they omit?

A detailed analysis of adult speech in Rhys' session at 14 months is presented first, as an indication of what frequently occurs in other books, in subsequent sessions. This synchronic view of a single session (section 3.1) is complemented by a more complete description of four recorded sessions (section 3.2) in which each child respectively hears the same material repeatedly discussed.

3.1 The construction of a paradigm

The material presented to Rhys at age 14 months comprises three boardbooks, each consisting of between six and eight single pages (three or four double pages), and an illustrated cover. One of the books, by Bruna, consists of a single item on each single page (fish, bee) set against a plain, but brightly coloured background. The other two are stories; each page is a scene. *Puffa on the Farm* (Brimax Books, 1982) depicts animals boarding a train for a ride. The front cover displays three animal types (horse, pig and cockerel), while the first inside page depicts a horse type and a duck type (four tokens in all), until on the final two pages, eleven different animal types (twenty-three tokens) are shown aboard. The illustrations in *The Happy Bunny* (Brimax Books, 1983) depict a (naughty) bunny and a range of other creature types in a variety of different settings (e.g. a ploughed field, a farmyard). Featured in addition to the creatures are a farmer (driving a tractor), two children, and an adult female figure, coded as 'the Mummy'. Overall in the session there exists a printed resource of some thirty-one different animate referents.

Examination of the material shows considerable reduplication of content. Of a total twenty-eight different creature types depicted, thirteen are common to two or more books; in addition, of course, some animals recur on different pages within the same book. Taking the materials as a whole, the animate referents (human and non-human) may be divided into two groups. Group one (N = 13) consists of those which appear in the illustrations with considerable frequency (3+ times each) for example, rabbit or cow. In group two (N = 18) are those animate referents which appear relatively infrequently (on average 1+ appearances), for example, fox, deer, or Mummy. This is consistent with material which, in published form, is loosely organised within a narrative structure.[1] This numerical data is stressed in order to indicate just how discriminating the adult linguistic presentation of these pictorial facts eventually turns out to be.

Foreground versus background

Inevitably adult readers are, to a degree, always constrained by the pictorial material to hand; they are unlikely, with a young child, to speak of the hospital when the scene is of a farmyard. This said, what is omitted from a linguistic description can be as significant as what is included in it (Whorf 1936 [1956:72]). Contrasting the avoidances with positive behaviours, it is apparent that much of the available pictorial material is missing from this father's descriptions. His speech makes almost no mention of setting, or background referents, be they flora (flowers, grass, trees), vegetables or fruit (turnips, apples), farm buildings (stable, pigsty, hutch), implements and equipment (broom, pitchfork, watering can, water barrel) with which details some scenes, in the 'bunny' book particularly, abound. Almost totally excluded too, are references to humans, and the interactive relationship between one character and another (surprise and shock of the 'Mummy' when the 'rabbit' eats the turnips).

In other words, judging by the language of this adult, the presentation is manifestly about animals. But it is possible to go further, and note the terms in which these animals are discussed. The organisation of the pictured material is uniform in that creatures are identified individually on each page, almost always without reference to any activity in which they are shown pictorially to be involved: 'running away' (from the Mummy) or 'climbing aboard' (a train) or 'eating carrots' (in the farmyard), and almost totally without a qualifying description involving an adjective or preposition. Utterances of the form 'naughty bunny', or 'bunny's under the logs' or 'doggie in the water', if sometimes present, are quite exceptional. Similar observations were made for the 9-month session.

Systematicity of presentation is further to be observed at a lexical level. Each creature is identified by means of a (usually) invariant word form: 'horse' does not become 'gee gee'. The only variation here is the occasional prefacing of the noun with 'Mr' as in: 'Duck – Mr duck'. Again, as has been found in many studies of picturebook reading, certain individual creatures are associated with their characteristic sound (e.g. 'woof woof, doggie say'). As with lexicalisation, the animal sound is formally invariant: 'woof woof' does not become 'bow wow'.

Degrees of salience

Consider now the organisation of adult speech at a discourse level. Nouns enjoy differential status. There are those which are included following a child initiative; Rhys spontaneously draws attention to them by pointing, and the adult responds: 'tractor' is an example. And there are those which are introduced spontaneously by the parent, often in a frame of the following type: 'Horse, there's horse'. However, such nouns may acquire a heightened degree of salience by being featured, in addition, as the focus of a question:

Where's the [Noun] (e.g. horse)?
Show Daddy the [Noun] (e.g. horse)!
Can you point to the [Noun]?

Rhys is also invited to produce the characteristic sound, within a syntactic frame of the following type:

What does [Noun] (e.g. horse) say, Rhysie?

That is to say, Rhys' cooperation is actively being sought for the purposes of identifying referents, and producing the corresponding onomatopoeic attribute. These findings are entirely consistent with observations of picturebook work with a child of a similar age (and sex) (Ninio and Bruner 1978).

Selectivity versus exhaustivity

Let us now enquire further and ask: which of the creatures pictorially available does this adult elect to talk about? If the nouns present in this father's speech are considered as a function of the frequency with which the corresponding referents occur in the illustrations, two possibilities arise. Either this father can return to the same animals again and again, or he can opt to ignore those previously presented in the interests of maximising coverage of those not encountered hitherto in the session. If the cow (picture of) appears again, does this father ignore the cow on its second appearance, and talk about the caterpillar? Proponents of the view that picturebooks aim to teach children a 'maximum number of words' might incline to this latter hypothesis.

In reality, it is the former consideration which prevails. Of the frequently appearing group one referents, ten (of the thirteen) receive mention on two or more of their appearances at least (e.g. cow, horse). Conversely, of our eighteen group two items (those which occur twice or less), six (e.g. caterpillar, donkey) are ignored completely, and a further ten are referred to once only (e.g. butterfly, snail). In simple terms, when the page is turned, the tendency will be to ask the infant to point again to the cow (already identified on the previous page) rather than disregard the cow on a subsequent appearance, and ask the infant to seek and locate the donkey instead. In other words, in this session, the interaction turns on a subset of animate referents (of the total potentially available) being consistently presented, and represented.

The identification of a selected set of creatures, some twenty in all, together with, for some, their characteristic sound attribute, thus dominates Rhys' 14-month session. Active child participation, too, is sought for precisely the same purpose. Table 3.1 lists a subset of the animate non-human nouns which feature in this father's discourse in this session. Asterisks in column one denote gestured responses by the child consequent upon an adult request to identify the referent, while asterisks in column two denote a child's responses to an adult request for the corresponding sound, sometimes more than once per page. Comparable items featured in adult speech, but which do not elicit infant participation, are unstarred.

Table 3.1 Father's references to animate non-human nouns, Rhys, 14 months

Designation of item	Sound	Appearances on different pages	Different occasions item referred to (N)
(Mr) Duck	Quack***	Six	Four
Birdie****	Tweet tweet*	Five	Four
Piggy***	Nasal fricative****	Five	Four
(Mr) moo cow	Moo*	Four	Four
Doggie****	Woof woof	Four	Four
(Mr) Owl	Hoot hoot***	Three	Three
Horse*	Pphh (bilabial fricative)*	Three	Two
Pussy cat***	Miaou*	Three	Two
(Mr) Turkey	Gobble gobble***	Two	Two
Baa lamb*	Baa*	Two	Two
Frog	Croak croak	One	One
Buzzy bee	Bzz	One	One

Base: Nouns associated with an onomatopoeic feature in Rhys' 14-month session. Total N = 12

Active child participation is purposefully directed by this adult, and is to be distinguished in its focus from a larger number of nouns which Rhys is required only to listen to. Rhys' involvement is not, on the whole, actively solicited for the purposes of identifying those items (the tractor, or the (male) farmer) which are potentially attractive to him, and even though they are mentioned within the adult discourse. Almost without exception, Rhys' attention is here oriented by adult questioning towards the construction of a particular paradigm.

The principle of the paradigm

Recurring rituals of presentation in which syntactic frames are held broadly constant create here a category of animate non-human nouns in paradigmatic association sharing a set of common features. Both the pictorial context (farmyard background) and linguistic context (inclusion and juxtaposition in a common framework) implicitly link the animals presented within a category (for now unspecified) whose (implied) shared feature is a living creature (found in the farmyard or country) and whose main attribute is the production of a characteristic sound. Distinctions of wild versus domestic animal, of two-legged versus four-legged are for the moment blurred or ignored. What is for the moment important is the classification of a number of nouns into a single group with a set of shared characteristics.

As has been noted in many studies of book reading, and sometimes to researchers' surprise, onomatopoeia has an important place in reading to young infants. Referents are readily associated with the noise they make. What is 'surprising' is that parent readers so frequently choose to specify what sound a creature makes even though those sounds cannot be represented visually. In the illustrations, cows have horns, and horses have manes, but these features, although visually perceptible, are rarely specified. Describing the physical appearance of an animal, or even its location (in the hutch, on the train) might seem the most obvious course in book reading, yet it is not one that this adult takes, at least not initially. Why not?

Several reasons have already been advanced. For Ninio and Bruner (1978), as for Lakoff (1987) and Golinkoff *et al.* (1994), the importance of the early recognition of the whole form, the outline or gestalt precludes focusing on parts (mane, horns or tail). There is the issue of perceptual salience (Adams and Bullock 1986:169). Sounds are both perceptible and demonstrable by a parent and, presumably, readily imitated and acquired by the infant. They engage and sustain infant attention. In addition, noises are fun (Urwin 1978:96). And there is, of course, the symbolic function: sounds are an effective word substitute. An infant may not be able to say: 'Start the story, Mummy!' but, as in this study, a child may (with effect) produce a 'sound' (brrm brrm) to prompt mother into reading the first words of the text: 'There was a ring at the front door.' Further, as Bruner suggests, with animal sounds in particular, the infant is encouraged in a process of identification; both reader and animal character are attempting to 'speak'.

The view to which I would incline, however, derives from the theory of semantic relations outlined in section 2.1. Sound features have the advantage of being both context-independent (horns might identify the particular cow in this particular picture, but not always; cows can be polled), and, at the same time, with regard to the remainder of the items in the category, uniquely specifying. Horses may be distinguished from turkeys by the number of legs they have, but horses and sheep cannot be differentiated on this basis. A further advantage is the commonality of the members of a particular group: co-hyponyms of a superordinate term must be not only different, but similar. The living creatures (the implied superordinate term of the category here created) all make sounds. In sum, what at one and the same time both groups together and yet distinguishes all the members of the paradigm (living (farmyard) creatures) is not physical attribute, but characteristic sound. In terms of semantic theory, we could say that when we hear 'moo', we think 'cow'.

Thus, with reference to an unspecified superordinate term (farmyard creatures) a paradigm is created within which a set of lexical items, or hyponyms, are both identified one with another (each produces a characteristic sound), yet also distinguished one from the other (here, each makes a different and quite specific sound). This is close indeed to Barrett's hypothesis of how children acquire meaning: the semantic field is suggested; the contrasting items within it listed; a typical, non-contingent, yet uniquely specifying attribute for each item is quoted.

An infant's powers of perception

A second issue to be considered concerns the repetitive nature of adult questioning. Why should this adult expend energy asking Rhys to identify time and again an animal he apparently already knows? As previously (see Chapter 1) denotation plays a part. The horse on the front cover of book two (a grey) is not the one (coloured brown) on the inside page, for example. This adult is, still, inviting the child of 14 months to ignore such differences and to recognise instead each individual token as a member of the same general category type: 'horse'.

But there might well be other reasons, though these can only be speculative. The reading of text by sighted children is dependent not only on linguistic knowledge, but also on visual perception. In this connection, invariance is a principle of written text which all sighted readers must master. Two-dimensional (letter) shapes appear in different guises, yet all the variations of (for example) 'a': upper versus lower case, script versus print, well-formed or smudged, wholly or partly formed must be perceived as an instance of the same underlying general category (Garman 1990:8). Recognising an item as a particular instance of a more general category is not of course specific to reading, but what is significant here is that the forms to be recognised in picturebooks, and in written texts, are two-dimensional. Could it be argued that picturebook activity is an early exercise in perceiving similarities in difference?

There is a further perceptual argument for repetitive questioning. The reading of text requires the reader to distinguish individual forms as salient, not in isolation, but when set within a variety of different backgrounds (Garman 1990:23). Again the relevance for reading print of a challenging linguistic activity based on pictures may be observed. Although it might seem simple to identify and re-identify the same animal, in fact, as a greater number of items appear on the page, the task of identifying the correct one, from the infant's point of view, appears (to these parents) to become progressively more difficult. Selecting the pig partly obscured, and huddled together with ten other animal types in the train (at the end of the train ride book), requires more discrimination than to select it from among a choice of just three (at the start). The cognitive challenge is greater (and more interesting for Rhys); this task he apparently experiences a degree of difficulty in managing. Purely as a hypothesis, then, the suggestion is put forward that practice in distinguishing shapes in an increasingly complex environment in picturebooks acts as a precursor to pattern recognition of a kind required when children learn to read text.

3.2 The construction of an event archetype

In the above example, the pictorial material available is organised linguistically into a paradigm with a specifiable structure but neither the superordinate term which governs the paradigm (farmyard creature), nor the event setting or location (countryside) is explicitly stated. The paradigmatic approach continues to be used, however, but in much developed form with both these children up to the age of 2 years, by both parents, using a very much more detailed type of material. The blueprint of presentation to be described below is manifest in the speech of both parents, and applies if not to all, then to a large number of pages of two entirely different picturebooks presented to Ceri, and to Rhys respectively, between the ages of 11 and 27 months. The very homogeneity of these parents' behaviour, even despite such methodological variation, is for this precise reason that much more instructive.

The structure of each page description comprises the explicit specification of an overall location or event, defined by a single lexical term, for example, the 'park' (i.e. playground), the 'supermarket', or the 'zoo', and a set of specifically defining attributes (in the form of nouns) associated with that event: 'swing', 'roundabout', 'mincemeat', 'marmalade', 'camel', 'elephant', etc. Between the event and the specifics (or hyponyms) is interposed, whether lexically specified or not, the superordinate term under which the specifics are grouped: 'equipment', 'shopping', 'animals', and which in turn is itself a canonical attribute of the event to hand. Finally, the lexical hyponyms are themselves often qualified by one, or several, traits. The event, its superordinate term and the specifics with their defining features together form an event archetype. As constructed by these adults, event archetypes convey, through language, norms of perception of the events or scenes presented in picturebooks; they are representative (i.e. characteristic) of the culture concerned.

Two books are reviewed here, each read at four different sessions. Ceri's book, *My Day*, presented at age 11, 13, 14 and 18 months, consists of routine occurrences, getting up, getting dressed, eating, visiting the park, the supermarket and, less typically, a visit to a zoo, which together make up the contents of a day in the life of a toddler. Rhys' book, *On Holiday*, presented at age 20, 21, 23 and 27 months, depicts the sorts of activities a small child might take part in on a holiday (e.g. outing to the beach, zoo, campsite, or circus), as well as more home-based pastimes (playing musical instruments or craft activities). The two children in this family, had, at this age, only rarely, if at all, visited a beach, a campsite, circus, or zoo; for Rhys particularly, much of the book's material is unfamiliar from everyday experience.

Theme: event, location or activity

The theme for each page is apparent to the adult, who may convey this to the child in speech by specifying linguistically the nature of the event, the activity or its location.[2] In some instances, the theme for a particular page is, in addition, related to the book's overall purpose:

Mother 11-month session	Mother 14-month session	Mother 18-month session
(Turning to page 29/30)	*(Turning to page 29/30)*	*(Turning to page 29/30)*
Oh, and the *zoo*, Wezzy!	Oh, we're at the *zoo* Wez!	Oh Wezzy, *zoo*!
	At the *zoo*! Yes darling.	Here's the *zoo*, darling.

Father 20-month session	Father 21-month session	Father 23-month session
(Page 1/2)	*(Page 1/2)*	*(Turning past inside cover)*
Here is another thing to do on holiday.	This is the holiday story. All the children going for a *picnic*.	This is all the things people do on holiday ...
The *picnic*.		This is a *picnic* Rhys.

These adults also order the information for each page. If it is mentioned at all, the theme is assigned chronological priority (i.e. it is cited first, as soon as the page is reached). Furthermore, if these parents do designate the theme, that lexeme (here 'zoo' and 'picnic') remains formally unaltered on subsequent occasions. Finally, if specified at all, the theme is usually cited each time the page is read, even though other items on the page may be omitted on a second or subsequent reading.

Human interest

Human beings, when included, are mentioned, if not first, then very early on in the particular page description. Thus, after announcing the theme of the seaside, Rhys' father moves immediately to 'little boy got his finger caught by a crab', although he might equally well have described, but does not, an inanimate referent: 'there's a boat' (for example). Often the human beings mentioned are canonical with respect to the event (i.e. define it uniquely). On the zoo page (Rhys, 21 months) for example, the 'zookeeper' is mentioned within the first three items (no fewer than fourteen creatures are cited subsequently), while on the circus page (Rhys, 21 months), the 'ringmaster' is first out of seven items. People, and what they are doing, are rarely an afterthought in picture description.

Hyponyms in paradigm

These parents further construct a paradigm, citing for this purpose hyponyms: aspects of the illustration which are both canonical with regard to the event, and specific to it (i.e. which distinguish it from other events of a similar nature). Thus, at the funfair, the 'big dipper', 'dodgems', 'heltersketter', and 'swings' are grouped, and introduced by the adult in preference to 'icecream', 'goldfish' or 'flag' (also depicted). At the circus, 'juggler' and 'clown' are mentioned; also pictured, but excluded from the discussion are: 'band', 'crowd' and 'icecream lady'. Using Cruse's formal test, it could be said that the typical circus has a juggler and a clown (and a ringmaster), whereas a circus remains a circus without the crowd (e.g. in rehearsal), or without icecream ladies. In the same vein, electronic music can nowadays substitute for a band. Alternatively it might be said that 'juggler' and 'clown', together, presuppose a circus, in a way that a 'band' and an 'icecream lady' do not. Over a number of sessions, the constituents of a canonical paradigm may vary; hyponyms are substitued one for the other (cf. Fivush). At the picnic, for example, 'eggs' and 'tomatoes' (savoury items) replace the sweet items ('cupcakes' and 'gingerbread') mentioned at a preceding session. Thus, while the same superordinate category (food) features at both sessions, the repertoire of items belonging to that category is diversified and/or increased at each individual session.

In addition to the canonical aspects of an event, these adults may include more marginal ones, in which case there is a priority with regard to order. For a given session, the tendency is for the canonical aspects to be presented before the less prototypical wherever possible (but see Chapter 4). Thus, in the picnic scene, the food and drink to be consumed are itemised first, before turning to less characteristic features of a picnic (the presence in the picture of e.g. a fox and a rabbit, of ants and wasps). When reading with an older child, it is very unusual, however, for these adults to include marginal aspects without referring, also, to prototypical ones. Tiredness might lead to the adult's highlighting only the features a child might particularly enjoy (e.g. 'balloons' at the funfair); this, however, is a rare example taken from the last page read in the 21-month session to Rhys.

Superordinate terms

Thus, the lexical items which are characteristic of the event (items of food and drink at the picnic scene, various types of animals at the zoo, items of play equipment in the park) are, if there are several of them, grouped into paradigmatic sets. The basis of the paradigm is, from a linguistic point of view, not random; underlying it may be a specific lexical relationship, for example, each member of the paradigm may stand in a part:whole relationship, or, alternatively, be a hyponym of a superordinate term. The superordinate term itself (italicised in the example below) may actually be specified:

Mother	Ceri (18 months)
Oh Wezzy, *zoo*.	
...	
	[hello, hello]
Hello *animals*.	
Hello!	
Oh, Wezzy, where's giraffe?	

Lexical traits

Individual lexical items are, in turn, almost invariably subject to further qualification. Qualification is often explicit, and, most typically, specifies at least one if not more criterial traits of the lexeme in question: supermarket – 'trolley'; lemonade – 'to drink'; lion – 'grr'; camel – 'hump'; elephant – 'trunk'. (Less frequently, non-essential traits of nouns are cited, as in: jam tarts – 'scrumptious', but here the qualification evokes perhaps an affective response in the infant (see Chapter 4, section 2.1.) Consider this description of the zoo:

Mother	Ceri (18 months)
Where's *giraffe*?	
	Points to book.
Good girl.	
	Points to book.
	[*ang neck*]
Yes.	
	[ang neck]
It's long neck hasn't he!	
Yes! (*laughs*)	
And where's the *lion*?	
	Points to book.
	[*aargh*] (roaring sound)
Aaargh.	
There it is	
(*pointing*) *Panda*, yes?	
And *monkeys*.	
See monkeys?	
	Points to book.
That's right	
And *camels*.	
Where's camels?	
There's the camel!	
Look at him, *with his big hump*.	

However, picturebook presentations are not always as explicitly straightforward as the above extract suggests. Groupings may also be governed by an unspecified superordinate term. For example, the superordinate term 'circus act' governing 'jugglers' and 'clowns' is not cited. Likewise, lexical features or traits might be inferred, rather than explicitly quoted. One might hypothesise, for example, that the food items in Table 3.2 are organised by contrasting two traits: a lexical trait: 'sweet' versus 'savoury' food items, and a grammatical one: 'mass' versus 'count' nouns. Similarly, the grouping of 'ants' with 'bees', or of 'dog', with 'fox' and 'rabbit' is perhaps suggestive of an unspecified superordinate term, insects and animals respectively. (Brackets { } indicate terms not explicitly cited.)

In most instances, descriptions contain a variety of features, some of which are implied, whilst others are explicit. Consider the following description of a park scene:

THE SEMANTICS OF PICTUREBOOK READING

Father	Rhys (21 months)
	(Bottom left-hand side of double page)
	Rhys points to fish
	[aaha]
Fishies. Swimming in the *water.*	
Shwsshws *(onomatopoeic rendering of fish swimming)*	
And the *ducks (adjacent to fish, excludes mention of boat and fishing rod, also pictured)*	
What do ducks *say?*	
	[du du]
Quack quack.	
(points to different ducks at top of page)	
Flying. Ducks flying.	
(kite flying adjacent to ducks)	
That little boy's got a *kite*	
And this little boy's playing with a . . . *ball*	

Table 3.2 Organisation of 'picnic' page, Rhys, 20 months

Superordinate		Hyponyms	Grammatical feature
{Human participants}		Little boy	
		Little girl	
{Food}	{Sweet}	Piece of cake	
		Piece of pie	
		Gingerbread men	{Count nouns}
		Jam tarts	
		Cupcakes	
{Drink}		Lemonade	
	{Savoury}	Cheese	{Mass nouns}
		Bread	
		Butter	
	{Sweet}	Icecream	
{Insects}		Ants	
		Bees	
{Animals}		Dog	
		Fox	
		Rabbits	

Note: Lexemes are listed in chronological order of citation in adult speech.

Table 3.3 Organisation of 'park' page, Rhys, 21 months

Superordinate	Lexeme	Explicit traits	Implicit traits
{Living creature}	Fish	–swim–water	{Water}
	Duck	–say–quack	
	Duck	–fly	{Flight}
{Toy} (Boy)	Kite		
(Boy)	Ball		

Paradigms and features in the above sequence may be represented as in Table 3.3. Explicit traits are indicated by –, and implicit lexemes/traits which are common to more than one referent, by { }.

As already indicated, the hyponyms of a superordinate may change from one session to the next. In a reading of this same page one month earlier, hyponyms of the superordinate term 'toy' were, not 'kite' and 'ball', but 'kite' and 'balloon'. The commentary runs: 'and running, with a balloon ... or standing, flying a kite'. The common trait (in the picture) is a toy attached to a piece of string, which a boy holds in his hand.

Over a number of sessions, the features or properties of a noun become accumulated; taken together they contribute to the noun's meaning. Over just two sessions, the (implied) superordinate category 'toy' includes within its membership 'kite', 'ball' and 'balloon'. However, 'kite' (in the adult's train of thought) also shares features with other nouns which are not toys. A kite 'flies', just like a duck. Moreover, although 'kite', 'ball' and 'balloon' are all members of the toy category, within that toy category, constituents can be more or less similar. The (pictorial) feature which kite and balloon share, and which distinguishes them from the bouncing ball also pictured, is that they, and only they, are attached to a string and can be flown from a child's hand.

The point to be emphasised is this. The meaning values which attach to an individual word form can be altered simply by manipulating the linguistic contexts in which that word form occurs. As may be seen in this small example, even though the actual term, or label, 'kite' which refers to the referent kite never alters, the linguistic environments surrounding this word form do change. To rephrase Cruse, the meaning of a given lexical term derives from the sum of the actual or potential linguistic contexts in which that term might appear.[3]

Thus far, the emphasis has been on the manipulation of a single word form within a variety of linguistic contexts for a single page. Consider now the recurrence of a single referent in different material environments (i.e. from one page and/or one book to another). If it is true that a superordinate term, on one page, gathers to itself a range of hyponyms (of which the listing of 'kite',

THE SEMANTICS OF PICTUREBOOK READING

'ball' and 'balloon' as hyponyms of the superordinate term 'child's toy' is an example), it is also the case, in picturebook reading, as nowhere else, that a single lexeme functions as a hyponym, not of one, but of several (different) superordinate terms. Take the example of the 'elephant', a favourite of Rhys between 17 and 27 months.

This referent recurs in two different picturebooks: *On Holiday* and *It's Fun Finding Out About People and Places*, and in three different scenes, at a zoo, in a circus, and in India. It is noticeable that on each of his appearances, the elephant is pointed out and labelled. If this activity is construed as an exercise in teaching the referential meaning of a linguistic term (i.e. recognising, each time, that the representation of the grey creature with the trunk corresponds to the word form 'elephant'), the exercise might seem overworked to the point of futility. Such, I believe, is not the purpose of pointing out the elephant each time. Rather, what is now being learned is that 'elephant' contracts a different set of relations on each page, depending on the nature of the paradigm or description of which the elephant forms a part. In other words, the importance of the elephant lies not so much with him, but with his neighbours of circumstance.

'Elephant' appears first of all as an instance of a 'zoo animal' and in this capacity is allied with 'penguins', 'flamingoes', 'lions', 'tigers' and 'seals'. On a subsequent page however, the elephant features again, but as an immediate hyponym of circus animal, alongside (performing) 'dogs' and dancing 'bears' (see Table 3.4). At an even higher level of description, both 'bears' and 'elephants' (animals) are hyponyms of the superordinate term 'circus act'. In this capacity, elephants rank not merely with 'bears' and 'lions', but also with 'jugglers' and 'clowns' (people). In a third scene, in the second picturebook, the elephant appears again, but this time as an example of 'animals which work for us' (e.g. in India), shifting logs, or transporting persons. In this usage 'elephants' are juxtaposed with 'donkeys' and 'llamas'. All these meanings coalesce around the single word form 'elephant'.

What is true of the superordinate level, is also true, at a lower level, of traits and features. Attributes of the 'elephant' vary upon each of his appearances, as had been the case with 'kite'. At the zoo he has his 'trunk out' . . . 'taking the little boy's icecream'. At the circus he 'holds hands with his mummy by the tail'. In yet a third book the elephant is 'giving the baby elephant a bath' (i.e. by squirting water from the trunk) and so on. In this way, associations of words are built up. Each individual speaker has, of course, different associations for different words. Speaker A's main association for 'elephant' might be 'circus', Speaker B's 'zoo', or the 'African bush'. But all these must be acquired if children are to broaden their knowledge of the network of meaning relations peculiar to their own language and culture (and ultimately help themselves with the task of reading which lies ahead). Picturebook illustrations are particularly well placed in the opportunities they offer a child to learn the varying sets of contextual relations into which a given lexeme might enter, and the different specific features which may qualify it.

PICTUREBOOK READING AND WORD MEANING

Table 3.4 Constituents of the event archetype

1	Lexicalisation of event/location/activity e.g.	(a)	Zoo
		(b)	Supermarket
		(c)	Circus
		(d)	Picnic
		(e)	Park
2	(Canonical) human participants of (1) e.g.	(a)	Zookeeper
		(b)	Butcher
		(c)	Ringmaster
		(d)	Little boy/little girl
3	Canonical superordinate terms with respect to (1) e.g.	(a)	Animals
		(b)	Shopping
		(c)	{Circus act}
		(d)	{Food/drink}
		(e)	{Playground equipment}
4	Hyponyms of superordinate terms quoted in (3) e.g.	(a)	Giraffe/elephant/camel/monkeys
		(b)	Mincemeat/sausages/marmalade
		(c)	Juggler/clowns/elephant/bear/horse
		(d)	Cheese/bread/butter/lemonade
		(e)	Swing/seesaw/slide
5	(Explicit) criterial or other attributes of hyponyms quoted in (4)	(a)	Long neck/trunk/hump
		(c)	Spinning hoops/funny face/balancing ball
		(e)	Onomatopoeic sounds/songs (e.g. ssw, swim); see saw marjorie daw (as the swing moves)

Let us recall now Barrett's thesis of how word meaning is constructed, a thesis derived, not from observations of parental speech addressed to infants, but from the linguistic behaviour of his own child learning to speak. Cognitive psychology, perhaps more than any other discipline, concerns itself with categories and category formation (Lakoff 1987:7); it emphasises particularly the relationship obtaining between a hyponym or set of hyponyms and the corresponding superordinate term. Such a relation explains, for example, how a child comes to understand that elephants and camels are classed, or categorised, as animals. Following this, Barrett hypothesises that there must be a specification of '*the* semantic field (emphasis added) to which a noun belongs'; this is an essential aspect of learning the meaning of a word. Thus, to return to the example quoted earlier (section 2.2), the word form 'duck' is grouped with 'goose' and 'swan' yet, at the same time, must be understood as distinct from both of these.

What this view fails to capture however, is that the same lexeme may be a hyponym not of one, but of a variety of superordinate terms. Take the example of 'duck'. This term might denote the feathered creature on the pond (in

111

which case it is aligned, let us say, with 'swan' and 'goose'). But might not 'duck', as Barrett himself reports, also refer to the orange and yellow plastic toy which floats in the bath. In which case 'duck' shares features with, or so one might speculate, 'beaker', 'cork' and 'shampoo bottle'. All, for example, are bath toys. As such their attributes differ in some respects from those of a feathered duck; they can be stored on the edge of the bath, for instance. Much of Barrett's contribution to our understanding of how infants develop word meaning is thus endorsed by this analysis. The lexical item, its neighbours in paradigm, and its features are specified. However, from this study of adult linguistic input, it would appear that these parents, in the course of their reading, may specify, not one, but several superordinate terms of which a particular noun might constitute the hyponym. Linguistically, nouns are not assigned to a single category; they are simultaneously members of a variety of different superordinate terms. Adults, seemingly, spare their infants nothing of the complexity which underlies a human being's understanding of entities and events in the real world.

Summary

The picturebook scenes described in this chapter, whose page contents are arranged thematically, are subject to an unprecedented degree of hierarchical ordering with regard to the lexical input of the adult language.

Quoted first or very early on in the page description is the overall theme of the event and activity ('zoo', 'supermarket', 'circus', 'picnic', 'park'). Defining or canonical aspects of the event are also cited. These are in the form either of the human beings associated with the event ('zookeeper', 'ringmaster'), or an object ('trolley'), or a superordinate term ('animals', 'shopping'). If the canonical superordinate term is not explicitly cited, it is implied in the paradigm of hyponyms which accompany the event (e.g. in the case of the picnic, {food} and {drink}).

With respect to the superordinate terms, a number of hyponyms are, without exception, quoted in paradigm, or, failing this, at the very least, a single member of a paradigm is cited ('cupcakes' or 'tomatoes' for food at the picnic, and 'lemonade' for drink). While superordinate terms are optional, especially with younger children, hyponyms are almost always quoted, and may form the bulk of the description in the early stages.

Finally, features or traits of hyponyms are specified, often explicitly, as in the 'long neck' of the giraffe, or the 'trunk' of the elephant. Such features are very often what distinguishes the particular hyponym from other co-hyponyms grouped within the same superordinate term. Additional features are suggested, by, for example, judicious sequencing of presentation (e.g. 'duck' – {water}, {flight}). Taken together, the various aspects of these adults' descriptions of picturebook pages constitute the event archetype.

Diagrammatically page descriptions may be represented as in Table 3.4.

Examples (a), (b) and (e) are taken from the mother's speech; examples (c) and (d) from the father's. Featured in brackets { } are the lexemes not explicitly quoted in the sessions recorded.

4 DISCUSSION: CONTRIBUTIONS OF PICTUREBOOK READING

Picturebook reading has been shown to enhance an infant's knowledge of the semantics of their language. Lexemes are defined both with reference to a pictorial scene and also in terms of other linguistic forms. They are units which are invariably accompanied by one, or more, specific features (implied, if not formally specified), and governed by one, or a number of, structural relations, for example, hyponomy. The meaning of a word is constituted by, and derived from, its relations with other words.

Something of this view is captured in the following remark concerning the acquisition of verb forms: 'The function of an action is thus defined partly in terms of the objects involved, just as the function of an object is defined partly in terms of the actions it is involved in.' (Tomasello 1992:213). But Tomasello here alludes to the perceived interrelation of objects and actions in the (extralinguistic) world; in this enquiry, the emphasis is upon the interdependence of word forms within language. Although a picturebook scene necessarily forms the starting-point for linguistic description, real-world experience of that pictured event is not a prerequisite; neither of these children at this age, for example, had ever visited a 'real' circus.

Consider now the issue of the relevance of picturebook activity for literacy. In a small study such as this one, no causal relationship can be proven between the activities of early childhood and developments in language and literacy in the long term, but three hypotheses as to the 'value' of picturebook activity are now put forward.

The nature of the stimulus

Learning in a young infant derives in part from practical circumstance. Picturebooks form part of that circumstance, and a most obvious quality of a picturebook is its capacity to present infants with an accumulation of visual material representing a variety of events whose components may be simultaneously viewed and discussed. The provision of a number of different pictorial scenes further allows lexemes to be employed in a range of contexts, which in the normal course of everyday life may well be restricted to a single context. In one study, 'kill' was used only in the context of exterminating bugs (Tomasello 1992:115).

In addition, the presentation of lexemes is multi-sensorial as perhaps in no other area of a child's life: substantives may appear in acoustic form, in iconic form, and in association with a parental pointing gesture. An adult pointing gesture constitutes a visually perceptible marker of the phonological boundary between one word and the next. As the parent introduces a substantive ('horse'), there is a pause in which linguistic form, visual form and gesture coalesce before the adult visually signals a 'change' of visual referent and a 'change' of acoustic form (to 'moocow') by demonstrably moving the finger to an adjacent image (of a cow). Syntactically too, word boundaries are clear. A noun is often cited in isolation, before it occurs in association with other word units: 'Horse! there's horse'. Adult speech, at the beginning at least, is strongly lexeme (word) oriented (see section 3.1).

What, however, is the connection with the written word? Written language is dependent on the separation of the stream of speech into individual units, and in English, the basic orthographic unit is the word (Garman 1990:41). The emphasis on phonological boundaries perhaps arms a picturebook reader with an acoustic awareness of where one word 'ends' and another 'begins'. Certain contemporary reading recovery programmes are designed precisely to heighten a non-reader's awareness of the relationship between (acoustic) word boundaries and the spaces which surround words in print. A word counter is placed into its own (graphically represented) separate word box (one of a sequential series) using a finger movement. All the senses are canalised in an effort to promote, in non-readers, a type of linguistic knowledge without which proficiency in reading can never be established (Dolan 1993).

Semantic relations

Contrary to many assumptions, early picturebook reading is not exclusively concerned with the referential meaning of individual word forms. Unconstrained by the practical demands of daily life, the adult reader is free to integrate lexemes within a clearly definable set of hierarchically ordered relations, to specify those aspects of a substantive which are uniquely qualifying, and to identify lexemes in a variety of different pictorial and linguistic environments. These environments, taken together, constitute the meaning of that lexeme for an infant.

There are important implications here for how parents help children to arrive at an understanding of what words mean. In section 2.2 of this chapter, word- and event-based models of meaning were opposed. From this enquiry it emerges, however, that parents approach lexical development from different angles simultaneously. Through the explicit specification of judiciously selected hyponyms (camel, elephant), the overall event (visit to a zoo) assumes linguistic shape and form, while the structured description of the event contributes reciprocally, and in turn, to the meaning of those same lexicalised hyponyms. In such an approach, individual word meaning at hyponym level, and the linguistic description of the event as a whole, are inter-dependent.

However, despite the importance assigned to intra-linguistic relations, knowledge of the real world remains an indispensable part of understanding language (Palmer 1976:56). Some reading comprehension difficulties in adolescents have been attributed not to difficulties with deciphering the text as such (the 'words' can be 'read') but to a lack of knowledge of the events described. The empirical example cited is of a bird which nests over the weekend in a letter-box. The point of the passage can only be appreciated by referring back to the shared context of life to which the writer implicitly refers: letter-boxes remain undisturbed on a Sunday (Nonnon 1992:112). Picturebooks often depict more public settings, some of which (a hospital, or factory) may be unknown to a young child from private experience. Through their reading children may enhance their knowledge of real-world events, knowledge which arguably equips them for all types of linguistic encounters, reading included.

Discourse

Consider now, from a different perspective, the relationship obtaining between language use and pictured event. Certain key features characterise the adult linguistic descriptions analysed here. Selectivity is one; neither adult describes a picturebook scene exhaustively. Relevance is a second feature; the elements selected are not random, but central to that picture's meaning. These are integrated within a linguistic description offered as an interpretation. Third, by virtue of this description, certain pictorial features are rendered more salient than others, which, in turn, recede into the background. Fourth, of those topics discussed, some (human beings) are judged to be more central than others. The presentation is ordered. Fifth, through description, referents stand, not in isolation, but in meaningful relation one to the other; the description is coherent. Last, for any given page, the page description has clear phonological boundaries. It often begins on a high pitch and tails off to a lower pitch as it reaches its conclusion – the acoustic equivalent, perhaps, of a paragraph.

What is the linguistic importance of such event descriptions? As will be argued in Chapter 4, pictures in books are the iconic representation of a discourse topic: they are what adult and child talk about together. Eventually the visual element disappears and the topic assumes a purely linguistic form. But there remains, in that pure (discourse) form, a title (event specification), the choice of (relevant) topics in relation to the title, salience (centrality of certain features), the logical ordering of presentation of those topics, and so on (Brown and Yule 1983:71 ff.). Children are introduced as early as the second year of life to some of the most fundamental principles of the organisation of discourse.

How might early descriptions of picturebook scenes connect with the reading of stories particularly? Just as stories later on, they depend for their interpretation upon an ability to simplify, highlight, create patterns, ignore (Rabinowitz 1987:19). In paving the way to literacy, picturebook scenes offer more than an opportunity to learn vocabulary and syntax (Crain-Thoreson and Dale 1992); underpinning these parents' interpretations of picturebook scenes are some of the very principles which govern the understanding of narrative text itself.

5 CONCLUSION

The 'traditional' emphasis upon the presentation of lexical items as isolated units has obscured the contribution which picturebook reading may make to the development of word meaning as defined with reference to theories of lexical semantics. Semantic knowledge of this kind is of intrinsic value to a developing infant. In the longer term, access to literacy for children read to in early childhood will have been preceded by a period of intense oral language work, in which the need to distinguish acoustic and visual patterns, the development of an understanding of reference, sense, contextual relations, and discourse organisation, together with enhanced knowledge of events in the real world constitute the perceptual and linguistic foundations from which the ability to read (and write) derives.

4
PICTUREBOOK READING AS EVENT INTERPRETATION

1 INTRODUCTION: DIFFERENCES OF PERSPECTIVE

The dialogues described in this book take place with reference to a particular illustration. A page in a picturebook depicts a scene which forms the locus of attention between the two participants, and a starting-point for discussion. Described in the previous chapter is how these two adults typically view that scene. Selecting a feature or features of the tableau as a topic, these parents talk about them in a particular way. Their descriptions are frequently dedicated to issues of archetypal event interpretation and individual word meaning. How do people know that a ('picnic'/'camel') is a ('picnic'/'camel'); because of the ('food'/'drink'; 'hump'). The formula may be extended to 'elephant' ('trunk'); 'supermarket' ('trolley'); 'cat' ('miaou') and so on. What is not discussed is, for example, whether the dog scraps with the fox, or if the ants devour the food. As pointed out in the Introduction, children may learn about events of the real world from their reading, but equally they gain access to their parent's (subjective) position with regard to that world. They gain access, that is, to parental values.

But what about the child's viewpoint? A child's standpoint, at the outset certainly, is different from that of the parent. Not only because a tableau may be semantically indeterminate and we often need to be told 'which aspects ... are relevant and how they are to be interpreted' (McGinn 1984:7), but also because what people perceive is very much a function of their previous experience of what they are looking at (Lakoff 1987:129). Initially, children may not even be aware of the central (adult) interpretation of a scene. Infant understanding appears to be less integrated than that of the adult, and even at times fragmented; Rhys or Ceri may focus on a small detail in an illustration, at the expense of the whole. Whereas his father highlights the canonical aspects of the picnic, namely, the food and drink available, Rhys himself is captivated by the fox hiding behind the tree. This I call marginal, or peripheral focus – which does not mean unimportant. Affective investment in aspects of a scene is often what motivates infant readers.

Infant and adult are further differentiated by their linguistic knowledge.

Adults, unlike children, possess the terminology which enables them to describe, in language, any, or all of the aspects of the illustrations chosen. Nor will these infants necessarily have had first-hand experience of some of the events, or referents, presented to them in pictorial form. Ceri may have been to the beach, but never to a hospital. Rhys may have seen a penguin, but never a flamingo.

A final difference is infant emotional investment in recurring items. Of the tendency to return again and again to the same referent(s), book illustrators are well aware; on different pages of the same book is to be found, somewhere displayed, for instance, a mouse, an elephant, a cat, or a duck. Some of these items, possibly, will be remarked upon, by child, or adult. Some may be related to the central meaning of the whole. But they can affect dramatically the view which an infant expresses of a particular scene.

The description of Chapter 3, then, omitted all mention of how children themselves construct a scene: the achievement of a jointly negotiated interpretation is thus a first consideration. Second, the event archetype, a schematic description of the structure of parental discourse, in fact telescopes linguistic events which occur over a period of some six months or more. Time is therefore a second consideration. Third, the structuralist account of Chapter 3 fails the data in that it belies the complexity of the interactive processes via which the archetypal description is achieved in practice. It offers a linguistic picture of events, much as a work of art might hang in a gallery. But what are the various stages of the composition of this picture? Movement, shifts of position, oscillation between viewpoints, all of these underly the final static version painted in Chapter 3. If adult and infant have different perspectives on a picturebook scene (and it is taken as axiomatic that they do), what is the reciprocal impact of the one upon the other? In other words, and this is to be the main focus of the discussion for this chapter, how, in the dialogue, are the points of view of each speaker dynamically interrelated through time?

2 ACCOMMODATING THE INFANT

The reading dialogues of this study are characterised by a high degree of infant participation. Infant contributions may be solicited by parental questions, but equally they may be the vehicle for what these infants themselves elect to 'say' spontaneously (Chapter 2, section 2.2). Parental questions are formulated in such a way that the responses of their infant are generally appropriate, and actively received as such. Given these broad parameters, consider now some of the approaches used by these parents as they interpret a picturebook scene for their infants.

PICTUREBOOK READING AS EVENT INTERPRETATION

2.1 Adjustments in face of new material

The introduction of new material – new in the sense of not having been read before, has a major impact on session dynamics. To aid with the identification of referents, items, generally speaking, are pointed out by these parents, at a first reading, in a carefully ordered sequence round the page, moving slowly from one juxtaposed item to the next, rather than moving quickly and suddenly (say) from top right to bottom left. Contiguity of referents is thus often a factor. At the same time, the rate of delivery is significantly slowed up in initial readings, in order that the infant grasp the connection between word form and iconic referent: 'There's the carrots [pause] and the marmalade' (Ceri, 11 months). Thus 'known' referents on pages which are 'new' are presented in much the same way as lexical forms whose referents are totally unfamiliar from first hand experience: 'oilrig' or 'astronaut' (see Chapter 2, section 3.3). The implication here is that the more frequently a picture is discussed over a number of successive sessions, the earlier a sentence structure of complete type will appear in the adult discourse, with its appropriate intonation: 'Getting sausages and carrots and icecream!' Instead of isolated labels, the infant will come to hear sentences.

Reading and rereading the same book is thus significant from a developmental standpoint. Once infants know where items are (on the page), the adult reader is free to develop not only their syntactic but also their semantic understanding. Freedom from the constraint of contiguity, for instance, leads to the juxtaposition, in speech, of referents which, in the illustrated material, are widely separated; members of paradigms are regrouped, and features alter (see Chapter 3, section 3.2). There is a limit, however, to which lexical items can vary in paradigm. For any given page, once the viable possibilities are exhausted, the page is dropped, unless it retains a particular affective or humorous importance for these infant readers; in which case, in all likelihood, they will go on to produce the lexemes for themselves (see Chapter 2, section 5.2).

With regard to the construction of the archetype, certain items in a scene are invariably presented first. Unless the children are either tired, or very young (under 13 months) these adults always denominate, in a first reading, for any given page, and even if no other aspect is mentioned, the hyponyms characteristic of a particular setting. That is, the animals on the farm, the specific (food) items at the picnic, the equipment at the playground, the items of shopping at the supermarket, will be stated. At the earliest sessions, too, hyponyms are qualified, either with specific features, especially onomatopoeic sounds, and/or references to personal experience.

These parents may, in addition, in an early session, identify the setting or event; superordinate terms on the other hand are generally introduced after mention of the event and its defining hyponyms. In the following example, the hyponyms ('lion', 'elephant') and setting ('zoo') are mentioned early on, while the introduction of the superordinate term ('animals') occurs only much later:

Ceri (11 months)	(14 months)	(18 months)
Oh, and the zoo, Wezzy! (*points*) Mr lion! Grr, Mr lion say!	Oh, we're at the zoo Wez! At the zoo! Yes darling. See the elephants?	Oh Wezzy, zoo! Here's the zoo, darling. Hello animals! Hello! Oh, Wezzy, where's giraffe?

However, it should be stressed that the introduction of superordinate terms is never purely a function of a child's age, linguistic capability, or 'cognitive stage'. Accumulated knowledge of the material, both linguistic and pictorial, plays an important part. In the next example, infant familiarity with food items (as opposed to zoo animals) presumably leads to the early introduction (at 13 months) of the superordinate term 'shopping'.

Ceri (11 months)	(13 months)
And there they are. In the supermarket. With the trolley.	Where are they now? (*Ceri points to the trolley*) Trolley! Yes! they're going in the trolley to the supermarket.
There's the carrots. And the marmalade. And the sausages. And the soap.	Doing the shopping. First there's the butcher with the meat. And here's the sausages. There's marmalade, and here's mincemeat.

It follows then, that the more a child is read to, and becomes familiar with basic hyponyms, the earlier, possibly, will the activity, location or event and corresponding superordinate terms be specified. Lexical knowledge is augmented, not only by presenting a very wide range of materials, but also by returning to read the same page over and over again.

Judicious ordering, and a slowing down in pace of delivery characterise presentations of 'new' material. Consider now the presentation of lexical terms for referents which may be unknown even in real life (astronaut, whale, parachute). Here procedures seem quite precise, involving the choice of clear exemplars, the specification of essential features, and the inclusion of affective connotations.

Clear exemplars

Describing a 1-year-old's understanding of the meaning of the word 'umbrella', Anglin (1986:86) makes the point that his daughter recognises an umbrella as an umbrella if it is open, but not if it is closed. Evidence from this study seems to support the view that reading adults acknowledge and accommodate this aspect of infant perception. The first written mention of the word form 'parachute' in Ceri's book accompanies a picture where the parachute is shown strapped to the pilot's back (i.e. unopened). It is only when the parachute is pictured in flight that the corresponding word form 'parachute' is introduced. When reading, these adults assist their infants' learning of totally new referents by associating the label for an unfamiliar referent with a clear exemplar of the referent it denotes.

Essential features

Verbal explanations which explicate essential features may also accompany new word forms. Consider this example. On his daily walk in his pushchair, Rhys, as a small baby, would cross a railway bridge bordered by high stone walls but 'bridge' if familiar in experience, had never been linguistically coded as such. When reading, Rhys meets the unfamiliar lexical form 'bridge' in this way:

Father to Rhys (18 months)
And look, there's a bridge.

(*points to bus approaching the bridge*)
With the bus.
Ptptptpt (*makes bus sound*)

(*points to lorry on the bridge*)
And a lorry. It's a milk lorry isn't it?
There's the milk lorry, hmm.

(*points to water beneath the bridge*)
See the boat going underneath.
tttttttttt (*makes boat sound*)

The 'labelling' of the bus, lorry, and boat, respectively, should not, I believe, be construed as an instance of identifying procedures one independently of another, but, on the contrary, as a deliberate specification by this adult, in series, of the core semantic features of 'bridge', namely that transport can pass both over and beneath it. The reduced scale and unique vantage point which a two-dimensional representation of a bridge affords make possible the exposition of such traits; in 'real life' they are very difficult (except with a model) to demonstrate, for a baby cannot, at one and the same time, be both on top of a bridge, and underneath it. What the 'bridge' and 'parachute' examples indicate is that these adults, albeit unconsciously, refrain from labelling 'new' referents until such time as some of their quintessential properties can be made readily apparent.

Experiential correlates

Adults may go further than this. First, the introduction of a new lexeme may be afforded prominence (prefaced, for example, with the word 'look' as the adult points) whereas the 'givens' of this infant's lexical repertoire, 'boat' and 'lorry' are subordinate, both chronologically and phonologically. Second, onomatopoeic renderings are again in evidence. The 'bridge' is here endowed with qualities which arouse pleasure in the infant (just as the bee, unfamiliar to both infants at 9 months, had been made to 'buzz' round the book); Rhys' father breathes life into the unfamiliar word form 'bridge', as the bus drives towards it, or the boat chugs under it.

This 'elaboration' of substantives (to borrow a term from DeLoache and DeMendoza) lies at the very heart of picturebook reading. When analogies with the real world are drawn ('socks – like Rhysie's'), when nouns are dramatised, through the 'pretence' of munching an apple, or by 'roaring', as a lion might, these enactments do more than help the infant to understand the word form 'cognitively'. They convey a 'feel' for the word in question. This is achieved in a variety of ways, by appealing to the different senses. The sound of a boat chugging up the river is just one way. The potentially frightening experience of an encounter with a lion: 'Grr' is another. The taste of food: 'Jam tarts! scrumptious'; the atmosphere of peace as a baby sleeps: 'Sshh! baba's sleeping'; perhaps simply a pleasurable incident from the child's real-world experience: 'Yoghurt! Wezzy's favourite!' are yet other instances. What seems clear is that picturebook reading is not simply about acquiring word meanings devoid of all affective connotations. In this respect book reading may be contrasted with television images, where often what is before children are simply 'words' and 'pictures' without their vital experiential correlates.

2.2 Investing in the infant viewpoint

Various types of adjustment are thus made in face of a child's unfamiliarity with pictorial material. Moving now from difficulties with individual lexemes, towards a construction of the event archetype, it may be observed that these parents attend carefully, not only to what their infant does not know, but also to what they do know, or rather what they both know and like.

In the literature, much emphasis is given to the internalisation of the adult viewpoint by the infant; the suggestion is that an infant moves gradually towards an end point represented by the adult position. One hypothesis with respect to infant development might thus be that, in order to arrive at a reading of a semantically inert picture, the adult consistently and repeatedly restates their own (adult) position, in the hope that with time the infant will 'make their own' whatever their parent's particular interpretation might be.

The approach of these parents is, however, at times, quite the contrary. They very often actively take up the viewpoint of the child, particularly in early readings (Ceri, 11 months), to the extent that sometimes only the infant viewpoint is articulated. The adult position may even be excluded from mention altogether. Pleasure is derived, not from the degree of convergence between

PICTUREBOOK READING AS EVENT INTERPRETATION

Table 4.1 Readings of four pages of a single picturebook* to Ceri aged 11 months

pages 5–6	19–20	27–28	31–32

Central meaning which eventually attaches to page in adult speech

| Early morning: parents in bed, infant plays/dresses | Daytime play activities: reading, painting, etc. | Adults and children have tea | End of the day: children watch television |

Linguistic coding by mother at first recorded reading at child age 11 months

Oh Wezzy! Where's pussy on this page Wezzy? Where's the pussy?	Can you see pussy on this page Wezzy? Can you see the pussy darling? Show Mummy pussy. Show Mummy the pussy.	And there's pussy again! See pussy?	And there's pussy again. Trying to get the mickey mouse isn't he, hmm?
(*C points to cat*) There, yes, Wezzy got pussy! Good girl, Wezzy! She pointed to pussy haven't you darling! Yes, that's right.	(*C vocalises* [e]) Where is he? Show Mummy then! You point to pussy for Mama. Show Mummy, Wezzy, look. There he is darling. (*C points to cat*) (*vocalises* [e])		
Pussy, darling! Miaou pussy say.			
There's teddy, having a cup of tea. And dolly. And Daddy pouring the tea.	Yes, that's a better girl! You show Mama pussy.		

* *My Day* (Ladybird books)

infant and adult viewpoints, but from the difference of perspective between the two participants. In other words, at the beginning, and this point must be stressed, these adults on some pages may not attempt to encourage their infant towards any point of view at all, other than their (the infant's) own. Instead, they invest predominantly in the infant viewpoint.

Consider two examples. The first concerns initial readings with Ceri of four double pages of a picturebook dedicated to life at home. The double page pictorial scenes are, in a 'grown up' version: getting up in the morning; daytime play activities; having tea; and watching television, respectively. However, in the dialogue, Ceri's mother: (a) attends as a matter of priority to a marginal detail (the 'cat'), which recurs on repeated pages, and (b) foregoes mentioning her own understanding of the picture to the extent that, on three of the four double pages (19–20; 27–28; 31–32) the scene's central theme does not feature at all (see Table 4.1).

Why, if the intention is to arrive at an adult view, should the central meaning not feature in the adult discourse? The incorporation of infant experience is part of the answer (see section 3.1). But child age, and session dynamics are also factors. This mother 'allows' interest in the cat following a period during which Ceri has been looking at preceding pages from an 'adult' perspective. Book reading, in other words, includes moments during which Ceri, in a relatively quiescent state, seemingly concentrates hard upon the adult point of view, and others, often of intense pleasure, during which she is in a relatively high state of arousal emotionally, and activity in the form of gesture or vocalisation, ensues.

The second example illustrates how this father cedes his own position to that of the reading infant. In this case, he begins by articulating his own viewpoint, but then breaks into this (adult) account, in the interests of inviting Rhys' perspective on the page. This inside cover contains figures representing scenes from the book: a little girl returning from the funfair with a fish, or a child going to a picnic carrying things to eat. The interest of the example is to show how this adult, even in stating his own position, actively acknowledges that of his infant reader:

Father	Rhys (20 months)
Here we go then, let's see what's in this book.	
Oh Rhysie, all the things to do when you're on holiday!	
Dressing up isn't it?	
The queen, and the . . . mo . . .	
The little boy dressed up as a monster using the cornflakes packet for a mask, hmm.	
What else can you see?	
	R points to dog.
The doggie.	
	R points to football.
And the football.	
	R points to cat.
And the pussy cat.	
	R points to mouse.
And the mickey mouse, little mouse.	
	R points to picture labels.
That's the words.	
What about fishywishy.	
	R points to fish.
And the gingerbread man (*points*).	
And the polly parrot (*points*).	
	R points to balloon.
And the balloon, yes, balloon, balloon, hmm.	

As may be seen from both these examples, picturebook interpretation is a matter of joint construction between adult and child, and never the imposition of one person's viewpoint upon another. What deductions may be made, at this juncture, about adult–infant interaction in picturebook reading dialogues? Mutual engagement is one feature: the child listens to the adult's viewpoint, and the adult listens to the child. However, it is seemingly not sufficient for these parents, with respect to any chosen page, to adopt, and express their own particular point of view, while offering tacit approval (only) to the infant's voice. It is not enough for example, at the picnic scene, for Rhys' father to continue referring to the food laid out on the table cloth while Rhys insists on referring to the animals in the bushes. These adults adopt and articulate the infant point of view at least some of the time. They enthuse about the 'cat' (as in the first example), or (as in the second) introduce a topic of interest to the child reader (here the 'fish', the 'gingerbread man', and the 'parrot'), however marginal (to the adult), by talking about it spontaneously. In so doing they invest emotionally in the infant's point of view; there is an expression of affect. These adults match infant interest with a display of pleasure and enthusiasm of their own. These adults, then, both see the position of the infant logically (note the topics to which they are drawn), and engage with them emotionally. In other words, they empathise with the infant.

The second deduction to be made with regard to interactive processes over time is this. The evidence of the citations at 11 months in Table 4.1 (and cf. also the adult behaviour described earlier, in Chapter 1), suggests that, with a younger age child, adults may invest very extensively indeed in the infant point of view. Later on, it is apparent that both these parents more readily put forward a point of view of their own (the details of which were described in Chapter 3). How and when, then, does this come about? One can only speculate with regard to the evidence, but it might be that, as Rhys and Ceri are increasingly able to participate (through the development of the ability to vocalise and point), so their parents, freed from the need to express their infant's perspective, are placed in the position of being able to offer a different interpretation: their own. The dialogue, from being in some senses largely unipolar, becomes genuinely bipolar. Parent and infant take up their own positions with respect to a scene, even though, as will now be demonstrated, their respective positions, on occasions, coalesce.

3 MODIFYING INFANT PERSPECTIVE

Reading dialogues thus rely upon each of the participants adopting and expressing their own, sometimes very personal, point of view. Rhys for example will be interested in the 'tractor', Ceri in the 'teddy' or 'cat'. The adult view on the other hand incorporates aspects which are totally new to the infant. How then are these respective points of view to be related?

My hypothesis regarding processes of change (in the infant) runs as follows.

If communication between two partners in dialogue is to occur at all, the perspectives of both participants must at some point overlap. That is to say, while emphasis has until now been given to points over which the perspectives of the two participants diverge, there are occasions when perspectives intersect. Aspects of the illustration are sometimes of almost equal significance to both parties. This area constitutes a common topic of interest; adult and child are interested by one and the same topic, simultaneously, though possibly for very different reasons. What purpose might this (momentary) convergence of perspective serve in the construction of the archetype? The answer has to do with how children, over time, shift position, and come to see the picture from a different point of view.

3.1 Incorporating infant experience

If the adult objective, at least in part, is ultimately to present the infant with a semantically organised interpretation of a happening or event, that adult must (in my view) ensure that their description intersects in part, if not wholly, with aspects of their young reader's experience. These adults draw for this purpose on the knowledge which they have of the child listener: his, or her, emotional responses, linguistic knowledge, experience of real-life events. In other words, the event archetype must, if it is to be adopted by the infant, articulate, either totally, or in part, with the synchronic reality of the child's own life. To cite a simple example, this father, knowing from first-hand experience that Rhys enjoys eating tomatoes, and aware that the linguistic archetype is composed of food items, selects the 'tomatoes' in the picnic picture as the point of intersection between adult and child perspective.

The overlap between adult descriptive purpose and child experience is an absolutely dominant aspect of picturebook description. Parallels between infant experience and criterial features of the archetype are occasionally explicit, as in the breakfast scene: 'Boiled egg – like Wezzy has' (13 months); or the zoo scene: 'Polar bear – like your Brumas (a reference to Rhys' own soft toy); or, for the musical instruments: 'Piano – we might be getting a piano soon' (20 months). Such explicit references to infant first-hand experience in reading settings are already well documented in the research literature (Adams and Bullock 1986:188; DeLoache and DeMendoza 1987; Dockrell and Campbell 1986; Snow and Ninio 1986).

Much less frequently recorded, however, are the multiple, non-explicit references to the familiar in a child's experience. Familiarity may be derived from two sources: the shared experiences of real life, which then become incorporated into the archetype (as in the example of the 'tomatoes' in the picnic scene), or previous experiences of book reading. Consider some further examples. At age 14 months the living creature paradigm comprises both the 'dog', which in Rhys' real-life experience is a well-known and well-loved animal, and the 'turkey', a creature both formally and referentially totally unfamiliar.

PICTUREBOOK READING AS EVENT INTERPRETATION

The familiar 'dog' features alongside the unfamiliar 'turkey', the one a springboard to the other, even though this difference between known and unknown is not specified in the adult discourse. Or again, at age 17 months, Rhys' ongoing real-life experience had included a visit to the local wildlife park, where two birds in particular, the toucan and the penguin, had captivated his interest and attention. At the next reading sessions, these two items are among the first to be presented on the zoo page, but without any reference to the previous weekend visit. They feature among a range of other creatures (walrus, hippopotamus) of which Rhys has scant knowledge. It is as if the adult reasons on his behalf: 'A lot of this is new, but some of it makes sense already – let's start there!'

In the next examples, familiarity with, and enjoyment of, an item derives not so much from real-life experiences, but from repeated experiences of reading the same book. Again these parents use enjoyable features in order to expand an archetypal interpretation. For instance, to present the construct 'adult activities in far-off lands', the Red Indian, a well-established picturebook favourite, is used as the bridge for the introduction of the (less familiar) South American gaucho. Neither of these referents had been encountered in actuality. Or again, in reading the 'early morning activities' page with Ceri over a period of several months (11–18 months), this mother always begins with the baby having its nappy changed; this is at one and the same time part of the archetype, and the item which, in consecutive readings, generates a consistently positive emotional response from Ceri. The advantage of such references is, of course, that on reaching that page, infant satisfaction is immediate, not deferred; these two subjects do not have to wait to find something interesting in their reading. However, only close contact on the part of the adult with the ongoing events of an infant's 'real', and 'reading' lives makes such points of intersection possible. There is benefit in the infant being read to by somebody who knows them well.

The important point about these examples is that these adults frequently do not stop at those aspects of life with which the infant is simply familiar (DeLoache and DeMendoza 1987:117); they go beyond this in order to select topics which in addition have given pleasure. Adults may be explicit on this point: 'There are your favourites – the penguins!' And what is the function of affect here? It seems that the pleasurable aspects of real life (the 'dog', or the 'penguins') form the bond between infant and picture, and at the same time, constitute the jumping-off point for the introduction of less well-known, possibly totally unfamiliar aspects of the archetype, the 'walrus' (in the zoo scene), for example. Thus do adult and infant oscillate between the known and the unknown for the purposes of the construction of the archetype; affect is yet again in the service of cognitive growth.

As a final example, Ceri's mother describes what the child in the book has for lunch. Disregarding the plate of roast beef and vegetables, and the icecream, she opts instead for the sausages and beans, and yoghurt: 'Oh! having lunch, Wezzy! Got sausies, and beans, and yoghurt. Wezzy likes yoghurt, don't you darling!' (13 months). This presentation is at once culturally determined: had it been in a Japanese picturebook it would not have included sausage and beans, nor would it have consisted essentially of a 'main savoury course' followed by one 'dessert' course. It is, from a linguistic standpoint, ordered. But it also builds as a priority upon what is personally significant; Ceri relates more strongly to yoghurt than to icecream. The skill, perhaps the very power, of parental language is the reconciliation, within one archetypal description, of cultural, linguistic and individual concerns.

3.2 Transforming infant perspective

In the preceding section it was observed that the event description intersects at some, if not all, levels of infant experience at least some of the time. In the zoo example, infant enthusiasm for the 'toucan' coincided with the adult's intention of telling the infant about the 'zoo'. In cases such as these, infant perception seemingly becomes structured, but not qualified, by adult intervention.

There are, however, moments in the dialogue where infant and adult perspectives diverge. Those moments occur when the marginal takes over from the central, the part replaces the whole, or a peripheral detail, rather than the overall theme, predominates. In instances such as these, the articulation of an adult central purpose, as earlier defined, may be considered to be influencing the infant's perspective on a scene; the view which an infant has of that scene becomes modified. Here adult language may be said not just to structure, but to transform these infants' view of their picture (Todorov 1981:87). How, in the dynamics of the discourse, is this achieved?

Subtle pressure to shift viewpoint is exerted upon these infants in three ways. The first indication of adult priority is discourse position: both adults attempt gradually to place the most important elements of the page (to them) first in their description of a page. The page reading begins with central, rather than marginal, elements. Second, these parents increasingly assume responsibility for the introduction of the central elements where possible, but are more and more disinclined to direct attention to the marginal elements. It is the infant reader who, in the long term, introduces the marginal elements, which the adult certainly accepts by responding by name, but little more. The third subtle pressure is the amount of talk time devoted to the marginal elements compared with more central ones. Just as in the very early sessions, when both adults used the technique of emphasising in speech those aspects of infant behaviour which are to be encouraged, while ignoring those which are to be discouraged, so here the feedback which lateral elements receive is minimal compared to the extensive exposition of those aspects more germane to adult purpose. The behaviour of adults, as well as of infants, exhibits systematic patterning.

Consider the page readings with Ceri cited earlier (Table 4.1) in which the

PICTUREBOOK READING AS EVENT INTERPRETATION

'cat' features. Although marginal from the standpoint of the adult, the 'cat' was totally dominant in discourse terms at age 11 months. It was (then) afforded exceptional priority by this mother both in terms of discourse position (being the first, and sometimes the only item cited on the page where it occurred), and in terms of talk time (no other item in this book, at this age, be it the 'car', the 'horse' or the 'swing' received such lengthy attention in descriptive terms). But most important of all are the intensity and extremes of pitch range in this mother's voice, which, presumably, act as a mirror to infant interest and enthusiasm for the item at this early encounter.

Over a period of some seven months, however, the status of the cat becomes a matter for negotiation between adult and infant. The cat's position, in this picturebook, is to be gradually downgraded in the discourse of this mother; its very inclusion becomes an increasingly precarious matter. For, as the number of topics per page discussed by the adult increases, those which are more central to adult purpose assume pride of place on each page, entailing a shift downwards in priority accorded to the 'cat', from initial to a medial position in the adult discourse at 13–14 months. Talk time devoted to the cat is also reduced; the 'cat', if present, receives just scant mention in adult speech. Eventually 'cat' is eliminated altogether from each page, with only the adult interpretation being cited: 'There they are, watching TV' (on page 32 at age 18 months), unless Ceri, that is, not to be beaten, of her own volition reintroduces the cat as a topic for discussion, seizing her chance at the end of the page, after the adult view has taken precedence (page 5 and page 27 at age 18 months). But by now the emotion in the adult voice has gone; the response, now, is no longer to excitedly enthuse over 'cat', but to mention it almost as an afterthought 'and pussy cat again, yes', and then, as indicated above, only when Ceri introduces it with an initiative of her own. Thus is Ceri's favourite, the cat, displaced by the scene archetype in picturebook reading, if only to return, however, as main protagonist in some storybooks (see Chapter 2, section 3.3).

However, where picturebook referents correspond with the event archetype, they are retained through time; the 'elephant' discussed in Chapter 3 is a case in point. And what is true of an individual item is also true of a whole event. As a final illustration of the process of prioritising selected archetypal features, which are eventually adopted by the infant reader, consider four complete extracts of readings of a picturebook scene with Ceri at 11, 13, 14 and 18 months. The particular double page shows small children (participants) engaged in various play activities (superordinate term) in a garden (the event location) (see Table 4.2).

This example is instructive in two ways. It shows clearly the consistency of parental discourse structure which sometimes obtains for a given page over a period of many months. It is likely that Ceri becomes used to hearing the 'story' of this page, and can understand it, eventually, without the need for iconic support. Second, Ceri eventually intervenes quite spontaneously to identify precisely those aspects of the picture ('horse', 'car' and 'bike') which had

THE SEMANTICS OF PICTUREBOOK READING

Table 4.2 Readings of a double page from one picturebook to Ceri (11 to 18 months)

11 months	13 months	14 months	18 months
Little boy on his trike.	Oh! little boy on tricycle.	And little boy ride the bike. Show Mummy the bike . . . the tricycle. Hmm?	There they are in the garden. Wezzy got garden, haven't you Wezzy?
		(*C points to sun*) The sun, darling, yes. Good girl, the sun	(*C points to horse*) There's horsey, yes. Little girl pushing horsey (*C* [push push]) Push little horsey and Push little horsey!
Girl pushing the horsey. And there's a little car again, See! Little boy in a pedal car.	Little girl pushing horsey.	There's the pedal car, See. There's horsey.	(*C points to car*) [what's that?] Little boy and his car. It's his pedal car. (*C points to bike*) [what's that?] Little boy riding his bike like Wezzy got.
Little girl push the horsey.		There's the pram with the toys in.	

featured so consistently in the adult descriptions of the preceding seven months, even though the double page contains other items potentially of great interest to her: soft toys, flowers, and so on. The point has been reached where infants look with their parents at what those parents perceive.

But, just as in speech acquisition, infants do not take over parental speech entirely, but ignore aspects of it, or coin their own formulations, so too with picture interpretation. Infants may adjust their perceptions in line with their parents' view, but they move just as readily from a state of convergence with the adult view, to divergence. They swing their attention away from the archetypal view, and interest themselves in yet other elements of a particular scene. To new departures such as these let us now turn.

4 TURNING POINTS: COGNITIVE GROWTH IN THE 18-MONTH-OLD CHILD

Picturebook interpretation is a cyclical process; developments are not static. With time, these parents are again drawn to reflect in their presentations the more mature view which these infants, at around age 18 months, seemingly have of the events in their books. The developments described are not necessarily associated with linguistic capability (Ceri was into the one-word stage at this age, whereas Rhys had barely five words in his active vocabulary). Three changes in child, and adult, behaviours are briefly presented.

4.1 Intertextual comparisons

In the previous chapter, word meaning was said to derive from the sum of the linguistic contexts in which a word appears. Rhys' cross-referencing of lexemes heard only when book reading offers empirical corroboration for this theoretical view. Consider this data. Hearing: 'The knave of hearts *stole* some tarts', Rhys spontaneously says: 'Tom', thereby expressing the connection with another nursery rhyme in which the verb 'stole' also features: 'Tom, Tom, the Piper's son *stole* a pig and away did run.' Rhys here not only connects the acoustic shape of stole (2) with that of stole (1), but, more than that, the main association is not with other acoustic shapes (roll, coal, hole) but rather with the precise (linguistic) context of occurrence of 'stole'. What is remembered is not only the word form itself, but also the linguistic context in which that form has previously appeared. Intertextual comparisons of this kind suggest that children, when mastering their native language, notice, compare and explicitly interconnect linguistic contexts in which lexical terms occur.

4.2 Departures from ostensive definition

A second development concerns the move away from ostensive definition in some areas of parental speech. Up until child age 18 months approximately, observable phenomena are selected as markers of events, while abstractions, for the most part, are avoided. 'Trolley' rather than 'self service' is chosen as the defining feature of supermarket; edible components, rather than the time of day, define a meal. At the same time, events and locations are clearly distinguished from other, similar ones: 'trolley' defines a 'supermarket' specifically, whereas 'shoppers' (also featured) might also apply to a small corner shop.

Gradually, however, there is a move towards describing the illustrations in terms which cannot, and do not, involve ostensive monstration. The early introduction of some superordinate terms ('shopping') has already been discussed. But now, explanations and reasons for happenings feature increasingly – in the form of references to (past, or future) actions, which are implied, but not actually shown in the illustrations. In 'Mummy getting dress out of cupboard, yes. Little girl *going to have dress on today*' (Ceri, 18 months), where a small child is shown in a state of undress, this mother refers to the little girl's future state, not depicted. The account of 13 months had stated simply 'little girl got pants on', without reference either to the actions of a second protagonist or to the little girl's imminent change of appearance. Certainly at 18 months the connection between what the two characters depicted are doing is increasingly apparent in the discourse.[1]

But parents go even further than this. As well as references to what characters are about to do, there are, as we saw in Chapter 2, increasing references to internal states or emotions: why people do things. Why is a little child crying/cross/throwing a doll from the cot? In other words, characters are more and more described with reference to their intentions and motives, and in relation to one other. Protagonists and events, instead of being simply juxtaposed, are now quite explicitly interconnected, and motivated. In this aspect of language use Ceri particularly shows an early, and very marked interest. What can be inferred from the picture, as well as what is literally displayed in it, is an aspect which links both picturebook work and narrative.

4.3 Norms versus deviations

A third and striking innovation at 18 months concerns modifications to the event archetype itself. Presented in the 12–18 months period is, most usually, a version of events in which things are normal, and going well. Children play in the playground without incident, infants eat their food uneventfully, the shopping takes place according to plan; there are no mishaps. Once the archetype has been established, however, exceptions to the norm start to appear. At around age 17 months, both infants become increasingly interested in the discrepant. Details of pictures are now included which suggest conflict, disorder, chaos. The world begins to have defects. Children of around 20 months of age, it is said, experience a sense of panic at the realisation that all in the world is not right (Trevarthen 1992). In picturebook activities: a boy refuses to eat his supper; an egg smashes on the supermarket floor; a man hurts himself while building a house; a little girl's dress gets splashed with water – these exceptional happenings are now included, against the backdrop of the comparatively uneventful presentations of the preceding six months. It is as if the adults in this study are intent, first, on creating for the child a normal version of events, leaving for later the need to address departures from that norm. One may speculate as to whether such a position does not also have important implications for a young child's moral development.

Summary

This chapter has been concerned with how the adults and children in this family negotiate an interpretation of a picturebook scene. Findings suggest that these parents, in constructing an event archetype, rarely disregard the infant viewpoint. On the contrary, appropriate allowances in rhythm and pace of presentation are made during first readings; in particular, the infant perspective is both adopted and explicitly articulated. Simultaneously, however, by exploiting their knowledge of their infants' likes and preferences, the adult 'central' viewpoint is merged with the affective concerns of each child reader as individual. Having bridged the potential gap between infant and picture, unfamiliar material, both pictorial and linguistic, is introduced in order to further expand the event archetype.

Over a period of months, these infants' often initially divergent standpoint takes second place to the archetype in the adult discourse. Synchrony between adult and child viewpoints is momentarily attained, but only until new departures and interests in both children, at around 18 months, precipitate further changes in perception, which, in turn, the adult once more accommodates in the discourse. The process is one in which the perspectives of both infant and adult diverge, converge, merge, and rediverge, in a ceaseless cycle of interpretation and reinterpretation.

5 DISCUSSION: THE NEGOTIATION OF MEANING

In this chapter, some of the processes which, over time, lead to changes in both infant and adult readings have been described. A subset of the features which have accompanied changes in infant understanding will now be discussed: the presence of a consistently available adult within a shared routine of reading whose attitude to the infant is characterised by empathy. The discussion is concluded by a brief review of further possible benefits to the infant of the linguistic descriptions which accompany picturebook reading.

5.1 Processes of growth and change

What has been suggested here is that, from often totally different starting-points, a commonly negotiated perspective on a picturebook scene is evolved, which, potentially, forms a fresh starting-point for a new engagement. In this discussion, attention is drawn to two apparently conflicting, almost paradoxical aspects of infant development, namely the fluctuations in perspective which occur either between partners synchronically, or within one partner (the infant) diachronically on the one hand, and the remarkably consistent, sometimes unchanged linguistic behaviours of both these adults, and through time, on the other. The two poles, movement and flux, versus stability, continuity and predictability, are as the warp and the woof which together make up the longitudinal fabric of parent–infant picturebook exchanges.

The fluctuating nature of picturebook interpretations

Reading here is viewed as a dynamic construct. Dialogue is not simply a matter of imparting information in the sense that Speaker A transmits a message analogous to that which is in his own mind, to be registered as such by Speaker B. Nor either, does communication here resemble information processing in which Speaker B extracts the meaning from a stream of speech uttered by Speaker A. The meaning of a picture is jointly constructed in a collaborative process involving both parties.

Much of the discussion in the literature suggests that, as the child grows up, he or she moves in the direction of the adult. With respect to book reading in particular, children, it is said, are not yet in possession of adult 'rules' of interpretation as such, but they can be 'trained' to adopt a particular point of view (Snow and Ninio 1986:133). Useful as such statements are for emphasising the difference of viewpoint between adult and infant, they have, in my opinion, one major drawback, which is this. The viewpoints which adult and infant have of a picturebook tableau are not static. In other words, what is omitted from much debate on growth and change in the infant is the ceaseless and reciprocal impact which infant and adult have one upon the other, and the considerable degree of oscillation, in both, towards, and away from, the point of view of the other. These adults begin by leaning heavily towards the infant point of view. But as development takes place from within these infants, for example the development of the capacity to point, so these adults become free to diverge. Then these children take on more of the adult perspective. However, the obvious preoccupation with the deviant and exceptional in pictures on the part of both Rhys and Ceri causes their parents yet again to shift position. In other words, with respect to any given pictured event, there is not one view, but a constant appraisal and reappraisal by each participant one of the other, and of the picturebook scene, leading to the articulation of a dynamically evolved construct of that event to which each participant synchronically and diachronically contributes.

The linguistic significance of stable routines

The shifting patterns of event interpretation described above take place over a very long time scale, some six months or more for each child respectively. The emphasis has been precisely on change, as these parents and infants together reach a degree of commonly negotiated understanding of what picturebook scenes might be about. Let us now turn to the opposite pole, the place of stability and permanence. Shifts in (infant) perspective do not occur as it were overnight; rather they evolve within a structured exchange routine whose salient characteristic is consistency. As observed in Chapters 2 and 3, there is predictability: in the referential use of lexis, in the nature of the questions asked and answered, and above all, in the use and reuse of the same book, within which the same pages return, and within these, the same favourite pictorial items are almost always mentioned.

Consistency of presentation in book reading is, in my opinion, central. Not only because repetition, from one session to another (according to a behaviourist model), breeds success, nor, either, because the infant is afforded a repeated opportunity to tease out the relationship between linguistic form ('parachute') and two-dimensional reality (picture of a parachute). Rather it is the case that, through increasing familiarity of the infant with the material (linguistic or pictorial), the internal organisation of parental speech alters, both phonologically, syntactically and lexically. Utterances may lengthen, the semantic system attain greater hierarchical depth. The discourse, in becoming familiar, increases in its degree of independence from iconic representation; the linguistic description stands more completely alone, without the pictures. And in the process, perceptions, slowly, are restructured.

Affect

Consistency of presentation is but one factor. Growth in the infant also depends, fundamentally in my view, upon affect. I refer not so much to the affective bond existing between parent and infant, though this, of course, is important (Bus and IJzendoorn 1988), but rather to the emotional relationship which seems to obtain between Ceri or Rhys, on the one hand, and aspects of the illustrated material which s/he contemplates, on the other. By this I do not mean that these infants simply learn what they 'like'. Affect is the very engine of growth at a whole variety of levels.

Adults draw on their knowledge of their child's ongoing experience to involve them emotionally in their reading, selecting topics which are not only familiar but also meaningful to their child. Various reasons have been given in this chapter: a parent's pleasure in the differences of perception which their infant may have; an infant's sense of relief at being able to indulge their own subjective perceptions freed from the strain of attending to the objective adult view. New words, new pages, as well as new skills are all, in some sense, rooted in the affective response of the infant, which the parent recognises, shares, builds upon and extends. These parents may exploit their child's emotional involvement for their own adult purposes, to enhance that infant's lexical knowledge, to merge individual child experience with that of the wider speech community. Further evidence for the importance of meaningful items for infant aesthetic and psychic development will be adduced in Chapter 8. Suffice it to note for the present that the process of picturebook reading is as much about the pleasure which these infants derive from finding in their book something that they already know and like, as it is about the joy of learning new items.

Empathy

Growth and development in the infant, it has been argued, are necessarily contingent upon these two adults having a different point of view from that of the infant and expressing that – but not only that. In this family, change also has to do, it seems, with the ability of those same parents to engage with, and articulate the point of view of their infant interlocutor. In other words, it seems that not only do parents have a point of view other than that of the child (otherwise how could development occur); it is also the case, in this study, that they engage affectively with the spontaneous response of the infant (from which then derives an ongoing process of growth and change).

To summarise, from a communication point of view the utterances of adults in this family, in their culture, it seems, contain markers of the following:

- a capacity (of the speaker) to find common ground with the interlocutor, as, for example, choosing the tomatoes in the picnic scene, instead of the bananas;
- a capacity (of the speaker) to mark their discourse with the perspective which they have on a topic (e.g. a mathematical perspective involves counting all the tomatoes one by one);
- a capacity (of the speaker) to shift viewpoint to that of the interlocutor (but without losing sight of their own) in order to see the world from the interlocutor's vantage point (the ants on the table cloth are included in the discussion);
- a capacity (of the speaker) to engage affectively with the interlocutor, to acknowledge and express that engagement in their own discourse, lexically, or phonologically, or both (the adult gets excited about the ants).

These principles bear some resemblance to the review of dialogic principles proposed by Linell and Jönsson (1991). What I would stress, however, is that dialogues between these parents and their infant (and, in my view, therapist and client, and not least, teacher and pupil) depend crucially on the second two of the aforementioned parameters – the capacity on the part of the adult to engage (affectively) with the viewpoint of their interlocutor, and to take this as their starting-point.[2]

For Winnicott, the capacity to view the world from a perspective other than one's own is essential in health: 'a sign of health in the mind is the ability of one individual to enter imaginatively and yet accurately into the thoughts and feelings and hopes and fears of another person; also to allow the other person to do the same to us' (Winnicott 1970 [1986:117]). Empathy (on the part of the adult) is an aspect of early parent–infant interaction which has received scant attention in the research literature. Yet the capacity of the parent to get into their child's skin and see things from their point of view, and articulate it, seems, in the context of the observations made in this family, to be a feature not so much of emotional health, as Winnicott believed, but of cognitive growth.

5.2 The impact of language

Even as one observes what the parents and infants in this family 'do' in their picturebook reading, and how they do it, one question remains paramount. Of what benefit is it to the child that a parent behave in this way? It is a question to be answered at a number of different levels. From a linguistic standpoint, semantic and discourse development are parameters which receive especial endorsement in picturebook settings (Chapter 3). The importance of early picturebook reading for infant psychic growth has yet to be discussed (Chapters 7 and 8). Addressed below, albeit very briefly, is the qualitative contribution to the cognitive development of the infant of a picturebook description. The value to these infants of a linguistic description, in my view, has to do with what they actually perceive in picturebooks, how much they understand about what they see there, and the use which they make of that knowledge to interpret happenings in the real world.

Structuring infant perception

Human beings view the world, not only with the eyes, but with the mind. Seeing is more than a matter of stimulation of the optic nerve; it is a mental act of perception (Gombrich 1960). This is a cumulative process; Western twentieth-century man perceives and represents the human body very differently from the ancient Greeks. Let us then enquire as to whether or not the possession of linguistic knowledge conditions what these two infants perceive in their picturebooks.

While children's perceptions are clearly not entirely contingent upon language, whether in reading or everyday life situations (they perceive their mother's face irrespective of any linguistic label they may or may not possess), linguistic knowledge does seem to play an increasing part in reading discussions. In the early stages, up to the age of 13 months (approximately), when pointing to pictures spontaneously, it is strongly the author's impression that both Rhys and Ceri selected images for which they already knew the corresponding word form, and some for which they did not. However, when asked (after about 14 months) by the adult: 'What can you see on this page?', these children almost invariably located a referent for which they already possessed a word form. (Closed adult questions of course were always directed at what the child knew; these adults never asked either child to point out something they felt s/he did not know).

As time went on, however, the cases where these infants, even spontaneously, drew attention to an aspect of their book for which they had not already been provided with the corresponding linguistic term became less frequent. Having noticed a referent (e.g. a dog) they might then go on to notice differences between individual dogs for which they did not know the exact word form (dalmatians as opposed to terriers). But the trigger to noticing the referent in the first instance seemed to be linguistic in kind. Certainly, there were exceptions; the butterfly is an example of an item noticed at 19 months without its label having been fully acquired, but such instances, it seemed, were rare.

Could it be then, that these children somehow internalised that what is the focus of attention in books is in some way connected with the language used to describe it? Did they learn, in some social sense, that 'what it is appropriate to talk about is what has already been talked about', the rest being, as it were, off limits, even taboo? Or could it be that linguistic experience itself genuinely does determine in some perceptual sense what Rhys and Ceri noticed about their picturebook world?

A tentative conclusion might run as follows. With time, adult linguistic input appears to structure these children's perception of their picturebook world to a quite significant degree, though why this should be so is unclear. If children possess a label for a pictorial feature, that feature, over time, apparently enjoys an enhanced degree of salience relative to other (unlabelled) referents. It might be the case, too, although I have no firm data on this point, that pictorial distinctions which are not the focus of discussion risk passing unnoticed (cf. Brown *et al.* 1958:7). This study can offer no definitive conclusion on this issue, but it possibly merits further research.

Making sense of a picturebook scene

Referents in a picturebook scene not only acquire salience by virtue of having been discussed; they also become interconnected, and begin to make sense. This is a further advantage of adult comments made to the reading infant. That is, entities which are available to visual inspection, become, through the language of picturebook reading, hierarchically organised and interrelated. Referents of all kinds, be they human or animal, animate or inanimate, gradually come to form a coherent whole, by virtue of their integration within a paradigm, or event, linguistically mediated. At the same time, the behaviour of human protagonists is rendered 'sensible', because of the position they enjoy ('ringmaster', 'zookeeper', 'waiter', or simply 'Mummy' or 'Daddy') or the motives, thoughts and ideas which are attributed to them. To this kind of understanding of events, infant readers become introduced via language.

It is far from clear whether, without such a linguistic construction, any understanding of illustrated events could be reached independently by the infant. Indirect support for this view comes from research into the perception of pictures by children with language difficulties, or who are severely disturbed emotionally. Such children describe the different aspects of an illustrated event, or set of events, not as an interrelated and meaningful whole, but in fragmented, dissociated form. A tree in the background is, in the discourse of such children, on the same plane as the protagonist; both are juxtaposed as isolated entities. 'That's a man; there's a tree'. The protagonists, if they are mentioned at all, are themselves seemingly perceived as unrelated; at least, in the discourse, they are not connected (Préneron 1994). Linguistic description is possibly an indispensable part of allowing children to apprehend the nature of the connection between different pictorial representations.

The transfer of knowledge to real-world events

A final question concerns the extent to which these infants use the knowledge gleaned from reading as a basis for interpreting reality itself. The answer takes two forms. The first, already well documented in the literature, is that adults take the initiative, and introduce, into real-life situations, references to books. Passing a dog in the street, a parent may liken it to one known in a book (Heath 1982). In this study too, countless allusions to reading in the course of daily life are made by this mother – with Rhys particularly. He is encouraged, for example, to 'be like Tom' and put his boots on.

But do infants spontaneously use knowledge acquired in reading, whether linguistic and/or non-linguistic, to interpret the events of real life? Two anecdotes serve to illustrate that Rhys does precisely this. At 18 months old, before he could speak, Rhys, staring at a display of cakes in a bakery, identifies just the single one which he had met for the first time in his reading: the doughnuts! At 20 months the construction site in town is discussed using gestures in terms of the 'hammer' (gesture of monstration), 'banging' (downwards movement of child's arm) down (on the man's thumb), and the man 'holding his thumb' (infant holds own thumb) because he had hurt himself. This sequence, again, replicates exactly what had been first developed for him in a reading situation. It is as if two-dimensional images, and, most probably, their associated linguistic forms, serve as a basis upon which to construct a view of single items, and even events, in the three-dimensional world.

For both these infants, though in different ways, events of the real world, particularly those of which they have little first-hand knowledge, become endowed with a unity and coherence greater, one suspects, than if the complex interrelationships governing those events had not previously been discussed with reference to a picture. This is another way of saying that children's perceptions and world view may be strongly influenced by their experience of books (and possibly of other media as well). Whether, and which, children, as individuals, 'use' what they see in two-dimensional form as a schema for the construction of life's events, is also a topic which perhaps warrants further investigation.

6 CONCLUSION

Parent and infant turns in picturebook reading dialogues have, in this chapter, been examined to the extent that they contribute to a jointly negotiated, canonical reading of a picturebook scene. Picturebook activities have been viewed as more than an exercise in the development of word meaning; they may also take the form of an event interpretation involving mutual recognition of participants' differing perspectives. Part, if not all, of an adult's reading of a page is brought within the sphere of an infant's pre-existing, and changing, knowledge and affections. Instead of being imposed 'from the outside', the archetype which eventually unfolds takes on personal significance for the infant, and, I would suggest, is the more readily internalised in consequence.

Part III
THE ONTOGENESIS OF NARRATIVE

Storytelling, in spoken or written mode, is an undertaking of monumental importance in the history of man. Whether in the form of myth or legend, chronicle or biography, epic or novel, narrative has been described as one of the most basic human activities, reflecting every person's need to tell someone else that something has happened. What narrative tells about is a sequence of events in time, which, in the process become organised, evaluated, transformed. One of its functions perhaps is to defy the ephemeral nature of experiences, to hold on to occurrences by telling about them, that is, to retain, repeat and re-present for consideration 'what was, in actuality, a transient happening' (Whitehead 1990:98).

It is not just at a societal level that narrative assumes significance. Personal biography, that capacity to structure the world around an autobiographical event, allows children particularly to order and explain things which otherwise might remain random and inexplicable. Without this ability to reorganise and review their experience, people would, in Stern's view, be literally mad (Stern 1985). Narrative form, then, is a developmental turning-point in a human being's understanding both of the world, and themselves.

The construction of narrative, however, is not only a basis for psychic health; it is also, for some, the route via which a return to health may be achieved. The psychoanalytic enterprise itself is founded upon narrative – in this circumstance not so much the recall of past events, but the establishment of a coherent and plausible biography constructed by the patient in conjunction with the therapist. The patient's 'ragged story' is transformed with the help of the analyst into a convincing 'narrative' based, not on what did happen, but on what might have happened, in the patient's past: 'the transference neurosis is not a direct repetition of events, or even experiences, but a constructive fiction' (Klauber 1987:19).

In the life of an individual child, storytelling begins early; ask a child what s/he has done today and the chances are you will get a story (Meek *et al.* 1977:7). Language of course is fundamental in the ordering process; the events of the day are organised selectively. Herein lies a key difference between a narrative account and a videorecording; through language, our activities and experiences are given shape and pattern and events of emotional importance highlighted. The 're-presentation of experiences in order to understand them better is a marked feature of human thinking, occurring in children's play, in art and across cultures' (Whitehead 1990:98). Very early on, then, people's lives may become objects of reflection.

Storytelling is thus by no means an event which is confined to literature. It is a genre which every toddler might encounter to a greater or lesser extent in non-fictional form every day of their life. What then, are the essential features of telling a child a story from a book? What are the core features of narrative fiction, and how is a toddler first introduced to them at around one year old? How does the process of storytelling between mother and infant evolve between one and two years old? In this, and the next chapter, data which draw on the construction of storytelling experiences between Ceri and her mother are presented in an attempt to ascertain something of the contribution which storybooks make to the ontogenesis of narrative. (The exclusion of Rhys in this circumstance is discussed below, Chapter 6, section 5.2).

5

THE WORLD OF THE STORY

1 CORE FEATURES OF NARRATIVE

1.1 A definition of fiction

In order to understand better the essence of storytelling, take as a starting-point the distinction made by Bruner between non-fiction and fiction. Two fundamentally different but complementary approaches to ordering experience and constructing a view of the world are contrasted and compared. The first is the paradigmatic, logico-scientific view, which is concerned with the establishment of truth, objectively verifiable. This position is characteristic of the scientific essay. The second, more the province of the poet or the storyteller, is concerned, not with objective truth, but with lifelikeness. Well-formed argument, that is, is contrasted with literary fiction: poem, play, or novel (Bruner 1986).

While the central propositions of the former are verifiable with reference to empirical data and answer the question: 'Is this true, or not?', the storyteller answers to the criterion of verisimilitude: 'How lifelike is this?' Within the argument, the scientist is concerned with universal truth, with description, explanation and categorisation. The storyteller, dramatist, or poet, however, is concerned with a dual landscape. On the one hand, there is a preoccupation with actions and events – the 'grammar' of the story. On the other, the motives and feelings of the characters, on the basis of which events become connected, must be addressed. The protagonists, or rather, their beliefs, intentions and consciousness knit the events of the plot together; into their life and mind, the reader must enter. It is this concern for psychological truth which is so essential in works of literature.

From the point of view of the reader, too, the response to the two modes of writing must of necessity be different. A relative degree of certainty contrasts with much greater uncertainty. For whereas a scientific writer seeks to achieve identity of perspective with regard to the referent – the message must be received as it is transmitted, the storyteller represents their material from at least a dual, if not a multiple perspective, having in mind both the dual landscape and the response of the reader. Indeed, far from being invited to corroborate the standpoint of the author, as in non-fiction, readers of fiction are often recruited for the purpose of inventing the story for themselves, at least partially. The reader interacts with the text to construct its meaning. 'In the end, it is the reader who must write for himself what *he* intends to do with the actual text', since 'fictional texts are inherently indeterminate' (Bruner 1986).

Narrative text thus has two major components: a sequence of events explicable with reference to the psychological identity of the protagonists, and the author's viewpoint(s) on the events as they unfold. An interpretation of the text is the result of a three-way encounter between the text, the author of the text and the reader. The three-way exchange is neatly summarised thus: '*every actually spoken word* (or comprehensibly written one), and not one slumbering in a dictionary, is *an expression and product of the social interaction of three components:- the speaker* (author), *the listener* (reader), and *the one of whom* (or of which) *they speak* (the hero)' Voloshinov (1926 [1988:17]). In storytelling however, the contact between author and infant is not direct; the parent is interposed as storyteller. The parent is thus both 'reader' (of the original written) text, and 'creator' (of the story as actually told). He, or she, relates the (written) story for the listening infant.

1.2 Stories for children

What can be said of a child's response to a work of fiction? How does a 7-, or a 10-year-old, able to read for themselves, enter into a fictional world, and how might their response differ from that of an adult?

A children's story, is, by definition, not life, not true. But at the same time, for a child, a story may be so apparently real as to be barely distinguishable from reality itself. Authors create a 'Secondary World' into which readers enter, as if entranced, on becoming involved with the story (Tolkien 1964). Ultimately, however, an adult can pull back and realise that a story is just that: a story. But younger readers need to be reminded, even reassured, that what they have read is not real. This is far from Brecht's view that a relationship of distance must obtain between audience and protagonist, and from the need for the dramatist to be constantly reminding one of it. It is far, too, from the sophistication of a Virginia Woolf, whose changing perspectives leave the adult in doubt as to who, and where, they are as reader. The emphasis, with the child reader, is on increased belief. One of the issues which must be considered is the way in which a parent leads the very young infant into the magical world of the story and towards the belief that it is true.

Total absorption is one aspect of reading fiction. Generated, too, however, may be a more reflective and more critical mode of reading. Warlow describes it thus:

Really there appear to be two methods of reading fiction. Either the attention of the reader, particularly if a child, is focused exclusively on the Secondary World of the novel, his eyes are glued to the rapidly turning pages, his critical faculties are entirely suspended ... ; or else he reads more carefully, pausing to think, making mental notes of interesting points and considering whether the book is good or not. [The latter is] a form of mental 'flickering' between a commitment to the Secondary World and critical evaluation of it.

Warlow (1977:94)

A child reader of fiction thus enjoys a (sometimes unshakeable) belief in a world not of their own making, but there may be present, too, a capacity for reflective judgement. Consider now the position of the much younger child, aged two years or less, being read to from an illustrated storybook, and referred to in this chapter as an 'infant'.

1.3 The infant response

Ceri, as a pre-literate infant sitting at her mother's knee does not, as might an older child, have direct access to the written text. What she perceives directly are the illustrations of her book, which she may interpret in her own way, spontaneously and independently of the parent reader. This infant's perception of the illustrations may relate to the story as written, or it may not. Her attention may be drawn to the picture of the hero, but she may also be attracted by the train in the corner of the illustration whose presence is of no consequence to the author's written story at all. This parent (using not one, but a sequence of pictures, and with access to the written text if need be) is moved to construct her own adult version of the (author's) story. The parent's storyline, at the very least, focuses on the hero of the published text and a set of events in sequence. This adult version overlays the infant's perception of the pictures. But she remains mindful, always, of Ceri's point of view. As with picturebook reading there is, at the outset, a potential gap between the two viewpoints, that of the adult, and that of the child, a gap which is to be bridged by the intersection of the two viewpoints at certain junctures. This is the position in which this parent and infant reading stories together find themselves.

Psychological truth

For Bruner, psychological truth is the very essence of fictional narrative, yet it is a dimension of reading which is perhaps less frequently encountered in picturebooks. In narrative, motivation and intention are as the glue which binds together protagonists and their actions. Readers must be helped in the move both outwards from themselves into a world of action, as well as inwards, into the world of feelings (Meek *et al.* 1977). However, a storybook is the story, not of oneself, but of somebody else. On what basis, then, are child readers able to penetrate a story's content? They do so by relying on, even extrapolating from, their own first-hand experience of people, their thoughts and feelings, experience which, in the case of the child, is much more limited than that of the adult. There is a need for children's authors to take due account of the disparity:

> the writer is left with one obvious and inescapable difference between child and adult readers: the former have not lived so long, and in the nature of things they cannot have built up the same mental and emotional capital of background knowledge and first-hand experience.
> (Trease 1977:148)

The adult presenter is thus faced with something of a paradox. Book reading involves learning about the experiences of others. The difficulty is that first-hand experience of others is a prerequisite for entering the world of the book, and yet such experience is precisely what younger readers lack. How much more acute is this dilemma with a young infant. This is one of the challenges of storybook reading which the adult as presenter must meet.

The psychological dimension to reading brings with it a further, linguistic, challenge to the adult as presenter. If a story is to achieve lifelikeness in the Brunerian sense, then feelings and emotions must form part of the stuff of the narrative. But the move away from ostensive definition (in picturebook reading) does not begin in earnest until well into the second year of life (cf. Chapter 4). Abstract nouns: joy, sorrow, disgust, are not yet a feature. How, in that case, should the feelings of the protagonists be conveyed to a 12-month-old who does not yet possess an extensive linguistic repertoire in this domain?

Material truth

Alongside the psychological truth of fiction, there is material truth: the background, or environment, against which, or within which, personalities enact the drama of their lives. One may think of Dickens or Balzac, Austen or Zola. Physical circumstances, the material backdrop, are, I believe, as important for infant readers as they are for adults. How might this dimension of reading be approached with a pre-literate infant?

The response is to be found, in part, by recalling the premise enunciated in Chapter 1, namely, that parents build, when reading, upon what they know their infant to be. This includes their infant's cognitive capacities, emotional preoccupations, linguistic development, and, of particular relevance here, real-world experiences. Infants themselves live within an environment. There is never a baby (on its own) but, always, a 'nursing couple', an 'environment–individual set-up' (Winnicott 1952 [1958:99]). The environment, at the beginning, is represented largely by mother, and will include both the person of the mother and the ritual patterns of care, or techniques which she uses with her infant: 'the infant has come to know this technique as part of the mother, just like her face and her ear and the necklaces she wears, and her varying attitudes (affected by hurry, laziness, anxiety, worry, excitement, etc.)' (Winnicott 1954 [1958:266]).

Routines of handling, the mental and emotional disposition of mother, her appearance, which includes her body (here, face or ear), and her possessions (here, her jewellery) which infants can explore with all their senses, are constitutive of the infant's environment. The world of an infant, therefore, is not constituted by the infant only, but also by those around; by her possessions, and theirs; by patterns of care, and by sensations which are familiar. Infants' experiences of the outside world are more circumscribed, perhaps, than that of older children, but experiences they have nonetheless, of a particularly rich kind. This is the basis, perhaps, upon which mother and toddler together will be able to 'enter' the story, even the basis upon which a mother may mobilise her infant reader's response to the story she recounts.

Affect

Toddlers thus differ from children in that their experience of the outer world is more limited. The intensity of their emotions constitutes a further possible difference. Winnicott again:

> In this particular matter of seeing the world as it is, what can we say about the toddler? For the toddler, every sensation is tremendously intense. We, as grown-ups, only at special moments reach this wonderful intensity of feeling which belongs to the early years, and anything that helps us to get there without frightening us is welcome. For some it is music or a picture that gets us there, for some it is a football match, and for others it is dressing up for a dance. ... For the little child, and how much more for the infant, life is just a series of terrifically intense experiences.
> (Winnicott 1964:70)

Fiction, for many, is not so much a question of knowing, as of feeling; it has its roots in affect. The organising principle, from the author's point of view, is a story which feels right, not one that is known to be right (Britton 1977:108). As for the reader, the origin of their response is always affective, finding its expression in the form of criticism, or of a 'flood of tears' (Warlow 1977:96). Emotions and mood contained within or aroused by the story – joy, pleasure, fear, sadness or disgust – are a dimension of reading of particular relevance to a young infant. However, in order to experience certain moments as especially intense, there must be periods of relative calm. Incorporating these differing moments into their presentation is a task which confronts any adult who reads to a very young infant.

Activity

Active participation is a further peculiar characteristic of early infancy. Toddlers are not seated motionless while listening to a story, as they might one day be at a playgroup. They contribute actively (and sometimes unpredictably), indeed are encouraged to do so. There is a preoccupation with touching the book, meaningfully, which represents a further challenge to the reading adult, to reconcile her own 'adult' purpose in telling the story with the desire which Ceri, for instance, has to make incessant contact with the book herself, on aspects which are important to her. Storytelling takes the form, not of monologue, but of dialogue. What, however, is the nature of this dialogue? Active infant responses to illustrated stories are one of the aspects of early reading which needs to be considered.

Style

Last, narrative fiction is written in accordance with a set of conventions with which an infant, as yet, is unacquainted, and in a style of language sometimes very different from child directed speech. In sum four key aspects of storymaking with a one-year-old have been identified:

- The psychological experience and material circumstances of the protagonists must be conveyed to an infant whose linguistic understanding still relies heavily upon ostensive definition.
- Two apparently different worlds, that of a toddler, idiosyncratic and known intimately by themselves, and that of a wider world (of the story as written by the author) must somehow be bridged.
- The intense and active moments of infant involvement, often centred upon aspects of their choosing, must be integrated within a bipolar exchange whose purpose ultimately, from the adult point of view, is to tell the child the story.
- The 'grammar' of a story, and language in written, rather than spoken style, must be introduced to an infant barely able, as yet, to speak.

Given these constraints, how does this mother, when reading a story from a book, confront matters of realism, both psychological and material, and infant reader activity? (Story grammar and written text are matters for Chapter 6.) These are the two main issues now to be examined in an analysis of the presentation of two illustrated storybooks in which Ceri's participation was particularly active. The first was presented to her at child age 14 months, and the second at child age 25 months. Similarities and differences in patterns of behaviour in both Ceri and her mother at infant age 1 and 2 years old respectively are described.

THE WORLD OF THE STORY

2 A STORY WITH A 14-MONTH-OLD

The example of *Alex's Outing*

Alex's Outing by Mary Dickinson (Scholastic Publications, 1984) is the story of a little boy who, in the company of his (easygoing) mother, takes part in a children's outing by bus to the country. On the trip, which includes a picnic and blackberrying, Alex's mischievous antics contrast with the behaviour of an obedient little girl, Wendy, and her much more strict mother. On his return home, Alex cleans himself up by having a bath.

The book comprises sixteen double pages, with, printed on the left, the story, and on the right, a single scene illustration (picture of Alex falling in the mud, or of his peers picnicking, etc). The published text accompanying these illustrations comprises some seven hundred words, an extract of which is now cited:

> On the way home from the bus stop Alex's mother showed him the blackberries she had picked. Alex remembered the ones in his pocket. He slid in his hand. Ugh. His pocket was all wet and sticky. The blackberries were very squashed. There was a big patch of purple on his jeans. Will Mum be cross, wondered Alex.

2.1 Content

The 'adult view' in this narrative is represented by the storyline, an adapted parental version of the story as it appears in the original. This storyline, from the point of view of its content, cannot be considered familiar ground for this infant reader. At one level, the story has parallels with her own life: the choice of a small child, a boy, as the hero of the story, and his participation in an outing accompanied by his mother, is not dissimilar from Ceri's real-world experience, since she too is a small child with a Mummy who takes her out. However, the main event of the story, a trip to the country for a picnic by bus in the company of a group of other children and their mothers, is not an event Ceri had ever taken part in. 'Old' words are being combined to introduce 'new' content, that is, a storyline whose contents are largely unfamiliar. The premise that children will, in their reading, encounter events and experiences which are not their own is here fully borne out.

However, a remarkable feature of the telling of this story is not so much the complete absence of the original story as written text, but rather how little the author's story, either as originally written, or even in paraphrase form, dominates the live interaction. Instead, this parent's presentation is devoted almost exclusively to the evocation of a familiar world in which Ceri may recognise herself. This familiar world is constantly intercalated with the events of the storyline. The following extract makes clear the distinction between (unfamiliar) storyline (italicised) and familiar world (indented):

Mother	**Ceri (14 months)**
(Page turn)	
Now they're going home in the bus	
(page turn)	
Have to wash handies won't they Wez, hmm.	
There, what can see here?	
	[nasal fricative] *(her 'pleased' sound)*
Who's that Wezzy, who's that?	
	[dai]
Doggy, yes! What doggy say?	
	[heu heu] *(her 'dog' sound)*
Woof woof, that's right, Wezzy!	
	[keus] *(her 'delighted' sound)*
Yes	
(page turn)	
And there they are, getting ready for bathroom.	
	[pussy]
Pussy! Yes Wezzy, you can see pussy!	
And what else can you see in the picture?	
Can you see teddy? Where's teddy?	

Overall, in the presentation of this book, the storyline accounts for barely ten out of a total of one hundred or more adult utterances. 'Have to wash handies', for example, is all that is rendered of the fifty-eight word extract cited above. Instead, the parent, as creator of this story and Ceri, as listener, collude in the evocation of a familiar world. In Bruner's terms, the child (listener) – parent (narrator) axis is exceptionally strong, while the hero of the story (Alex), as new input, occupies, in quantitative terms, a relatively minor place.

But what is this familiar world? The world referred to is that envisaged by Winnicott, the 'total environmental set-up' in which the young infant lives and moves. The pictures in the book are described, not so much with reference to their importance to the story-as-published, but rather as a function of their importance to Ceri's personal preoccupations and circumstances. Thus, where her real-life favourites occur in the picture (here, the dog, the cat and the teddy), this mother is careful to include them in her presentation even though they bear little, or no, obvious relation to the storyline as a whole. 'Teddy, there's teddy' she says, as she turns the page over and teddy, pictured sitting on the floor of the bathroom, comes into view. Comparable examples are the plastic duck, the bottle of shampoo, and the bath hat in the bathroom; all these are included in this storytelling event. Ceri is excited by these illustrations, and enjoys them intensely, for their own sake, because they give pleasure, but not necessarily because they have anything to do with the ongoing action of the story-as-written.

Between the storyline, as told by this mother, and the highly emotionally charged items, of especial importance to the infant reader, but seemingly unrelated to the storyline as a whole, is an intermediate area. In the intermediate area, the storyline and Ceri's world intersect. This mother achieves the overlap by selecting aspects of the illustrations which are relevant to the story as printed, but, at the same time, coding them in a carefully constructed linguistic formulation of her own, in such a way that a relationship between (the story) picture and Ceri's own life becomes clearly, but implicitly, established. Some examples should make this point.

In the picture, Alex's and Wendy's respective mothers are shown. Wendy's mother is of importance to the printed story since, as stated earlier, she is the foil to her more easygoing counterpart, Alex's mother. This adult presenter alludes to the illustration of Wendy's mother, but not by using the words 'Wendy's mother'. Instead she calls her 'the lady with the glasses'. 'Oh! the lady with the glasses. Can you see her glasses Wezzy? Show Mummy her glasses!'

The storyline is thus arrested, ceding its place to taxonomic description. The concern is now: 'what is of interest on this page', not 'what happens next'. But, why should the glasses be selected? Because spectacles are an important part of Ceri's life; at this age, she loves putting on and taking off the spectacles which her own mother wears. Not only do they form part of her material world; they have, in addition, strong affective associations for her. This is the world which Ceri knows, her own, or her mother's possessions, which she touches and feels, the equivalent for this infant reader of Winnicott's necklaces, artefacts drawn from this particular child's own, very personal, environmental set-up.

The illustrations are thus designed, many of them, to be relevant to the story as written, but, in the telling, aspects of them are selected, and coded in a form of language which makes them relate to this infant reader's experience. However, 'experience' has a dual implication. The theoretical view, earlier quoted (section 1.3) was that storytelling appeals not only to the material capital of a child's experience, but to that child's emotional capital as well. Remarkably, this is precisely what this parent, when reading to a young infant, finds herself doing.

Consider a further example, in which children are shown sitting together on board the bus. Mother says: 'There they are on the bus, *going bouncy bouncy bounce*'. 'The children on the bus' is an integral part of the narrative as published; thus far, this mother is merely paraphrasing the text. The written text, however, does not specify that these children are 'bouncing up and down' on the seat of the bus, nor indeed does the picture suggest this either, yet this is the interpretation proffered by this adult reader. Why? Because she knows (as a mother) that Ceri's main association with 'buses' comes from a song which she dances to often, in which 'the people on the bus bounce up and down'. 'Bouncing' on a bus bridges the world of the story with that of the child; the two coalesce, to the extent that is not clear if this mother's words are to do with the story or to do with Ceri's life. In fact they are to do with both at once. Voloshinov's conception of the word as a two-sided act, determined equally both by whose word it is, and for whom it is meant, could have no clearer exemplification.

But there is a further noteworthy feature of this mother's use of language. She could have said, quite straightforwardly: 'the children are bouncing up and down in the bus'. Instead, she opts for the much more evocative incantation: 'going bouncy bouncy bounce' which, in Ceri's experience, is further associated with jogging up and down on her mother's knee in imitation of a bus jolting along the road, and in which she takes especial delight. By judicious choice of language, this mother conveys the excitement on the children's outing – but without explicit recourse to intangibles: 'enjoyment', or 'fun', a vocabulary which Ceri does not yet possess, but the experience of which she has encountered many times.

Comparable examples of the creation of mood and atmosphere abound. 'Alex having a cuddle in the towel' after his bath suggests warmth of feeling, while: 'Getting very sticky and dirty aren't they Wez! Have to wash handies' links not only with the reality of Ceri's own life, for she, too, washes her hands when they are in a mess, but also with the feeling of disgust caused by the wholly unpleasant sensation of a viscous substance (which Ceri, as an individual, particularly dislikes). The line between the experience of the hero and the experience of our child reader is a fine one, both objectively (the contents of their shared world), and subjectively (in that they share the same feelings). The words of Voloshinov are apt indeed (1926 [1988:19]): 'the poet selects his words, not from a dictionary, but from the context of real life where they are fixed and steeped with evaluations'.

These findings may be summarised thus. The pictorial contents of an illustrated story and its accompanying text are 'read' by this parent idiosyncratically. The story-as-written is transformed into a presentation with a three-tier, hierarchical structure. Something resembling a pyramid might be an appropriate analogy. Each tier of the pyramid has a visual and a linguistic element. The broad base consists in the identification of a large number of pictorial details frequently almost irrelevant to the story as originally written, but whose visual content and linguistic coding both carry a high emotional charge for the infant reader. In this tale, examples are 'teddy' and 'cat', neither of which are mentioned in the author's original story at all.

A second tier consists of visual details of relevance (potentially) to the storyline, but where the language of the parent draws upon and thus reevokes a familiar real-world experience for this infant. 'Wendy's mother' (of the original) becomes transformed (linguistically) into 'the lady with the glasses'. The orientation of the picture is towards the author's text; the orientation of the language is towards the child reader. In the longer term, one might envisage that the 'lady with the glasses' will become, linguistically, 'Wendy's mother', whereas 'cat' and 'teddy', one might speculate, could well be eliminated from discussion altogether.

At the third tier, illustrations are both selected and coded linguistically in accordance with the writer's original intention. This (parental) linguistic coding is a paraphrased, and much abridged version of the author's original written text. What I have called the storyline must represent for Ceri, or so I imagine, new and difficult content. In terms of the dialogue as a whole, this third level, in quantitative terms, is minimal.

This three-tier somewhat schematic account of how the distance between Ceri's perception of her storybook and the author's written version of the story is bridged has implications at other levels: for the interactive exchanges between parent and infant and for the discourse structure of this mother's presentation. The second of the two issues for this chapter will now be considered: the active involvement of the infant in the dynamics of the dialogue as it unfolds.

2.2 Discourse

The different dimensions of this mother's presentation are carefully orchestrated. As in an opera, there are moments in her account when the actions and the events of the story are moved forward, and there are others when advances in the storyline are arrested, even interrupted, in the interests of a more lyrical or taxonomic description of the pages, more as a function, perhaps, of Ceri's curiosity and excitement. It seems that this mother 'holds' the storyline for her child, as it were, in the background, while becoming involved in another, often quite separate, set of themes, in parallel to it. Here (as before in Chapter 1) the extent to which a one-year-old can concentrate is always a consideration. At 14 months, descriptions do not extend beyond a maximum of three or four different items per page, at which point the page is turned and Ceri's attention re-engaged by a different illustration. It is at this moment that this mother frequently seizes the opportunity to allude once more to the storyline, even if such moments are shortlived, as the excitement of Ceri's world again takes over. Winnicott's view of a child's life being a succession of intense experiences (during which, in narrative, Ceri involves herself in aspects of the illustrations of her own choosing), interspersed with a series of calmer states (during which, in narrative, her mother intercalates the storyline) here finds empirical justification.

Changes in content from storyline to description are matched by structural differences in the dialogue. These differences turn on questions of interactive responsibility: 'which' participant does 'what', 'how' and 'when'. Despite the very active involvement of this 14-month-old at different points in the session, it is apparent that it is her mother who almost always moves forward the events of this story; she has both the knowledge and the language with which to do it. Ceri, in this particular storytelling event, responds only very rarely to questions about the storyline: 'who', or 'where' Alex is or 'what' he is doing. The storyline is thus characterised by a relatively complex sentential structure cast in the affirmative. Pointing to the protagonists as they reappear from one page to the next, and with Ceri in a relatively quiescent state, this mother uses utterances of the form: 'there's x (y)' as a means of identification, followed by an -ing form to indicate an action in process: 'There's Wendy waiting at the busstop, yes, and all the boys and girls going to the country. . . . There they are on the bus, going bouncy bouncy bounce. . . . Oh Wezzy, the mummys having their lunch aren't they! . . . And there they are picking blackberries, and getting very sticky and dirty aren't they Wez. . . . Now they're going home in the bus. . . . Have to wash handies won't they Wez. . . . And there they are, getting ready for bathroom. . . . And there's Alex, look, he's having a cuddle in the towel.'

Questions to Ceri are most usually reserved for moments when the action is arrested, when describing details of the picture. Of the picnic page mother asks: 'What can you see on this page?', and Ceri points out a banana, the bread and the juice, which the mother then identifies in language, using for this purpose a single noun, with little or no further qualification: 'banana', 'bread', 'juice'. Alternatively, Ceri will spontaneously locate something of especial interest to her. In other words, the moments at which the action moves on are, on the whole, not the moments when Ceri is most actively participating. Vocalisation, pointing, both spontaneous and solicited, and intense excitement are reserved for when teddy appears, when the duck is spotted on the edge of the bath, or the cat on the bathroom floor. Taxonomic descriptions thus tend to be associated with the active participation of the infant, with minimal (feedback) structures and sometimes, though not invariably, with interrogative forms.

In other words, while a single noun phrase characterises description, an expanded (and equally consistent) form of utterance structure is associated with the storyline. The different moments in the story are thus formally marked and clearly distinguishable. Functionally, systematic variation of this kind acts perhaps as a covert signal to Ceri: 'You will know when the storyline arrives because the nature of the language which I use alters completely.'

Other markers of the storyline are its discourse position, reflecting its relatively higher status from the point of view of adult purpose. That is to say, on pages where the narrative moves on the storyline features immediately, as soon as the page is turned, provided Ceri does not intervene and introduce another topic first. The effort made by this mother, in the storyline utterances, to reach a degree of consensus with her child may also be noted; tag questions, or 'yes', are often included (see examples above). As storymaker, she appears to want to merge her perspective on the picture with the viewpoint of her infant as reader. There is here unity of perspective, rather than a multiplicity of authorial viewpoints, as might be found in the very much more sophisticated writing of, say, a Virginia Woolf.

Summary

In reading *Alex's Outing* this mother and her 14-month-old infant together establish an interactional modus operandi in which both adopt clearly defined positions. A clearly demarcated narrative mode with an abbreviated storyline told by the mother alternates with a taxonomic mode, again with its own structural characteristics, in which the interests of the child reader are particularly excited. The dynamics of the interaction involve frequent shifts between these two levels; they constitute, as it were, the warp and the woof of the exchange which here takes place between parent and infant.

This adult emerges not so much as a storyteller, but as a storycreator. Using her intimate knowledge of her own child's personal world, the settings, possessions and sensations which are familiar and meaningful, and the language with which these are associated, she bridges the world of the infant reader and that of the book. There is as yet little distinction or difference between the one and the other, rather the one is a reflection of the other. Indeed, the book's hero and the infant reader, in the language of this mother, are often as one.

Notably absent from this presentation is the story-as-published; sustained extracts of the author's original text are not included. Even the paraphrased account features quite minimally. This mother instead uses the pictures to involve Ceri in things of interest to her. There is no sense in which this infant is reflecting critically upon what she hears; her commitment to and involvement in the events of the story are total.

How then do the theoretical points of section 1 match the empirical findings of section 2? Briefly, it is as follows. Fictional narrative is, by definition, predicated not only upon events and actions related in sequence, but also upon the thoughts, feelings and intentions of the protagonists. Postulated, too, was the existence of a fictional Secondary World, characterised by psychological and material realism, possibly beyond the social, even linguistic, reach of a very young infant. The potential for active and intense involvement on the part of the infant was also noted.

The parental response to the challenge posed by reading to a young infant is the structural and functional reorganisation of the text-as-illustrated, in which none of the key elements of narrative as defined above are vitiated. This parent directs active involvement towards more personal constructs, while proposing simultaneously a succinct, abridged rendering of the story-as-published. The (potential) discrepancy between the infant's world and the world of the book is narrowed, through careful choice of both pictorial images and language, while the literary canons of psychological and material verisimilitude are simultaneously respected. A degree of synchrony between adult and child needs is again attained.

3 A STORY WITH A 25-MONTH-OLD

The example of *Maisie Middleton*

Consider now another favourite story, read to Ceri at age 25 months: *Maisie Middleton* by Nita Sowter (Picture Lions, 1982). Maisie Middleton is the name of the young heroine who, early one morning, gets up in the company of her soft toys. Without waking Mummy and Daddy, they wash and dress by themselves. After an unsuccessful attempt at making breakfast on the part of her Daddy, Maisie and her animal friends prepare their own feast.

3.1 Content

Maisie Middleton is remarkable not so much for the alterations, but for the similarities of narrative technique which persist over one year as this parent presents a story. Not only does this mother rely on current phraseology and her intimate knowledge of Ceri's life to bridge the world of the story and that of the child; the technique of alternating storyline (told by herself) and active participation (on the part of Ceri) is almost identical to the one adopted at 14 months.

What has changed, however, is the material content of this child's world, along with her preoccupations. That is to say, salient aspects of the 'environmental set-up' have evolved. While Alex, our hero at 14 months, never left the company of his mother, Maisie, the heroine of this tale, is almost never to be found in it. The emphasis all along in this story for a 2-year-old is on independence, doing things by and for oneself (or rather in the company of those compared to whom Maisie emerges as more than equal): washing, dressing, even preparing her own breakfast. Washing, dressing and preparing a meal are an integral part of Ceri's real-life experience, though the latter is, as yet, a fictional extension grounded in her growing sense of autonomy. And Maisie has the superior role. She dresses more quickly than teddy, who gets his socks muddled, and she makes her breakfast more effectively than Daddy, who burns the eggs and bacon. Maisie's performance both mirrors and enhances this infant reader's own real-life position.

Thus, as at 14 months, the world of the heroine and that of the child reader become merged. Life at home in all its domesticity, getting up, getting dressed and having breakfast have all been rehearsed before, in descriptions of picture- and storybooks. But — and this is where the adult account in 'Maisie' resembles that of 'Alex' at 14 months — the details of the description always have a contemporary significance. In a total departure from the written text, Maisie is described by the presenter as 'going to the loo', as by now, does this 2-year-old reader. The storyline is further arrested to underline Maisie's success at getting dressed by herself, as Ceri is just beginning to do. 'Oh, she is a clever girl! Look at her getting dressed, Wez. Teeshirt on. Trousers on!'

Likewise, in a further departure from the written text, Daddy, having been roused from bed, is described in these terms: 'Poor old Dad! Got his dressing gown on', this last at the expense of many other aspects of Daddy which might have been described: the slippers he wears, his tousled hair, his dreamy look. Why? Because, at the time, one of Ceri's great pleasures was to bring her Daddy his dressing gown in the morning when getting up. It may be seen how

THE WORLD OF THE STORY

this presenter is at pains to merge the world of the infant with that of the book. The environmental set-up may have evolved, but set-up it remains nonetheless; to this the adult's linguistic account invariably returns.

Again, as at 14 months, this mother uses the technique of arresting the storyline in order to respond to Ceri's spontaneous interest in pointing out things she knows, and which are of especial importance to her as reader (rather than to the author as writer of the story). At 14 months, such elements included the duck in the bath. Here they include the flowers on the windowsill, the milk bottles on the doorstep, the sort of pyjamas Maisie wears, and so on. As with picturebook reading, story reading is far from being a passive, receptive activity where this storytelling dyad is concerned. On the contrary, Ceri is being presented with parallels between herself and her heroine almost constantly.

3.2 Discourse

What, however, of the respective interactive roles of child and mother and the language which this adult uses to put across the storyline? Here, important changes have occurred. Not only does the storyline now dominate the interaction; the language used is, frequently, that of the author as well as that of the mother. (Just how this mother builds towards the use of written text is discussed in Chapter 6.) In a second development, this mother now directly involves Ceri in the elaboration of the storyline, by asking her questions about it. At the start of the book, mother asks: 'That's Maisie! What happens in Maisie?' Let us recall that Ceri is now able to speak, in utterances of up to nine words in length. The dissocation between taxonomic description (in which the infant actively participates) and the exclusive responsibility of the adult for the story which obtained earlier has now been blurred. In this sense the focus of the dialogue has altered considerably, evidence perhaps of greater familiarity with the material and/or maturity on the part of the infant reader. However, the give and take over more tangential matters still remains.

Two further new developments at 25 months may be noted. The first concerns adult questions which, because of their orientation, are of a quite different order from 14 months. Directives to: 'Point to the . . .' are not so much entirely replaced by as interspersed with questions which are answerable only by calling upon Ceri's general knowledge. Eying the food laid out on the table ready for the feast, mother asks: 'What happens when you cut an onion?' or 'What do bees make?' In addition, questions are now being asked which require evaluative judgements on the part of the infant: 'I wonder what toothpaste she (i.e. Maisie) has, Wez.' These early speculations about how characters of the book might act are perhaps a prelude to more sophisticated questions which also invite comparisons between reader and protagonist but which come much later: 'How would you feel if you were asleep in bed and you woke to find three big bears in your bedroom. What would you do?'

A second innovation at 25 months is Ceri's newly developed capacity to draw upon her previous experience of life or of reading, in order to judge her storybook. That is, her commitment to the story is no longer total; it is by now, as Warlow suggests (section 1.2), 'reflective'. She has a sense of the rules of book reading; she adopts an evaluative stance, distancing herself in some moments from her reading. Two examples illustrate this point.

The pictorial scene is of a bathroom. Maisie is there on her own with teddy, while Mummy and Daddy sleep on in their room. The discussion between parent and child reader centres on whose toothbrush is which. 'That's right, that's Mummy's and Daddy's toothbrushes darling, quite right. You can see things in the bathroom can't you!', says this mother. Whereupon Ceri realises that, despite the reference to Maisie's Daddy, he is not present in the picture. But, according to the 'normal rules' of bookreading, mention of a referent is made in the (illustrated) presence of that referent, and so she enquires: 'Where is Daddy!' (he should be here!). The adult presenter explains 'Daddy's in bed! We're in the bathroom now. Daddy's still in bed. We're in the bathroom now, with Maisie and teddy.'

A second spontaneous intervention on the part of this infant reader involves distancing herself from the story in order assess teddy's behaviour. Teddy is shown as having just one sock to put on, at which point Ceri realises, as a function of her own real-world experience, that he will need two: 'Where's other sock?' she asks. Such is the acquired ability of this 2-year-old to pass judgement upon the realism, or otherwise, of what she sees in print.

This I believe to be a significant turning point in the literary career of this young infant. The availability of illustrations, non-ephemeral, silent and lending themselves to detailed scrutiny, has enabled comparisons to be drawn between illustrations and an oral account, related in turn to previous experiences of book reading (on the one hand), and illustrations and real-life experiences (on the other). In short, contemplation of these pictures, informed by previous reading experience, has led to the development of comparative and critical powers on a scale hitherto unseen in this particular infant when reading. At the same time, answers requiring generalisations from specific examples also become a feature.

Critical awareness of inconsistencies between various accounts and abstract generalisations are two quite basic hallmarks of a literate public (Goody and Watt 1972). At an individual level, then, early reading paves the way to literacy, not only because it offers the infant, through time, multiple opportunities for personal acts of interpretation (see Chapter 8), but also because it promotes a capacity in the fledgling reader to stand back and criticise, rationally and objectively, the printed material to hand. The heady, pre-literate days of total and absorbed participation, of unconditional acceptance, are perhaps over for good.

THE WORLD OF THE STORY

Summary

Storytelling for this mother–infant dyad, at age one and two years, relies on mother's choice of topic and language, to bridge the gap between the child's life and the world of the story. Implicitly, the environmental set-up of this infant reader (settings, the minutiae of everyday life and their associated feelings) is evoked to the extent that the potential distance between the story as written and the world of the infant reader is narrowed, if not nullified completely. Whereas, at one year plus, the storyline is from a linguistic point of view quite distinct from more intense moments of active participation, at age two years there is a manifest interest in the story, and in its degree of conformity with what this infant reader now knows to be the canons of storybook reading. The more critical stance which she now adopts is the result, possibly, of increased cognitive and linguistic maturity, but also, undoubtedly, of previous experience both of life and of book reading.

4 DISCUSSION: THE CENTRAL ROLE OF THE NARRATOR

4.1 Psychological and material truth

The novel, as a fictional form, is inscribed within an autobiographical and confessional tradition of which the work of St Augustine, Pepys and Rousseau all form part. Novels portray 'the inner as well as the outer life of individuals in the real world'; in this sense, they are to be distinguished from myth and epic (Goody and Watt 1972:346). This chapter has also been concerned with the inner and outer worlds, with psychological and material truth – two basic components of narrative fiction. The question was posed in particular as to how infants, despite their more limited experience of life, and an inability, as yet, to comprehend a language which refers explicitly to feelings, could nonetheless enter into the inner world of the mind and the emotions.

The creation of a story world is here enacted as follows. The psychological realism, the context of situation, the sentiments and feelings of the hero and heroine of the stories, are in effect a composition constituted, in part, by the material context and, in part, by the language of Ceri's own, first-hand experience. The psychic reality of the characters (feelings of joy, or disgust, for example), so difficult to describe explicitly to very young infants, is evoked as a function of what this adult knows to be the experience of her infant reader, using language which is uniquely theirs. The book becomes a kind of screen from which and on to which the details of a child's life are at once selected and projected; the linguistic description evokes not so much a Secondary World, but the child's own. Early storytelling is indeed autobiographical, but from the reader's (not the writer's) point of view.

What conclusions may be drawn with respect to a very young infant's understanding of narrative? At what age may a story from a book be read? Access to stories, of which key features were cited in the introductory remarks to this chapter, does not have to wait until children are able to speak. Affective responses, the evocative powers of language and material and psychological truth are aspects of reading fiction in which Ceri, almost before she has learned to talk, may be observed to participate. Critical responses, on the other hand, seem to emerge later, with this infant, from about the age of 2 years old and upwards.

Understanding and participating in the construction of stories are thus activities of which a 1-year-old is seemingly well capable. What should be observed, however, is that the balance between the known and the new in early storytelling is carefully struck; the former is proportionately much greater than the latter. This is a feature, possibly, of all stories orally recounted, but it is particularly pertinent perhaps with a young infant. Burdened with too much new information all at once, there is the risk of loss of interest, or lack of comprehension, or both.

4.2 The mirror role of mother

This discussion is concluded by considering from a standpoint which is more psychoanalytic than psychological, the nature of the language which this mother uses in the two book presentations studied here. This language has its origins in the life of the child reader; there is a sense in which Ceri's own personal life, her possessions, the events of her world, her sensations and feelings are mirrored in this mother's storytelling account. Mirroring, however, is almost certainly an understatement; this mother's speech, in effect, not only reflects, but more than that transforms and reprojects onto the page, aspects of Ceri's life, using language with which she is largely familiar. The experience of the hero, instead of being different, is often assimilated with, even identical to, that of the infant reader, who thus enters not so much another world but her own.

Functions of maternal speech

What purpose(s), one might ask, does linguistic mirroring of this kind serve? First and foremost, a story told in this way is probably both intelligible and pleasurable; Ceri finds in her reading, as all of us must, something she recognises and enjoys. At another level, the narrative account (of the hero) has parallels with Ceri's own (as reader), and she is, in consequence, the more easily able to identify with the events of the book – see herself reflected there, at least in the language, if not the illustrations. She becomes acquainted, perhaps, with the notion that literature, even though ostensibly about 'other' people, in fact has something fundamental to tell us, directly or indirectly, about ourselves. The mobilisation of one's own experience in order to understand the behaviour of the main protagonist is an essential component of understanding narrative. Early storytelling by this account is, then, nothing less than a very early exercise in identification.

A possible third function of this form of storytelling has to do with the development of the imagination. Mental functioning is enhanced via a process in which intersubjective experiences become intrasubjective. This is, for many, accepted theory with respect to cognitive or linguistic functioning (e.g. Deleau 1990). It has also been shown that imaginative play in the infant is structured and supported by an available adult (Emde 1994). Might the same also be true of the origins of the literary imagination? Following Coleridge, Rycroft suggests that the imagination is rooted, in part, in the capacity to see oneself as other, to view oneself (in one's mind) doing things: 'the function of imagination is precisely that of being able to convert the self into an object' (Rycroft 1979 [1991(a):69]). Here, this mother projects (on Ceri's behalf) a linguistic account of her own experience of her, which, by implication, her infant reader may then ponder.

If the imagination is indeed predicated upon the notion of self-contemplation, it follows that what is (perhaps naively) assumed to be that most personal and private activity, the imagination of a young reader, is initially dependent on significant support from a mature adult. That adult takes up the happenings and language of the child's own world and uses them in the construction of a story to which Ceri can relate in an intensely personal way. Coleridge's view of the imagination as it reveals itself 'in the sense of novelty and freshness, with old and familiar objects; a more than usual state of emotion, with more than usual order', could not be a more apt description of what this parent has been observed to be doing when telling a story to Ceri.

Thus, in a sense, this early storytelling event may be viewed not so much as narrative fiction, but rather as imaginative biography. Mother, in part, creates a story not of the hero but of her own child as she sees her; she puts together a version of her child's life and relates it in structured form. But instead of talking directly to Ceri and describing to her what she does, as she might in real life, what this mother does, seemingly, is to project on to the page a version of her child as she knows her, but as if she were talking about someone else. Ceri possibly recognises herself in her mother's language, or rather the language that is connected with reading, in a way that is quite unlike any other account of herself she might be given. Recall at this juncture the importance (to health) of a personal narrative, without which, according to Stern, people run the risk of insanity. The process is one of integration, in which different components of a child's life are drawn together in a coherently articulated account. Such a view leads directly to the conclusion that a further function of early storytelling is, possibly, to facilitate emotional health and psychic growth. In sum, the 'mirroring' dimension to maternal language promotes within the infant an enjoyment of reading, a capacity for identification and for literary imagination and, lastly, an ability to organise the self 'internally'.

THE ONTOGENESIS OF NARRATIVE

Non-verbal origins of mirroring

Linguistic mirroring in storytelling further begs the question of the (non-verbal) origins of this form of language. Winnicott's belief is that in the first weeks of an infant's life a mother acts as a mirror to her child. In their mother's face, the baby, unless the mother is preoccupied, can see reflected back a version of him/herself: 'What does the baby see when he or she looks at the mother's face? I am suggesting that, ordinarily, what the baby sees is himself or herself' (Winnicott 1967(b) [1974:131]. These first exchanges are crucial in conveying to the baby a sense of who or what s/he is. If the baby sees sadness or depression (which might not even be of the baby's own making) he or she feels worthless. If joy, the baby experiences him/herself as worthwhile. In this process, apperception (seeing oneself) is as fundamental as perception (seeing the other). In Winnicott's view, then, a tiny baby 'reads' the mother's face and what is seen reflected back is an expression of affect.

Consider three implications. The first is that a baby is apparently aware of the face of another, almost, perhaps, before he or she is aware of him/herself. From the beginning, a baby's attention is directed outwards, toward somebody else. Second, that 'other' is an integral part of that baby's sense of who he or she is. From birth, each of us is inscribed within a relationship; it is through and within that relationship that we discover who we are. To know ourselves, we must first be held, and contemplated, by another being: 'When I look I am seen, so I exist' (Winnicott 1967(b) [1974:134]). Third, while Descartes' formulation 'cogito ergo sum' suggests that people need to 'think' in order to 'know' that they exist, Winnicott stresses the importance of affect. It is early affective relationship(s) which determine(s) what people feel themselves to be.

Winnicott suggests that the mirroring function belongs initially to the mother; she is responsible for conveying to the infant through the expression on her face an image of what she sees. The baby sees not an exact reflection of him/herself, as in a mirror, but a distorted or transformed reflection. The mirroring role has the capacity to both form and transform the infant (Bollas 1979). Could the language of early reading be seen then, in part, as a linguistic transposition of this first affective relationship? The type of reading described in this chapter constitutes a linguistic extension of a much earlier exchange which Winnicott believes takes place non-verbally in the first weeks of life.[1] When reading these stories, this mother (and here it is the mother), in effect, articulates her own experience of her infant. These storytelling events literally offer back to Ceri a (linguistic) image of herself. In which case, could it not be argued that the early mirroring function of mother becomes transposed – displaced, into or onto a book? If this is so, this infant reader may find or rather rediscover in her storybook not so much herself-as-isolate, but herself-within-a-relationship, the earliest of her life, that between herself and her mother. It is not only the 'private culture', the 'sequestered ambience' of early mothering that is recaptured in later years. Reading transforms – in the way that a first relationship might (Bollas 1979).[2] Thus it is, or so I believe, that reading is, or can be for some, an extraordinarily moving experience.

5 CONCLUSION

A discussion of the significance of narrative, both phylogenetic and ontogenetic, paved the way for a selective review of certain key theoretical aspects of written stories. Matters of psychological and material truth and reader involvement with or distance from the story have been considered in relation to two synchronic accounts of reading a storybook with the same infant at 14 and 25 months old. Psychological and material realism is achieved for this infant by fusing her life experiences with the pictorial contents of the book, using a form of language which has strong affective associations. The transforming power of language reaches back to the first relationship in which a mother's gaze had the power to form and transform the infant. Early reading, it is suggested, is, in part, a qualitative reenactment of the earliest phases of this first relationship.

In this maternal account, the infant reader is, to a major extent, offered nothing other than a linguistic version of herself. The language of the storytelling adult appears, indeed, to have a triple orientation. Dedicated, on the one hand, to constructing a coherent biography of the infant reader, it rejoins the narrative tradition of the novel. But, in addition, it suggests a process of identification with another (the hero of the story) while simultaneously confronting the infant with herself as an object of contemplation. It is here, perhaps, that the beginnings of the literary imagination are to be observed.

6
STORY GRAMMAR AND TEXT

1 INTRODUCTION: STRUCTURE AND STYLE

In the previous chapter, emphasis was given to two features of narrative identified as fundamental: verisimilitude in the (adult) narrator's account, and the active involvement of the (child) reader in a text's interpretation. This chapter considers two further aspects of narrative: the 'grammar' of the story (the plot, the characters, their actions), and the written language in which the story is cast. The issues are, first, the acquisition by the infant of what Warlow (1977:93) and Rabinowitz (1987:29) refer to as the conventions of narrative and, second, the presentation of written text and accompanying illustrations. The aim is to examine how this mother approaches these dimensions of storytelling with her 1-year-old child.

A child's understanding of stories depends, it is said, upon a knowledge of the conventions of narrative structure. The connection between structure and meaning is easily demonstrated by referring to sentence structure which in English (though not in Latin) dictates that 'John kicks Paul' has a different meaning from 'Paul kicks John'. Equally, then, it is argued, knowledge of narrative structure (the details of which are discussed in section 2.1) is essential to the understanding of a story (Rabinowitz 1987:27). Studies of oral language development have tended to indicate that the acquisition of complex adult language is facilitated, in the early months, by 'child directed speech'. The hypothesis for this chapter is that narrative, its structure and its written code may also be subject to careful modification in maternal speech, in the interests of comprehension and acquisition.

Discussion is based on one of the first major narrative events in the life of the second child. The example chosen is the story *Pig in a Muddle* by Winfried Opgenoorth and Mira Lobe (Oxford University Press, 1983) whose twenty-one pages are mostly subdivided into between two and six tableaux (illustrations), each with accompanying caption in verse. Three readings are analysed, recorded at child age 13, 14-and-a-half and 16 months respectively. It appears to be this mother's intention that Ceri should listen to and understand the text as originally written. As far as it is possible to ascertain, Ceri does, at the end of the period, appear to comprehend a significant proportion of the story recounted in its 'published' form.

2 LAYERS OF MEANING

In order to appreciate better how this mother approaches telling her infant an extended story for the first time, some of the parameters involved are now described. What is it that Ceri must acquire?

2.1 The grammar of a story

Consider first the framework of action and events which constitutes a story's basic 'grammar'. Detailed below are aspects of a story's structure which are considered characteristic of the genre, at least where young children are concerned:

- The existence of a central character whose place with regard to the whole is significant and extensively more so than that of other protagonists. The purpose of the title is often both to orient the reader's attention towards this main character and/or offer hints as to how the story is to be interpreted. Our concern as readers is with Cinderella, not the fairy godmother.
- Included alongside the main character are one or more minor characters: in Cinderella's case, the ugly sisters, the fairy godmother or the prince.
- A series of actions befalls the main character(s). Cinderella cleans the kitchen, prepares her sisters for the ball, witnesses the arrival of the fairy godmother.
- These actions take place in a variety of locations. Cinderella is seen at home; travelling in a coach; in the ballroom at the palace.
- These actions, moreover, take place in a particular sequence. The notion of sequence is important: event (a) does not merely precede event (b) in time; it is a logical precondition of event (b). The fairy godmother must arrive before Cinderella can go to the ball. In other words, the events of the story are subject to a strict chronology. The implication for infants is that the pages of the book must be turned over from front to back, and only in that order.
- A further principle is to bring about a development in the action, a crisis and its resolution. Or, as Bruner puts it, there is 'trouble' (Bruner 1990:50). In consequence, a story typically has a beginning, a middle and an end.
- Finally, events are recounted from a particular point of view. In Cinderella, for example, the story is told from the point of view of Cinderella, not the fairy godmother. However, the perspective of the narrator may not be that of the main protagonist; the narrator may comment upon, dissent from or even be absent from the story. The events of a story may be viewed from a number of different perspectives, introduced in particular through the evaluative

THE ONTOGENESIS OF NARRATIVE

comments of different protagonists. The prince's attitude to Cinderella is not that of her sisters.

Relating this general format to the particular example of the story used in this study, we have:

- the existence of a central hero, here, a humanised animal (a female pig), who is cited both in the published title, *Pig in a Muddle*, and in Ceri's idiosyncratic version: 'Piggy book';
- a series of actions in which pig engages in sequence: driving to market, parking the cart, etc.;
- a crisis and its resolution: a parking infringement committed by the pig is followed by a chase and her escape via a department store, a fairground and a plane ride, ending in peace and serenity, in a leafy wood, where pig goes on to found a family;
- the presence of other characters (most of them human) who counterbalance the actions of the heroine, for example, here, the pig's owner, a policeman, a waiter in a restaurant, a store salesman, a pilot of an aeroplane. These characters offer a varied perspective on the events of the narrative.

In sum, this story is the realisation of an underlying narrative structure which includes the existence of a hero, engaged in a set of interconnected actions, in sequence, in a variety of locations, and in which are engaged, too, a number of minor characters.

2.2 Written text

A second issue for this chapter is the nature of the language in which this particular story is written. The spoken language which mothers normally use when addressing their infants is, stylistically, quite unrelated to written verse. Written discourse is, by definition, not one with which a 13-month-old is familiar; the task for the adult telling the story is to introduce this form of language to an infant as yet barely able to speak. The first few lines of the written text as it appears in the book in question are cited by way of illustration:

> Here's a wife who has a pig that drives the cart to market.
> When they arrive, they leave it where they aren't supposed to park it.
> 'Hello, hello,' the policeman says, 'You can't leave that thing here.'
> He leads them off to prison, by the nose and by the ear.

Internal to this written extract, and/or to the remainder of the written text (not quoted), may be noted, at the syntactic level, the existence of a range of features which are only rarely employed in speech addressed to young infants:

- subordinate clauses: 'Here's a wife who has a pig that drives the cart to market';

- direct speech quoted as it occurs between two or more protagonists: 'Hello, hello,' the policeman says, 'You can't leave that thing here'; 'Why thank you, sir, how kind of you'; (with the identity of the speaker unspecified)
- passive constructions: 'There she is, caught in a jam.'

At the lexical level may be noted, with respect to the written text:

- unfamiliar (sometimes generic) expressions: 'sporting gear', 'I'm quite a belle';
- colloquialisms: 'bucking bronco';
- idioms: 'that's saved her bacon'; having no 'head for heights'.

All of these features are exceptional to the language used on a day-to-day basis with this infant reader.

2.3 Text and illustrations interrelated

Syntax and lexis are not the only dimensions which may be unfamiliar in the language of written text. There is also the issue of the meaning of the story which, in parts at least, is derived from a consideration of the text, not in isolation, but in conjunction with the illustrations, rather in the manner of a cartoon. In picturebook activity, words often stand with pictures in an isomorphic relationship: the infant sees a ball, and hears the word 'ball'. A form of language is used which, ultimately, could be understood without iconic support. Here, contrary to what is often believed to be the case in narrative, the language of the text is often far from self-contained and self-explanatory; it can only be understood with reference to the extra-linguistic clues provided by the illustrations. Our reader is invited to contextualise the following extract from this story: 'An open window, trousers too. "Why thank you, sir, how kind of you."' This excerpt becomes comprehensible only in the context of a sequence of pictures with accompanying captions, which show the pig flying towards (picture a) and then emerging from (picture b) an open window, and then (picture c) thanking a man whose trousers she has (presumably uninvited) taken, and used in order to clothe herself.

The matter is complicated yet further, for not only is the connection between text and illustration tenuous; the connection between the identity of a speaker in dialogic exchange, and the words which they utter in direct speech is often not rendered explicit in the text either. For example: (waiter in restaurant) '"Would Madam like to pay the bill?" (picture of pig escaping) "I think I'd rather fly."' It is left to the reader to deduce from the context, both pictorial and linguistic, which of the characters in the picture says which line, and from that to conclude as to their actions, motives and intentions. In short, the style of writing is, in parts of the story at least, highly elliptical.

2.4 Illustrations as semantic convention

Illustrations to a story are not self-explanatory; they can only suggest, but never state, meaning. They are not a complete record of an event in the sense that a filmed record might be; knowledge of the conventions which govern them is essential for understanding. Actions especially depend for their interpretation upon 'convention and conditioning' (Gombrich 1972:373). As mentioned in the Introduction, the initiation and/or completion of an action (writing a letter) might be depicted, but the detail of its stages might be missing. Adults possess the 'rule' according to which the lacunae between illustrations (and indeed between a series of events in a novel) are constructed (cf. Rabinowitz 1987:151). Part of the adult's task, then, is to explicate, not merely textual, but pictorial meanings — to elucidate the gaps between.

A final challenge of this particular text concerns the length of the story. The book comprises twenty-one pages, each subdivided into a set of tableaux (up to six per page). There are fifty-eight tableaux of this kind, each with an accompanying section of text, or caption. The task for the presenter is to retain a young infant's concentration on the development of a story of considerable length, as well as to ensure that the storyline is understood by an infant whose knowledge of narrative structure, of the syntax and lexis of the text, and of the semantics of illustrations is scant indeed.

The choice of complex data on which to base this discussion of the acquisition of narrative is instructive from two points of view. First, the story chosen is a favourite one. There is, then, the opportunity to observe an aspect of reading so characteristic of infants — the reading of a single text 'again and again' — this time, however, not a picturebook but a story. A second advantage accrues from the very complexity of the published material. The intention here is to demonstrate how infants are helped towards an understanding of the structure and written language of narrative. Just as in oral language acquisition, adjustments are frequently made as a function of an infant's age and ability, so, here, it may be seen how a difficult text is modified in the interests of facilitating the acquisition of its narrative structure. The storybook selected enables a comparison to be drawn between oral story version and published (written) text which, for literature, is somewhat akin to the comparison made between child directed speech and adult oral language. A 'simpler' text might not have been so revealing of adult purpose; the 'work', in a sense, would already have been done.

3 READING FOR MEANING AT 13–14 MONTHS

Ceri does not come to storybook reading without previous experience. Formally, a measure of socialisation has already been achieved. Sequenced presentations, the discussion of a particular image, the reappearance of the same

STORY GRAMMAR

referent from one page to the next have all been rehearsed in picturebook activities (Chapter 1). Picturebook descriptions often resemble a 'little story' with a systematic beginning, a middle and an end (Chapter 4). Songs and nursery rhymes – narratives without iconic support have been sung. So, given these very general aspects of Ceri's literary background, how is this fairly complex narrative presented?

A comparison of this mother's oral presentations in three sessions with the 'original' written text and pictures (as published) reveals five main areas which are subject to special explanation or modification: the overall length of the story; its characteristic structural framework; the meanings implied by the illustrations; the lexical and syntactic adjustments to the language of the written text; and the intersection of the text with the infant viewpoint.

3.1 Brevity

With an older child, a story too long to be recounted in one reading can be started, left and then continued at a subsequent session (during the next evening for example). A quite different approach is found here. This mother, at each session, 'reads' the book from beginning to end. But while every page of the book is included at each reading, the story is 'shortened' in that not all the illustrations contained on each page are discussed. It is at the 13-month session that references to the whole range of illustrations are fewest; as time goes on, however, the number of pictures referred to at each reading increases. In tabular form the development is shown in Table 6.1.

Table 6.1 Pig in a Muddle: illustrations discussed out of total available

Ceri's age	13 months %	14 months %	16 months %
First 29 illustrations	69	79	90
Second 29 illustrations	55	55	73

At each session, it is the illustrations in the first half of the book which, comparatively speaking, receive most attention. This is consistent with the adult expanding the story, as it were, from the beginning outwards and 'skipping' the end of the book.

3.2 A complete experience

What, however, of the story's structure? It is essential to note that, from the first reading onwards, a complete if abridged version of the whole story is told each time. That is to say, the core feature of narrative, its tripartite structure, comprising a beginning, a middle and an end is regarded in some sense as

THE ONTOGENESIS OF NARRATIVE

fundamental, and this structure (however shortened the story) is found at each reading, even the earliest. At each session then, this infant receives what Winnicott might call a 'complete experience'. Whatever else might be altered by this parent in the interests of infant age and maturity, the basic framework of a story is always present and respected.

Linguistic emphasis is given from the outset to two other core features of narrative. The first of these is the clear identification of the main protagonists, in particular the central character, pig. This is undertaken quite explicitly, immediately the book is begun, either on the front cover, or on the first page. Thus: (Adult, 13 months, page one) 'Where's pig?' 'There's pig.' Infant readers are not inclined to wait several pages, as older children might, to find out 'who' the story is about. As with picturebook reading, satisfaction is immediate, not deferred. Recall, too, that this book is 'named' after the main protagonist: 'Piggy book' – which of itself is an indication of 'who' this infant reader should listen for.

However, in the early versions, pig is identified not only the first time she appears, but at all her appearances. In all 'stories' for children there is a main character and, in all narrative, events occur in a particular setting (i.e. something happens somewhere). One has only to think of little Miss Muffet sitting on her tuffet eating her curds and whey. The difference with a text based on a sequence of illustrations is that particular attention is given to linking the name of the pig quite explicitly with the picture of her each time she is mentioned. Pointing to the images in turn, this mother repeatedly uses the word 'pig' to ensure that the link between language and image is understood, draws attention to pig's reappearance by saying 'look' (i.e. there she is again), and seeks agreement from Ceri via the inclusion of tag questions: 'isn't she', 'doesn't she'. In three consecutive illustrations on one page, the commentary at 13 months runs as follows: picture (a) (adult points to pig) 'Piggy runs away, and hidies in there, doesn't she Wezzy'; picture (b) 'Look! Woman sees the piggy'; picture (c) Look! Piggy running away now darling.' Even a connection as 'self-evident' as the reappearance of the protagonist from one picture to the next, on one page, is explicitly drawn out by this adult presenter.

These extracts connect with a further finding. Throughout this first recorded reading, the spotlight in the adult version is narrowed to fall mainly upon a single main protagonist (pig), while excluding a number of minor characters. In instances where a small subset of the minor characters is introduced in this first session, as in the example above of the woman, this is done only within the context of an explicit relationship to pig. Subsidiary characters are mentioned, not in their own right, but because they do something with pig, or to pig (piggy and cat go to the fair together; the policeman leads her off; the woman sees the pig). Pig, at the earliest session, might not always be the grammatical subject, but she is nonetheless the constant focus of attention, whatever other characters might be involved.

The second core feature of narrative to which emphasis is given in the earliest session is the plot: the 'who' does 'what' and 'where' in the story. Again parental discourse signals quite clearly these features of narrative; formal markers are used in particular to herald a change:

- of person: 'Who comes now?'
- of event: 'What happens now?' or 'What she do now?'
- of location: 'Where she go now?' or 'Where they go now?'

This mother gives help, that is, with understanding either that the same person (usually the pig) is undergoing a change of place or activity, or alternatively, that someone different is momentarily to become the subject of the narrative, as in: 'Who comes now? Oh! the policeman!'

In the 13-month session, these markers are of especial importance. Events in sequence within the page are marked either by a question form, and/or by the use of the word 'now':

(*Page turn*)	What happens *now*?
(*Picture (a)*)	Piggy says: Oh I'm going to have nice dress on *now*!
(*Picture (b)*)	Here's piggy, got nice dress on, see!
	Got hat on,
	Looking in the mirror isn't she.
(*New page*)	She's going to have her icecream *now* Wez!

Continuity (or change) in the identity of the protagonist, a change of action and a change of location are three aspects of the structure of narrative to which this adult devotes quite explicit attention. It would appear, then, that this infant needs support in comprehending that a story turns as it were 'by definition' upon the 'same' protagonist recurring. She has difficulty, too, with comprehending a change of action involving that same protagonist, or the introduction of new protagonists. Or rather, she will comprehend these, provided the adult draws attention to them. In other words, Ceri's understanding of plot and structure apparently relies not only upon her mother eliminating much of the detail of narrative and reducing it to its 'kernel elements'; these elements are, in addition, the object of a significant degree of metalinguistic comment and clarification. It may be concluded that these procedures are in the interests of pointing up the structures which govern narrative, facilitating thereby Ceri's understanding of this particular text and possibly a more generalised narrative acquisition process as well.

3.3 Inference

Efforts to clarify Ceri's understanding of a complicated narrative text based around pictures are directed, first and foremost, towards explicating the basic structure of a story and what the elements of a story, by definition, comprise.

Also of concern in the early stages are the semantic conventions of illustrations and, in particular, the serial relationship which obtains between one picture and another. That is to say, this mother focuses extensively on elucidating the nature of the activity which is contained in visual form, using whatever language she feels to be appropriate. This is seemingly more important at this point than any attempt to introduce the words of the text as originally written. Put somewhat differently, whereas for an older child the language of the text is paramount in conveying the meaning of the story, with the illustrations functioning as a kind of 'optional amplification', the direction for Ceri at 13 months is the other way round. It is the meaning conveyed by the pictures which is first drawn out, with the text introduced as it were much later, and only when the 'meaning' of the pictures is fully understood.

But illustrations are not semantically explicit (as stated in section 2.4). They require interpretation. With small infants, inferences are not left unspecified. Extensive time is devoted to clarifying meanings – both the meaning which pictures contain and, especially, what must have happened between them. This is particularly the case in respect of the initiation of an action and its follow-through to completion. For example, mother presents two pictures: picture (a) in which pig is shown adjacent to but positioned outside an upstairs window of a building; and picture (b) in which pig is shown inside the building. An adult reader might deduce that between these two pictures pig has in fact used the window to enter the building, but not so an infant. This mother, in pointing to the window in the first picture, draws attention to the fact that piggy will be 'going in there'. In other words, where adults rely on inference, a mother will spell out explicitly.

At a formal level, syntactic and lexical parallelism is frequently used to draw attention to the start of an action in a first picture and its sequel or consequence in a second, adjacent picture. In the next example (see also the example quoted in section 3.2) pig decides to put on someone else's clothes; mother specifies not only that pig puts them on but points out, with respect to the next illustration, that she is dressed differently (i.e. having put items of clothes on, pig retains them). Adult speech has a janus-like quality to it, looking forwards and looking back all the time.

(*Picture (a)*)   She goes and puts trousies on, yes. She puts man's trousies on.

(*Picture (b)*)   Look and she running away
(*points*) got trousies.

An action and its consequence are also the subject of two other pictures. In the first, pig is shown with a clean face, with an icecream on the table in front of her, while in the second pig is shown with cream almost completely covering her face. In between, pig has (it is inferred) gobbled the icecream. Again this mother's speech highlights what it is that will occur 'between the pictures'. Her personalised commentary to picture (a) runs: 'She's going to have her icecream now Wezzy!' while that to picture (b) draws attention to the 'outcome', a kind of retroactive confirmation of the statement accompanying picture (a): 'She's got cream all over her face.'

Since so much of the adult talk of the first session is devoted to teasing out the links between pictures, would it not be true to say that understanding illustrations in sequence is not a task which infants can achieve unaided? Rather it is an activity which is environmentally facilitated, requiring, at times, considerable support from a concerned adult. Indispensable to the activity of storybook reading with very young infants is the presence of an older reader who can make inter-pictorial connections absolutely explicit. Without such a reader, the pictures, indeed, might never make sense at all.

3.4 Text modification

In the first two recorded readings of this story, at 13 and 14-and-a-half months, three major types of modification to the original written text have been noted. The first concerns the need to adapt to a young infant's concentration span: the story is abridged. The second concerns the help given by this adult to understanding the structure of the story: all kinds of pointers are used to help Ceri grasp the main orientations of plot and structure. The third has to do with clarifying the sense conveyed by the pictures: a number of supported inferences with regard to the interconnections between pictures must be made. A fourth type of modification has to do with the syntactic and lexical changes to the written text as published.

At the syntactic level, extensive adjustments to the original written version are made, inclining in the first instance towards a consistent, third person, sentential structure comprising (animate subject)-main verb-complement (either animate or inanimate) construction. In addition this mother specifies explicitly the locations and actions, which, in the published version, can be deduced from the illustrations and/or direct speech within the text.

The adoption, by this mother, of a descriptive mode in the third person as a means of elucidating the 'allusions' of the published version is demonstrated in Table 6.2.

Syntactic changes, then, lead this mother straightforwardly to identify pig by name and to transform into 'context-independent' utterances those aspects of the original text which rely on deictic or elliptical reference (Lyons 1972:61). It may be noted that, even as the meaning of the original text is explicated, the narrator's version makes little use of it at a formal level.

As may also be seen in Table 6.2, the omission of the direct speech from the captions accompanying the illustrations is a particular feature of the early readings of this story. There are many other examples. Pig's arrival at the fairground scene is introduced in the published text with: '"Roll up! Roll up! Let's have a go!"'; this is transformed, in the adapted version, to a third person description: 'Going to the funfair' (13 months); 'And they go to the fair don't they' (14 months); 'Going to the funfair' (16 months).

Table 6.2 *Pig in a Muddle*, modifications at 13 months and 14 months

Written text	13 months	14 months
	(*Page turn*) Where we go now?	(*Page turn*) Where they go Wezzy?
'There she is, caught in a jam. She jumps a car! She jumps a van!'	Piggy in the cars, isn't she Jumps the car, Jumps the van.	Look! in the cars. Jumps the car, Jumps the van.
'"Look out, Pig!" That pole's too long. Too late. It's Allez oop! and Boinngg!'	Look, piggy goes up into the window, Wezzy. Right up in there, doesn't she (points).	Up into the window.
'An open window, trousers too. "Why thank you, sir, how kind of you."'	She goes and puts trousies on, yes. She puts man's trousies on.	What she do Wez? Look put trousies on, yes!
'The man's amazed, and off she tears.'	Look and she running away Got trousies.	She puts her trousies on and runs away, doesn't she Wezzy!

In a second example, the pig joins the pilot in the aeroplane, which the text renders as: '(Pilot) "Just passing through?" (Pig) "No, dropping in!"' In descriptive mode this becomes (13 months): 'Up in the sky, whee, up in the sky! Look, sitting in the aeroplane aren't they!'

In the two instances where direct speech is used in the early sessions, the identity of the speaker is made quite explicit as in: '"Hello, hello," the policeman says, "You can't leave that thing here."' And, where, in the original, the text reads: '"I rather like this lovely dress"' (with speaker unspecified), mother glosses: 'Piggy says: "Oh I'm going to have nice dress on now!"' (13 months). What seems clear is that inferring the identity of a speaker from a textual quotation in direct speech is a task which a young infant is unable to accomplish without help, at least in the beginning.

What of the introduction of unfamiliar lexemes? These, unlike in much picturebook work, are only rarely the subject of disembedded or explicit teaching. The story is not 'held up' for the sake of such deviations. Instead, this mother generally starts with familiar words, selected as a function of the child's existing knowledge; these are used first to describe selected aspects of particular pictures. Then, in a carefully managed process, unfamiliar words are gradually introduced in the context of those self-same pictures, whose sense is already clear. The meaning of the 'new' words is derived from the contextual clues of the linguistic and pictorial environments in which they appear, often for the first time ever in the life of this infant. The process may be considered as similar to the introduction of superordinate terms in picturebook reading; only when the hyponyms are fully understood, and the meaning of the superordinate term is clear from the context, does the latter become introduced.

Sometimes changes take the form of direct substitution by a near synonym of an unfamiliar lexeme contained in the written text:

Adult (14 months)
Here's the *wife who has a pig that* pushes *the cart to market.*

Adult (16 months)
Here's the *wife who has a pig that drives the cart to market.*

He takes *them off to prison by the nose and by the ear.*

He leads them off to prison by the nose and by the ear.

But often the 'old' and the 'new' term appear simultaneously, juxtaposed in a tandem arrangement of near synonymy:

13 months	**14 months**	**16 months**
Piggy runs away!	There's piggy, running away!	Piggy *escapes!*
		There's piggy, running away!

Similarly, in the following extract, 'piglets' is the term used in the written version:

13 months
And they have lots of little baby piggies don't they Wezzy!

14 months
And they have lots of little baba *piglets*, yes? Little babies come!

Lexical adjustments may also involve a change in word class. Abstract nouns in subject position are not characteristic of speech directed to Ceri when very young. She is, however, getting familiar with the lexeme 'chase' in the constructions which follow: 'There's piggy, running away! There's the wife chasing her' (14 months); 'And she runs away. Everybody chase her' (14 months). This paves the way for the introduction, at 16 months, of the substantive 'chase' as in: 'Piggy's off, the chase is on.' Equally a 'whole' object description, used in the first instance, is later replaced by the (less familiar) 'part' object description. What begins as: 'The wife sees the piggy' (13 months) is transformed eventually into the full textual version: 'the woman sees her curly tail', but not until some three months later, at 16 months.

Finally it may be noted that the use of familiar terms in anticipation of their eventual replacement by an unknown one is a technique which applies both to synonyms, and superordinate terms. In the following example the already familiar hyponyms ('ball', 'bicycle') act as precursors to the unfamiliar term 'sporting gear', eventually introduced at 16 months, again in a tandem arrangement:

Adult	Ceri (13 months)	Adult (16 months)
(Page turn)		*(Page turn)*
What's she doing now?		*Tries out all the sporting gear*
Bouncing the ball!		Wezzy!
Bouncy bouncy.		Bicycle
Riding bicycle, yes.		and ball
Show Mummy the bicycle Wez.		and football.
Show Mummy bicycle.		
	(Ceri points to her book)	
That's the football.		
She's doing the football.		
Football, yes.		
Kicking the football, yes.		

What is clear from these lexical adjustments is that this mother is concerned initially with the sense of illustrations, rather than with the form of the published written text.

Just how extensive are the formal alterations to the original text at the earliest sessions? Two criteria have been retained here. The first of these is the extent to which the written text appears both lexically and syntactically unaltered in the adult's oral presentation at 13 and 14 months. It is apparent that this mother, at the beginning, almost totally eliminates the text as originally published; in only 10 per cent of cases are the illustrations selected by the adult accompanied by their corresponding written caption.

The retention of the lexemes of the written text in mother's oral presentation constitutes the second criterion (even if the sentence structure is adjusted). But at a lexical level, too, extensive modifications are to be observed. The lexemes of the original text are entirely omitted from more than half of the descriptions of the illustrations at 13 and 14 months. This mother totally changes even the content words of the original written text into an oral version which is entirely of her own making. (In the remaining 40 per cent of cases at least one lexeme appearing in the original is retained by mother). This is not, then, a situation where the adult 'reads' the written text several times over in a period of months in the hope that the infant will eventually grasp the meaning of unfamiliar words. In the interests of intelligibility, telling a story based on written text to this 1-year-old involves here, not simply a slight alteration, but an almost complete reworking of the original written text, both lexically and syntactically.

3.5 Moments of time out

Such changes to the written text are intended to clarify the structure and content of narrative for an infant reader who is as yet unfamiliar with stories. Their aim is to help Ceri understand what the picture story conveys, as a prelude to the introduction of written text, to which the adult alone has access.

However not all the modifications to the printed text are designed purely to facilitate Ceri's eventual understanding of the text as written. A disproportionate amount of adult speech time is also devoted to aspects of the pictures which often have little to do with the printed version which accompanies them. These 'details' may not be 'important' from the point of view of the final text version as it stands in the book, but they are of significance, even of overriding significance, at least initially, for Ceri's perception of the pictures.

The detailed characteristics of these moments away from the storyline are examined below, but first consider an example. The illustrations are of a fairground; the written caption reads: 'Roll up! Roll up! Let's have a go! Now see our friends enjoy the show.' In the story as a whole, the visit to the fairground is of relatively little import. But this is an example of how this adult chooses to deal with this event.

Mother	**Ceri (13 months)**
(*Page turn, referring to the pig*)	
Who she see now?	
Who can she see now!	
	[ball]
Ball, yes.	
	Points to balloon.
Balloon! Good girl! yes!	
(*points*) Another balloon.	
There they are on the seesaw.	
	Points to seesaw.
That's right! Seesaw darling!	
And look Wez, can you see up here . . .?	
Who's there darling?	
	[pussy]
Pussy, there's the pussy, yes.	
And who's in that picture, hmm?	
	[pussy]
Pussy, yes.	
Yes pussy.	
There they are, they're walking.	
They've got a balloon haven't they?	
Going to the fair, yes!	
Wezzy likes this page.	

From a phonological point of view, such moments are, initially, demarcated by heightened pitch and excitement on the part of the adult. In the first two recorded sessions, this degree of emphasis has the effect of driving the 'official version' of the story into the background, while more marginal themes seemingly dominate phonologically.

Second, in terms of time, a disproportionate amount of adult speech is devoted to them, given the marginal degree of interest they represent for the story as a whole. Pages upon which this mother spends an inordinate amount of time (the sports shop or the fairground scene in the initial sessions, for example) may be accompanied by the remark: 'Wezzy likes this page.' That is, they are of especial emotional significance.

Third, thematically, they frequently reflect closely the child's current 'real-life' interests, for example, at 14 months, ball, balloons, cat, seesaw, bikes, mess, washing, running away and hiding, clothes and getting dressed. Their source is often a detail of an illustration (e.g. balloons at the fairground or a train travelling in the background) rather than the published text.

Fourth, and most importantly, such topics do not occur only in one book; some of them recur intertextually in the same way, or in slightly modified form, in other books.

Finally, interactionally, moments of time out are frequently associated with active child participation, through pointing, vocalisation or speech. In this book, Ceri's participation is remarkably predictable, having the qualities of being comparatively infrequent (a maximum of six to eight child contributions per session), and thematically consistent (almost invariably the same half dozen or so topics excite active participation from one session to the next).

How do these topics function in the telling of this story? In the first instance, they may provide an entry point to the pictures. In some cases a degree of overlap is to be observed between the focal point of child interest and narrative content: the cat at the fairground, for example, is a protagonist and accompanies piggy in her antics. In other cases, the train and the smoke, for example, which in this tale are of no relevance at all to the narrative as written; these moments are seemingly allowed simply because they are of emotional significance to the child, and for no other 'reason'. Such arrangements were noted in the previous chapter and are not returned to here in detail.

But such topics may also play a special part in the construction of the storyline as a whole. In effect, the introduction of an 'unfamiliar storyline' (here, the story of pig) is achieved with the help of 'blocks' of language whose form and content are both familiar, and individually significant to the infant. As well as lexical familiarity, one might include here mother's onomatopoeic vocalisations: 'brrm, brrm, little car' or 'whoosh, up in the aeroplane'.

Comparisons with other texts read at about the same time reveal, however, that this mother, while presenting books, frequently inserts into a whole variety of (reading) contexts the very same capsules of language which are already known (or are in the process of becoming known) to Ceri. The two examples cited illustrate just how systematic these ritualised forms of presentation can be. The first example concerns the theme of clothes. At the start of her second year, shoes preoccupied Ceri (she had started to walk). Additionally, she was especially interested in a large chinese straw hat hanging on a wall in her home. The two extracts cited are taken from entirely different storybooks (*Alex and Roy* and *Pig in a Muddle*), yet the language of this mother, thematically and lexically, is almost identical.

STORY GRAMMAR

Alex and Roy (14 months)
Then they go to see Granny.

                        C points to Granny.

There's Granny, yes.

                        C points to shoes.

Granny's shoes, yes.
And can you see Granny's hat?

                        C points to hat.

Good girly, yes.
That's right.

Pig in a Muddle (16 months)
'Time to change. I'm such a mess
I rather like this lovely dress'

Wezzy! look at her!
Got dress on now!
And what's that?
What she got on her head?
Hmm?
Can you show Mummy?
Got hat on, hasn't she?
And shoes.

These extracts demonstrate the use and reuse, in different stories, of sequences which are entirely familiar. The next example is slightly different. Again it incorporates into reading a theme which is of topical interest in the real-life experience of this infant (getting into a mess) but in this instance the linguistic structure used is only in the process of becoming known. The structure runs: 'got (viscous substance) all over (a part of the body or item of clothing). Also specified is its consequence: having to clean up afterwards.

Alex's Outing (14 months)
There's Alex, stuck in the mud.
Got mud all over his trousies.
Got sticky fingers.
Have to do the washies.

Pig in a Muddle (13 months)
(Piggy) got cream all over her face.
Have the washies.

Pig in a Muddle (14 months)
Then she's going to have lots of cream, doesn't she.
Gets it all over her face, shwshw.
And the cream goes all over her face.

As to why this mother speaks with such remarkable systematicity from one context to the next one can only speculate, but several reasons suggest themselves. First, these building blocks of language are known from previous experience to be highly motivating for Ceri; they can be relied upon to engage attention. Second, they bring a sense of unity and coherence to a reading session, in the face of often overwhelming diversity. That is, despite the introduction of a wealth of pictorial material which may be quite new, at a linguistic level the child is frequently exposed to patterns of recurrence in language use, from one page to another, from one book to another. This was the case in picturebook reading; only a limited set of the total number of creatures available in pictorial form was actually discussed with Rhys at 14 months, and these were discussed repeatedly. Third, the repeated use of structures, especially unfamiliar ones, in a variety of different reading contexts arguably maximises the opportunity which Ceri has to learn what these (new) structures might mean. When reading, this mother is apparently, at times, practising language.

Following Chomsky, it has become customary, perhaps, to focus upon the creative aspect of language; language is capable of responding, in an infinite variety of ways, to changing communicative needs. Given this creativity in language, some observers have indeed wondered how infants come to tease out the relationship between language and reality. However, Bruner has noted that, even if utterances are novel, the extra-linguistic contexts in which they occur are relatively constant – a mealtime, or bathtime ritual, for instance – thereby easing the task for the infant of working out the correlation between utterances and extra-linguistic reality (Harris and Coltheart 1986:39). Evidence from this study of reading, suggests, however, that speaking with an infant does not consist of being endlessly creative. On the contrary, there is a clear effort on the part of the reading adult to remain, in certain respects, systematic with regard to the formal language used from one circumstance to the next. What varies in reading is the context of use of that language.

Consider this evidence. In picturebook situations, it was observed that irrespective of changing pages (i.e. contexts) the same lexeme was used over and over again: within the same book, and from one age session to the next. 'Doggie' never becomes 'bow wow'. In storytelling, it may be seen that such consistency of use is not confined to a single lexical item, on a single page, in a single book. From one book to the next, selected structures, even whole sequences of language, occur and recur with a remarkable degree of systematicity over a period of weeks, if not months. The often tenuous relationship which exists between language and extra-linguistic reality is, in reading, arguably much more transparent. Infants are offered the opportunity to discover and re-discover that, for example, the expression 'got' x 'all over' y is a structure which can apply to viscous substances such as mud and cream with an underlying implication that the experience is unpleasant. It is the 'covert' aspects of semantic usage such as these which are perhaps being suggested in repeated readings with young infants (Whorf 1945 [1956:89]).

Apart from the linguistic advantage of learning new words and structures, there is possibly a fourth reason for using and reusing the same modules of language when storytelling. It has to do with the comprehension of the text as a whole. Let us observe that Ceri is listening hard to her story; she has a lot to remember and take in. The inclusion of moments of time out allows for the presentation of an unfamiliar storyline to take place within a framework of fixed linguistic reference points. The load of understanding an unfamiliar story orally presented is probably considerably reduced by the insertion of instantly recognisable 'capsules' of language. Characteristic of individual learning in a reading setting, such language use – intercalating the familiar with the new – is also a feature of epic narrative in the medieval tradition. Perhaps it might be argued that the use and reuse of sometimes highly familiar language is in some sense fundamental to the construction of oral narrative itself.

Two final observations concerning the status of 'moments of time out' are these. It might appear, given the analytical emphasis placed upon subject, fabula and written text, that the storyline is in the foreground of this mother's presentation to her infant – phonologically, temporally, emotionally. In fact, as already stated, the converse is the case, at least initially. Evidence from the 13- and 14-month sessions suggests that the excitement and thrill of a story, from the child's point of view, reside in the 'moments of time out', in the (so called) details of taxonomic description. What (from the adult point of view) constitutes the 'story' is introduced, initially, almost as a matter of subsidiary interest, as a sideline to these highpoints of excitement. Not until the maturity of 16 months does a switch occur (see section 4.3).

The second comment about moments of time out concerns their distribution within the session as a whole. Their positioning is as striking as their prevalence. This mother's presentation of the storyline of *Pig in a Muddle* alternates with the active contributions of the child in a carefully organised rhythmical pattern which over time becomes steadily predictable. That is to say, Ceri's contributions, at 13, 14 and 16 months occur almost invariably on almost the same pages and are triggered by the selfsame pictures. They always occur, for example, at the moment when the cat appears (on page 14) or the train can be seen (on page 21), and so on. Mother and daughter seem to reach a modus operandi with regard to when and how Ceri comments on the events of the book. Once again there is evidence of patterning. This time the pattern, familiar to each participant, seems to allow this mother to explain for a while, virtually uninterrupted, some of the events of the story, while Ceri is content, at these same moments, to sit quietly and listen. The effect is to allow this mother to devote her energies almost exclusively to constructing a more complete version of the story.

4 PROCESSES OF CHANGE: 14–16 MONTHS

Thus far this description has addressed the initial modifications which this mother makes to the text as published in the first two recorded sessions of *Pig in a Muddle*. This final section considers some of the changes which occur between 14 and 16 months and which culminate in the introduction of the author's actual text. Of the extensive adjustments which take place in this period, four are considered in detail: the length of the story; its structure; the introduction of written text; and session dynamics.

4.1 The length of the story

From an abridged account, the story is gradually expanded into a more complete version. How is this achieved? It might be envisaged, for example, that in an early session mother attends (for instance) in detail to pictures a, b and c but, in the interests of brevity, neglects d, e, f and g. In session two, one might hypothesise that she attends to these latter four, while omitting the first three (since these have been discussed already), and then the sum of these two sessions allows her to build towards a complete rendering (a+b+c+d+e+f+g) in the final, 16-month session.

As earlier intimated, however, this is not what happens. Ceri enjoys a complete experience on each occasion. This adult presenter retains the same basic common core of pictures, in order to work and rework them over and over again, bringing the linguistic commentary associated with those pictures gradually more in line with the written original. In the process, more and more illustrations are included in the discussion (see Table 6.1). The corollary of this, however, is that a small minority of pictures, always the same ones, are omitted totally from all three sessions (i.e. they are never discussed at all). The implication, of course, is that the same person takes each and every session; otherwise how could an adult presenter know which pictures constitute the vital common core and what kind of language these pictures are associated with?

4.2 Narrative structure and written text

A fundamental principle of child development, already discussed in previous chapters, is that mastery of initially difficult tasks frees the infant to attend to new and more difficult sets of challenges (Vygotsky 1934 [1962]). Progress is a function not only of age and maturity but also of familiarity. It is a principle which can also be observed in early storytelling.

Increasing familiarity with the story's grammar and content over a three-month period leads first to a reduction in the markers of narrative structure upon which Ceri initially relied. The narrative, in consequence, becomes less fragmented and flows more easily. The presentation progressively acquires a greater sense of continuity and cohesion. For example, the identification of protagonists in each picture via ostensive definition, with reiteration in adult speech of the subject word ('pig' or 'she'), is much reduced even over a period of six weeks from thirteen to fourteen-and-a-half months. Ceri is able to carry the subject word over a longer series of actions. Likewise, the question forms which had been required to explicate key aspects of plot become progressively eliminated. At the page turn alone (when there is a risk of loss of concentration), the use of question forms decreases from a total of ten at 13 months, to six at 14 months, to zero at 16 months, where they are replaced by the use of 'and'. In the process, the subject of the previous page is carried over from one page to the next. This extract from 14 months occurs at the page turn: End page (17): 'Piggy and cat on horsey!'; page turn: 'Where she go now?'; new page (18): 'Oh! Piggy in aeroplane!' It may be contrasted with its equivalent from the 16-month session: 'Piggy flies up (end page 17) ... and (page turn) ... (page 18) into aeroplane!' Lastly, tag questions (isn't she, doesn't she) which maintain an identity of perspective between child reader and adult presenter gradually lapse. The withdrawal of these props introduces the child to a form of presentation more closely resembling continuous written discourse.

The elimination of these markers of support are associated with the inclu-

STORY GRAMMAR

sion of other features fundamental to narrative. At 16 months, in addition to the ones previously quoted, a wider range of subsidiary characters is to be found: the man whose trousers pig grabs, the crane driver whose cranehook she uses to escape, the waiter in the restaurant whose bill is left unpaid are now mentioned for the first time. With them, a set of perspectives other than pig's becomes introduced. That is to say, pig's extraordinary antics are evaluated by these onlookers: 'The man's amazed, and off she tears'.

A third aspect of narrative, hitherto absent, concerns the transition from one setting to another. Although in the earlier sessions pig had been described in different locations, how she got there was of little or no interest to the storyteller. One moment she finds herself in the street, and the next inside the store. What becomes of concern now, however, is the means by which she gets from one place to the next, by bouncing on a pole (into the window), or catapulting from a bucking bronco (into the aeroplane). The narrative, in effect, becomes more complete. Lexical developments outlined earlier are continued, while the amount of direct speech (whether in dialogue or monologue form) increases sixfold, from two utterances at 13 months to twelve at 16 months.

The build-up to text in written form develops over the 3-month period using many of these processes simultaneously. Four of them: lexical transformation, the replacement of third person description by direct speech, the introduction of minor characters, and a shift of viewpoint are illustrated in the following extract:

13 months	14 months	16 months
(*Picture* (*a*))	(*Picture* (*a*))	(*Picture* (*a*))
Piggy drops the plates. 'Crash!'	All the plates go crash.	'Watch out . . . china shop ahead. "Bang!" and "Crash!" and "Clatter!"'
(*Picture* (*b*))	(*Picture* (*b*))	(*Picture* (*b*))
(*Omitted*)	Piggy gets platter on her head.	'"Oh no!" The salesman shuts his eyes. "There goes my best soup platter!"'

Finally, one may observe an increase, not only in the number of illustrations discussed (Table 6.1), but also in the citation of the written text accompanying them, which occurs in upwards of 40 per cent of cases at 16 months, a fourfold increase over the previous two sessions. However, it is not merely the quantity of written text now available, but its status in the overall dynamics of the interaction which perhaps represents one of the most important shifts of all in this three-month period.

4.3 Dynamics: from background to foreground

Although prosody has not been a central preoccupation in the course of this research, in narrative it is impossible to ignore its role as an indicator of Ceri's move towards maturity with regard to storytelling. In the beginning, 'moments of time out' tended to dominate this presentation, with the storyline featuring, as it were, in the background, as an adjunct to these excited experiences. This adult apparently engaged infant attention by referring to detail, introducing the storyline almost by default. By 16 months however, in an extraordinary change of emphasis, it is the story-as-written (or paraphrased) which is delivered in an excited tone, with strong onset of delivery and high pitch and which commands the attention of the infant. The taxonomic details, of sporting gear, of clothing, even the cat, on the other hand, are now fewer in number and alluded to in low tones, as an aside, almost in parenthesis.

The transformation in comparison with the previous sessions is remarkable and testifies to a fundamental change in this child's relationship with her book. The metamorphosis from infant reader to young adult listener turns on the centrality of the storyline in the adult's presentation. At a phonological level, it is the storyline which at 16 months is dominant; taxonomic description has ceded its position, diminishing both in extent and emphasis. Moreover, much of this narrative is couched in written text – a form of language which is not habitually used by the parent. It is the author of the story, an 'unknown' third party, whose ideas and now words come to the fore. A personalised adaptation of the original story as written has to a great extent ceased to be necessary; in this sense this infant reader can be said to have reached a not inconsiderable degree of reading maturity.

Summary

The introduction of a young infant to an illustrated story in verse has been described. Four sources of difficulty of comprehension were initially identified: narrative structure, written text, the interrelationship between text and illustrations, and the semantic conventions of sequenced illustrations.

To this 1-year-old, unacquainted with the narrative genre, an extensive adaptation of this written text is proposed. A complete, if shortened, version of the original story is always presented, whose focus is a single central character, engaged in a set of actions, in sequence, in a variety of settings; these are, moreover, the object of explicit metalinguistic comment. This oral version is recounted in a form of language which is descriptive, using a standardised third person 'subject-verb-complement' sentential structure, familiar vocabulary and little direct speech. The meaning conveyed by the pictures, either individually, or in sequence, forms the entry point to a personalised version of the written text, and opens the door to its eventual intelligibility. Adult speech plays a key role in drawing explicit attention to aspects of continuity and discontinuity between pictures.

As the meaning of the story becomes apparent, then and only then does the written text (and along with it changing perspectives, dialogue and difficult lexis) become gradually introduced. Interestingly, perhaps, the inability to grasp changes of perspective within narrative has been identified as a major source of difficulty in adolescents classified as poor readers. These same readers are also unable to comprehend stories based, not on one central character, but a number of protagonists (Nonnon 1992). The study of this storytelling event suggests that parents of young infants may instinctively defer, but do not exclude, the introduction of the more difficult aspects of narrative which, in the longer term, will prove essential to the interpretation of more complex texts.

5 DISCUSSION: PATHS TO LITERACY

In this, and the previous chapter, some of the processes via which a 1-year-old infant moves towards a greater maturity in reading have been studied. What have these processes involved, and what does the term 'maturity' imply?

5.1 Access to written text

A first, albeit very obvious, comment is that adults and young infants do not rely on 'simple' texts, 'sparsely' illustrated; complexity apparently appeals to both participants. At a linguistic level, this infant reaches maturity in so far as she is able to accept listening to a text written in language which is quite beyond anything she normally encounters in everyday life. It has been seen, however, that this process depends on a single core set of pictures being worked and reworked. Building towards extended text rests not so much on linearity (the replacement of an initial set of pictures by a different set), but on circularity, rather in the manner of winding round and round a spiral staircase, going over the same ground again and again, but doing so each time slightly differently and in greater depth. The introduction of written text also depends on this adult initially using language drawn from the 'unuttered context' of the infant reader's life, in order to make clear the meaning of the story. That is, in this circumstance, the mother moves through meaning to written form, rather than the converse.

It is, of course, tempting to assume that complex ideas can only be expressed using complex language. Here it has been shown that Ceri is not required to grapple with these two facets of narrative simultaneously and that, in the very early sessions, it is the meaning conveyed by the pictures, rather than the complex language in which the story is originally written, which is afforded priority. It is beyond the scope of this research to speculate on the implications of these findings for teaching practice. It would appear, however, that the use of a form of language which is wholly accessible to a reading audience is infinitely preferable as a basis for the introduction of complex new ideas. Sadly perhaps this is not what is to be observed in many textbooks written for children.

5.2 Readers' responses

A second dimension to Ceri's move towards greater maturity in her reading has to do with the development what one might call a literary response, or set of responses. What is to be understood by this? The issue is complex; just two aspects are highlighted which warrant special consideration. The first is the question of evaluative judgement. At 13 months, Ceri is presented with a set of events to do with the main protagonist recounted from a single perspective. Lexical judgements on that protagonist's antics are limited to a single interjection by the adult reader (e.g. 'naughty piggy'). At around 16 months, however, these events become looked at from a different point of view, even a series of viewpoints, and with these differing perspectives comes a critical assessment of what that protagonist was doing. Here judgement on the events is conveyed within the story itself, in the responses of more minor characters. Stories, by definition, order and relate events using a particular form of language, but these events must also be evaluated; a succession of undifferentiated facts makes for monotonous reading. Changes of perspective within the story, at 16 months, and later, the development, in the 2-year-old, of the reader's own reflective powers are two manifestations of the evaluative function within storytelling. To such a function, infants even of a very young age may be introduced.

The second aspect of literary response has to do with the heterogeneous nature of the reading activity. The reading of stories is often described as inherently homogeneous; it is the place, for example, where infants have the opportunity to hear 'extended discourse'. But what, for instance, of reader participation? Evidence from this study suggests that different infant readers, as might children later on, react differently to stories when reading. In Ceri's case, her day-to-day experience is frequently merged with the events of the narrative. This infant reader brings something of herself to her reading, involves herself actively, intervening in order to construct an adapted, personalised version of the stories which she reads.

This contrasts markedly with Rhys. Active engagement alongside the reader in order to construct a personalised version of a written story is not a feature; from the outset (at around 16 months), the place afforded to the writer of the original text is much the greater. Comments are frequently deferred until after the story has been read, or he contributes a missing lexeme from time to time, sometimes in humorous fashion (see example Chapter 2, section 4). An almost exactly parallel variation in reading styles has been observed in a much wider enquiry. There, interestingly, the style used by parents was found to be 'in harmony' with the particular child reader (Crain-Thoreson and Dale 1992:428).

As in picturebook activity, at an interactional level, parents are drawn, perhaps, into following their child's preferences.

Rhys' storymaking activities have therefore not been analysed here in detail; from the beginning he seems equipped to 'take from the outside in'. However, it is perhaps of relevance to recall at this point the relationship between 'books' and the 'real world' discussed in Chapter 4 (section 5.2). In Rhys' case, it may be remembered, numerous references to book reading take place (to use Goody's formulation) 'in another setting'.[1] With Ceri, however, stories and picturebooks tend to be constructed by bringing real-life experiences into the reading sessions themselves. Thus, even though the discussion of Part III is based on a study of Ceri and her mother, the important point to retain is that a merging of the 'book' world, and the 'real' world forms an inherent part of early literary experiences for both these infants. The difference lies in the circumstances in which the merging of the two worlds takes place.

5.3 A systemic view of reading

At the beginning of this chapter, certain characteristics peculiar to narrative were listed; stories are, by definition, organised linguistically in linear fashion around a single hero and a set of interconnected events, in a way that picturebooks are not. I would conclude, however, by drawing attention, not to the differences, but to the interrelationship between picturebooks and stories. The centrality of pictures, and the need to attend to the 'right one' (cf. Chapter 1) is one aspect. A second connection is at the level of formal linguistic content. Both types of material form a backdrop against which capsules of language, whether familiar, or unfamiliar to the infant, may be rehearsed intertextually. The implication must be that an infant needs to practise new expressions in particular in a variety of different contexts before they are acquired, and that an adult reader may take advantage of these different contexts in reading to bring new expressions to the infant's notice. The language work which is present, consciously or unconsciously, in reading is thus considerable.

As well as commonality of language work, however, both types of material are subject to remarkably similar techniques of exploitation. Three types of content are invariably introduced. That which, at a cognitive level, is referentially and linguistically new to the infant (first) stands alongside material which referentially and formally may be of sideline significance (to the adult's purpose), but yet of great affective importance to the infant (second). Between the two, a third area exists where infant experience and the book's contents converge. In the third area, a topic is chosen which is referentially and linguistically familiar and of affective importance to the infant, but yet merges with or forms part of the story or picturebook event which forms part of the adult's purpose.

The implications are threefold. One, surely, must be that, independently of changing books and the variety of responses which this might engender, adult and infant in some sense remain the same (i.e. are recognisable to one another as individuals). This infant, wherever she is in her reading, always enjoys the 'ball' or the 'cat'. This mother, wherever she is, uses a particular technique and almost always the same one, to render texts meaningful. Second, consistency of presentation technique is of manifest importance to both Ceri and Rhys; observations of the author confirm that both would leave the chair if a visitor failed to read them their story in the way to which they were accustomed. Third, it is possible that systematicity of presentation has a bearing not only on whether children listen, but also on how they learn. Could it be that new and unfamiliar material is more easily assimilated if the angle from which it is presented remains consistent? Young children may well be attentive to perspective as well as to content.

It is perhaps opportune to ask nonetheless: is systematicity of the type described above stifling – do infant and adult become 'stuck' in a particular form of interaction? Or is it liberating – are these adults' habitual patterns of communication conducive to further development? It is an issue upon which this study, by itself, can permit of no firm conclusion, although evidence from work in other fields suggests that unpredictable or erratic responses on the part of a parent lead to disturbance in the infant. Consistency when discussing books possibly has a significance which is not yet fully appreciated.

6 CONCLUSION

Chapter 6 has been devoted to a description of this mother as facilitator of Ceri's comprehension of the structure, style and content of a single written story from the age of 13 months. This presenter's technique is characterised by the development of a set of routines common to both narrative and picture-book reading and by the constant reworking, in adult speech, of a sequence of pictures 'available to persistent scrutiny'. Such behaviours culminate here in the (apparent) ability of this infant at the age of 16 months to grasp the essential rudiments of a relatively complex narrative text. It is suggested that the provision of (a) favourite book(s), read repeatedly on a one-to-one basis, by the same caregiver, who is able to interpret and contextualise a book's contents and to foster and respond to infant enthusiasm and excitement, might be of benefit to any young child, in whatever form of day care they enjoy.

Part IV

FURTHER ASPECTS OF THE SELF

This story of reading began with a description how Rhys and Ceri become, in a general sense, readers (Chapter 1). This was a necessary prelude to a discussion of their individuality, that is, those attributes of individual behaviour which seemingly impose themselves upon the adult, and remain relatively stable over time (Chapter 2). Within the confines of their individuality, however, Rhys and Ceri nonetheless accommodate. They gain mastery of the linguistic system used by their parents (Chapters 3 and 4), and they learn how stories are structured (Chapters 5 and 6).

Part IV of this book returns to the notion of the self, the parameters of which were first outlined (using Rycroft's definition) at the beginning of Chapter 2. Chapters 7 and 8 start from the premise that the infant self is, from a linguistic standpoint, subject to different levels of construction and expression. Linguistic interaction is arguably indispensable to the constitution of the self: 'To study persons is to study beings who only exist in, or are partly constituted by, a certain language.' (Taylor 1989:34).

Part IV draws extensively on the theoretical writings of Winnicott, for whom the construction of the self cannot be assumed; it must, on the contrary, be the object of theoretical investigation. The focus of Chapter 7 is the (indirect) construction of the infant psyche by a parent. Chapter 8 is dedicated to an analysis of spontaneous self-expression by these infants, considered in relation to their psychic and aesthetic development.

But an analytic perspective inspired by psychoanalytic (as opposed to literary or psychological) theory is appropriate for a second reason. This has to do with the way in which some aspects of the data of these final two chapters have been accessed. Unlike the emergence of the self as described in Chapter 2, the linguistic subtexts which are revealed here were not present at a conscious level of awareness in this mother-as-parent, nor did they become available through a process of ordinary introspection. Only as a result of detailed analysis of the recorded data did the patterns described below become apparent.

The existence of the systematic patterns of communication described in Part IV is not, in my view, a matter of conjecture; they are formally observable and empirically verifiable. It is the interpretation of these data and of their relevance for human development more generally which is necessarily more tentative and speculative than has been the case hitherto. However, whatever the nature of the interpretation which attaches to the data, the centrality of the notion of the infant self, whose construction and expression dominates so many of the linguistic exchanges examined in this book (see Chapters 2, 5, 7 and 8), raises at the very least the following question. Can studies of cognitive and linguistic progress in the young child be theoretically justified without reference to the infant self? It might be appropriate to enquire whether the development of the former is not somehow contingent upon the development of the latter.

7

MATERNAL SPEECH AND INFANT PSYCHIC DEVELOPMENT

1 INTRODUCTION: LANGUAGE AND THE NON-LINGUISTIC WORLD

In Chapter 2 the expression by Rhys and by Ceri of preferred modes of engaging with a reading adult or with the pictures of a book led to the postulation of a distinct identity or character for each child; the emphasis then was on self-affirmation and on differentiation. In this chapter, the self is viewed from a slightly different angle. The prime concern is the construction by the adult, in speech, of Ceri's sense of who she is. The means via which this mother encodes actions and significant persons of a particular picturebook will be described. Since these actions are subtly coded in a form which suggests that they are either (1) not permitted to the child, (2) accessible if shared with an adult or (3) available to the child to experience autonomously, I propose that this mother is here concerned with structuring, albeit indirectly, her child's position in a moral universe. But since also this adult's use of language is suggestive of directions which a child might take with regard to certain attachment figures as opposed to others, one may also speculate as to the social (as opposed to individual and/or biological) origins of this infant's psychosexual development.

The theoretical construct adduced to account for the child's emerging self is that of the psyche, as defined by Winnicott, further discussion of which follows below. But at the same time, since the issue here is an infant's relationship to the world as mediated by a mother's use of language, a theoretical framework derived from linguistic theory is also appropriate. Many linguistic theorists concern themselves with the relationship between language and the non-linguistic world. Consider now the relevance of this construct to the argument of this chapter.

1.1 Language and external reality

An extraordinarily complex linguistic problem may be dichotomised in very simple terms as follows. Does the world itself determine the structure of a language system? Or is it the language system which determines a speaker's view of that world? Even with regard to the relationship between language and the external world (i.e. the world perceptible to the naked eye) linguists are not agreed. Often cited in support of the view that reality determines the structure of a language are studies of colour terms. Research has shown this aspect of extra-linguistic reality to be coded similarly across the world's languages (Berlin and Kay 1969). The arguments of Berlin and Kay and the research engendered subsequently are discussed by Lakoff (1987:24 ff.). Summarily resumed, the thesis holds that external reality (in conjunction with biological predisposition) is a crucial determinant of lexical structure, otherwise there could not exist such a degree of consistency between the colour systems of the different natural languages of the world.

There exists, however, the contrary position. A language system, it is argued, reflects not so much 'reality' as the values and interests of those who speak it and what is important to them (Palmer 1976:21). Depending on the language spoken and the cultural needs of its speakers, the system will be structured differently. Examples from lexical structure relating to the physical (and social) world abound. The Eskimo, for instance, have in their vocabularies a repertoire of terms for what, in English, is covered by a single lexical item: 'snow' (Lyons 1977:242). Or, topographical features in the desert may be lexicalised in great detail, so as to ensure that various locations of waterholes, vital to survival, are catalogued with fine precision (Brown *et al.* 1958). This is not to suggest, however, that such distinctions are not available in languages which have no such lexemes; if this were so, translation would not be possible (Lyons 1977:243). The point at issue here is that real-world distinctions which are not lexicalised are potentially more difficult to express, and may even be overlooked (Brown *et al.* 1958).

Whorf, however, takes the argument a step further. He maintains that, as different languages segment reality differently, so will a speaker's perception of the extra-linguistic world be contingent upon the linguistic structures used to code that world. Language does not merely permit people to view reality differently; it obliges them to 'think' in a certain way. A speaker of Hopi or Navaho does not think in the same way as a speaker of American English because the structures (particularly the grammar) of their respective languages are different:

> the background linguistic system (in other words, the grammar) of each language is not merely a reproducing instrument for voicing ideas but rather is itself the shaper of ideas, the program and guide for the individual's mental activity, for his analysis of impressions, for his synthesis of his mental stock in trade.
>
> (Whorf 1940 [1956:212])

Thus, for Whorf, language acts upon people's perceptions of the outer world, segmenting their experience of extra-linguistic reality, but it also acts inwardly, shaping both their ideas and their thought processes.

Although these theories have been evolved with reference to a language system, it may be noted, even so, that an individual speaker's use of the code (just as language structure in general) exhibits features which support both points of view. Maternal speech is heavily determined (with regard to its content) by the context of situation in which mother and infant find themselves. However, maternal speech is never determined uniquely or entirely by the extra-linguistic world; it has the potential to describe reality in a variety of different ways. Parental language addressed to young infants may have its roots in the here and now, but this does not tell us anything of what that parent chooses to talk about and how. The use of language, by definition, implies choice, although the speaker might not be aware of the choices being made.

1.2 Language and the psyche

Much more problematic even than the relationship between a language system and the external world is the possible impact which language use might have on the development of a child's psyche. Winnicott writes of the psyche in these terms:

> The psyche part of the person is concerned with relationships, relationships within, relationships to the body, to the external world.... The psyche (specifically dependent on brain functioning) binds the experienced past, the present and the expected future together, makes sense of the person's sense of self, and justifies our perception of an individual there in that body.
>
> (Winnicott 1988:28)

The psyche is thus a hypothetical construct, adduced to explain and justify that intuitive experience of a 'self-within-a-body' which (in the non-psychotic) binds together and makes sense of an individual human being's past, present and expected future. However, the phenomenon of psychic growth, even if an inherent process, is far from automatic; it is hugely dependent on the environment (Winnicott 1988:29). This environment is represented, initially at least, by mother. Maternal concern allows the mother to adapt to her infant and in the beginning the burden of adaptation is almost totally hers. A mother's nonverbal behaviour (holding, reliability) are key factors in this process. However, increasing failure to adapt leads the infant from a state of being 'merged' with mother to being separate and individual. It is the infant, now, who adjusts to the environment, though, of course, never entirely; lack of compliance is a sign of emotional health.

In this process the father plays an increasingly important part. Initially in the background supporting the mother, the father's presence helps the infant to disengage from mother and to form a unit of its own.

As the baby moves from ego strengthening due to its being reinforced by mother's ego to having an identity of his or her own . . . the third person plays or seems to me to play a big part. The father may or may not have been a mother-substitute, but at some time he begins to be felt to be there in a different role.

(Winnicott 1969 [1989:242])

While for the male infant the father figures particularly as the embodiment of conscience, for the female, identification with an adult male figure allows her to keep in touch with that masculine part of herself, permitting ultimately of the formation of a successful heterosexual relationship: 'Imaginative identification with the male enriches the girl's appreciation of the man's function and eventually strengthens her personal relation to a chosen man' (Winnicott 1988:45).

Let us explore the implications of this last citation in a little more depth, for Winnicott here raises three issues of crucial importance to the theory of infant psychosexual development: identification, object choice and (intrapsychic) androgyny. For Winnicott, as for all psychoanalytic theorists, psychosexual development is not solely a question of biological gender (whether an infant is born genitally male or female). Nor is it simply a matter of identification, the process whereby the characteristics (as an infant represents them to him or herself) of an adult member of the same biological sex (usually the father or mother) become assimilated. Certainly, identification, the process of becoming like or wanting to be someone, permits the sense of feeling male (usually in a genitally male body) and female (in a genitally female body). Nor may psychosexual development be restricted to issues of object choice: the sex of the person one would choose (eventually) as an adult sexual partner.

For while these three factors contribute to issues of gender and gender identity, Winnicott stresses in addition that infants of both sexes must maintain within themselves elements of persons of the opposite sex. It is as important for a young female to remain in touch with the male elements of her psyche, as it is for a boy to retain female elements. Intrapsychically, each of us is androgynous. This does not mean that females in consequence 'behave like' men; it is the imaginative identification with male characteristics which is the feature of emotional health. For the purposes of this discussion, the essential point is that, in the life of a female infant, the father assumes an increasingly important role: as the person who draws his infant daughter out and away from the mother–infant unit, as an object of libidinal affection but also as a source of identification.

The argument now to be addressed is the role of maternal speech as facilitator of the maturational processes outlined by Winnicott. To what extent are

- separation, individuation, and autonomy within the infant
- disengagement from the mother
- imaginative identification with the father

MATERNAL SPEECH AND INFANT PSYCHIC DEVELOPMENT

reflected in, if not actively facilitated by, this mother's use of language in a picturebook dialogue with Ceri aged between 11 and 18 months? The example to be described in section 3 reveals maternal speech to have the following characteristics:

- It is selectively oriented towards the child of the book, at the expense of other referents, animate or inanimate also available, potentially, for description.
- The child of the linguistic description is often coded as behaving with a degree of autonomy and independence quite at variance with the contents of the illustrations.
- Attention is deflected away from the adult female figures in the pictures (coded as Mummy) towards illustrations of adult male figures (coded as Daddy).
- Lexical–syntactic covariation presents to the infant reader a world view in which the child is clearly and systematically positioned.

2 THE GRAMMAR OF MATERNAL SPEECH IN RELATION TO THE TWO-DIMENSIONAL WORLD: AN EXAMPLE

The speech situation

From a researcher's standpoint, the choice of a book reading situation for a longitudinal study of psychic development has the fortunate peculiarity of stability through time. Whereas most speech situations ritually repeated in a child's life fluctuate (no two feeding routines, for example, can ever be the same exactly), a two-dimensional referent presents to parent and child alike the opportunity for coding and recoding, over a long period of time, a series of referents which are on each occasion identical. That is to say, biases which occur in adult speech are not due to alterations in the extra-linguistic context of situation (i.e. presence of Daddy on one occasion, but absence the next; the choice of one food as opposed to another). From Ceri's point of view, the book considered here is a favourite, read over and over again from infant age 11 to 18 months. The investment in this material was therefore considerable. The four videorecordings analysed here were made at child age 11, 13, 14, and 18 months respectively. On each occasion Ceri was reading with her mother.

The nature of the material presented

The external world, for the purposes of this discussion, is constituted by a set of illustrations depicting a typical day in the life of a toddler (*My Day*, Ladybird Books, 1983). This book is perhaps somewhat unusual among children's literature in that it is neither obviously a narrative (in which case getting across the storyline, in however simplified a form, might well have dominated this mother's presentation), nor is it a wilfully didactic set of materials thematically organised by page, each with a large number of labelled items to learn, in which case the presenter might well have been preoccupied with teaching vocabulary.

Rather, the book consists of a set of tableaux illustrating familiar and homely scenes (getting dressed, shopping, playground activities, mealtimes and bedtime), all of which form part of this infant's real life, and with whose corresponding vocabulary Ceri is largely familiar. The degree of latitude enjoyed by the presenter in organising this material linguistically is thus considerable, both from the point of view of the content of the illustrations (the vast array of referents, both animate and inanimate, in the scenes) and the absence of an accompanying text (this mother totally disregards in her presentation the small amount of text accompanying these pictures).

Linguistic analysis

How does this mother structure, through her use of language, this infant's perception of these pictures? Transcriptions of the dialogues which occur during the presentation of this book were examined for each one of the four recorded sessions. This mother's language was analysed, not only for its lexical content but also, if not chiefly, for grammatical structure. These two criteria were then taken together: vocabulary choice was considered in relation to grammatical content.

The speech of this particular mother was divided into a series of tone groups (utterances), that is, the (usually very short) phonologically circumscribed units with which many mothers habitually address their infants. Having first excluded those which concern Ceri's behaviour (for example, 'comments': 'Well done'; 'good girl', or 'directives' which encourage her to 'point to' an item: 'Show Mummy with your finger where's pussy'), each tone group remaining, which 'described' the book's contents, was individually categorised – according to the nature of its grammatical subject or head word, and according to its internal structure. The internal structure may be nominal (containing a noun, but no verb): 'teddy'; 'poor doggy', or verbal (containing a verb, or verblike structure): 'Mummy pour the juice out'.[1] For each tone group, the following criteria were retained:

- the internal structure of the tone group, whether nominal (e.g. 'teddy') or (pro)nominal/verbal (e.g. 'little boy running away');
- the form of the subject word, whether lexical (e.g. 'the little boy'; 'the little girl'; 'car; 'marmalade'), pronominal (e.g. 'he' 'they'), or deleted (implied) (e.g. '[. . .] going for a walk');
- the nature of the grammatical subject of the tone group, whether animate human: 'Mummy', animate non-human: 'cat', or inanimate: 'chair';

- for verbal groups, the lexical content of the verbal group in relation to the grammatical subject (e.g. what 'Mummy', or 'Daddy', or 'the little boy' is said to be doing).

Finally, the relationship between these criteria and the printed illustrations was considered in detail. In other words, the grammar of the adult language was examined per se and in its relation to the two-dimensional world to which it refers. It is the orientation of this description in the presence of the two-dimensional stimulus which is of most interest here.

3 THE WORLD VIEW OF MATERNAL SPEECH

3.1 Animate subjects

A most noticeable feature of adult language use in these sessions is the adoption of animate (predominantly human) referents as head words within a tone group — at the expense, that is, of inanimate referents. Of 273 grammatical subjects (explicit or implied), in approximately one quarter of cases only (N=70) do inanimate referents feature ('nappy'; 'swing').

Thus, despite a wealth of illustrated material which could allow these readers to focus on material realia in the tableaux, attention is here directed in a clear majority of cases towards illustrations of animate (predominantly human) interest. No attempt is made exhaustively to describe the book's contents; on the contrary, this adult reader's attention (and with it, presumably, Ceri's) is selectively focused. For example, a picture is 'about' the little boy riding his bicycle and not the flowers, which also feature in the same illustration.

As observed in Chapter 3, for both these parents, humans are a central consideration in picturebook descriptions. But the emphasis on humans must also, in part, be a consequence of Ceri's seeming reluctance to interest herself in names for things (already noted in Chapter 2) and the concomitant concern of this mother to reflect her own infant's reading preoccupations. Nonetheless, given the absence of written text in this book, this mother's lexico-syntactic choices are particularly illuminating. For within the category of 'human interest' this mother has a particular method of coding these pictures in her speech. It is this coding 'method' which is now described.

3.2 The centrality of the child

It is immediately apparent that what this adult presents as the subject of her discourse is, predominantly, infant activity. No less than 60 per cent of this presenter's animate subject references have as their focus either a child, or children, acting alone, or in joint activity with an accompanying adult. Table 7.1 gives the breakdown of the 203 tone groups in the adult language whose grammatical subject is animate.

Table 7.1 The animate grammatical subjects of adult speech

	N	%
Child as sole subject of tone group (e.g. little boy, little girl)	99	48.8
Child as joint subject of tone group (with adult)	22	10.8
Adult subject only (e.g. Daddy, Mummy)	28	13.7
Non-human animate subject (e.g. cat)	54	26.6
Total	203	100

Base: All descriptive adult tone groups with animate head word (N=203) in adult speech addressed to Ceri at 11, 13, 14 and 18 months, respectively, when reading one picturebook: *My Day*

It is noticeable, in addition, that tone groups with a child subject only are, for the most part, lexicalised ('the little boy riding his bike'; 'the little girl's doing the painting') as opposed to having either a pronominalised ('he', 'she' or 'they') or implied subject ('sitting on potty'). Second, such tone groups, when they are lexicalised, usually have a grammatically singular, rather than a plural, subject. Statements of the type 'this little girl's got book' (singular subject) are very common. Equally, 'joint' adult–child activities, which form 11 per cent of the total animate subjects, never have a lexical subject. Sentences of the type: 'the Mummy and the children are having their breakfast' never appear. Multiple referents are either coded in pronominal form 'they', as in: 'There they are, having breakfast' (where the picture shows a mother and two children at the breakfast table) or have an 'implied' subject (i.e. the grammatical subject is deleted) as in: 'Oh! [. . .] going for a walk with the buggy' (where the picture shows an adult female figure and two children walking to the park).

Nonetheless, within these dialogues, counter-examples are to be found. For instance, at 11 months there is plurality of lexical subject within one tone group: 'The Mummy and the Daddy are in bed'; 'little boys and girls going to sleep'. At 14 months, a collective noun: 'people' denotes plurality of referent. At 18 months, there is one example of the indeterminate noun 'someone' to denote a single referential subject: 'Someone's dropped an egg there.' Such counter-examples are, however, in the overall scheme of things, quite exceptional.

It appears then that the animate 'subject' words of the 11–18 months age range, in this book, are predominantly (though by no means exclusively): lexical; determinate; singular. If the referent is multiple, then the use of a pronoun (they), or subject deletion ('watching TV') is usual. What is of interest, however, is the lexical content of the verbal activity associated with these different grammatical subjects (considered in section 3.4).

With regard to content, the predominance of the child in the discourse reflects in part the material (the book describes a day in the life of a toddler). This fact does not, however, dictate that the child should be in a (grammatically) subject position. Child referents could equally appear in complement position, as in: 'the Mummy's feeding the baby'. In fact, with this book, human animate nouns (whether adult or child) never do occupy such a position in this mother's account (see section 3.3).

3.3 The adult as grammatical subject: a minority role

In this presenter's description, the adults of the illustrations are coded almost without exception as 'Mummy' or 'Daddy', even though the pictures are non-specific; grown-up, adult, lady, man, aunt or uncle, are terms which might equally have been selected. That is to say, the world of grown-ups, as linguistically presented, is constituted almost entirely of Mummys and Daddys. But, apart from this formal feature, how frequently do references to adults occur in the extensive group of animate headwords in this presenter's speech?

Analysis of the data (see Table 7.1) reveals that in only 14 per cent of cases does 'Mummy' or 'Daddy' feature as sole and explicit grammatical subject of this presenter's discourse, as in: 'Daddy pour the tea out.' To this 14 per cent may be added the 11 per cent of activities undertaken jointly by adult and child, in which adults are, as it were, 'present' in the discourse either pronominally: 'There they are, having breakfast' or by implication: 'going for a walk'. Multiple referents, it may be recalled, are generally coded pronominally or by implication; in such instances, adults feature in the linguistic account, but do not receive explicit lexical mention as tone group subject. They are 'present' but somewhat in the background.

But do the 25 per cent of adult 'mentions' reflect the pictorial data? It could be, for example, that adults feature only very marginally in the illustrations. What is to be observed, however, is the converse. The low frequency (25 per cent) with which adults occur in the discourse does not reflect the illustrated material proportionately since here (with the exception of the inside cover pages) adult and child referents occur, overall, in much more equal proportions. In a total of some 195 representations altogether, representations of adults total approximately 40 per cent, while the remainder (60 per cent) are of children.

Clearly the 11 per cent of 'joint' mentions of adults, together with 14 per cent of 'exclusive' mentions do not account for the 40 per cent of actual pictured appearances. How, then, might the minority status of adults in the discourse be explained? The shortfall must be due to presenter editing, that is to say, this presenter, in some instances, simply avoids mentioning the adults of the picturebook. Compared to their prevalence in the pictures, adults, in discourse terms, are assigned a minority role.

This latter finding is particularly striking when related to the illustrated material, which offers multiple opportunities for coding the child as a recipient of adult action, for example, at suppertime (the child is being spoon fed), change of nappy, getting dressed, lifting the child from the cot, helping the child into the bath, pushing them along in the supermarket trolley. All these activities are pictured unambiguously with an adult agent and the child in a passive, recipient role. The dialogue, however, does not present the activity with an adult grammatical subject, for example:

- Daddy's feeding the little boy.
- There's Mummy, changing the baby.
- Mummy's dressing the little girl.
- Mummy's getting the baby up.
- Mummy's lifting the little girl into the bath.
- Mummy's pushing the little girl along in the trolley.

Instead all mention of the adult is excluded and the child is cited as subject. This finding is constant for the whole of the period from child age 11 to 18 months. For example:

'Little boy having supper.'
'Baba having nappies.'
'Little girl having bath.'
'Little girl having ride.'

Thus, where this presenter elects to exclude the adult from the discourse, this has much to do with the status of the adult in the illustration. If adult and child are pictured together and if the picture, so to speak, depicts the adult as helping the child (to ride a bike, eat, bath, get dressed) this presenter focuses attention solely on the child (to the total exclusion of the adult) and portrays the child (linguistically) as grammatical subject, even as agent, of the activity in question. That is to say, the language of this adult reader confers upon the infant in the picture a degree of autonomy well beyond that actually depicted in the illustration itself.

3.4 The adult as subject: a minority, but significant role

Judicious editing out from the presenter's discourse of the number of actual appearances which 'book' adults make results in these adults occupying a minority role overall. Their low number of linguistic appearances is, however, offset to an extent by the qualitative significance of their role when they do appear. Here again, systematic variation is found, depending on the nature of the pictured material.

First, adults, when they do appear in speech, are frequently associated with specifically adult tasks. That is to say, a lexicalised adult appearance (Mummy or Daddy) in the discourse 'marks' an activity as being 'exclusively adult'. In the examples given below, the activities quoted as being carried out by the Mummy or the Daddy are, in actual fact, in the real-life experience of this child reader, the exclusive province of the adult, and the adult alone.

'Mummy pour the juice out.'
'Daddy reading the paper.'
'Mummy doing the ironing.'
'Daddy doing the cookies' (i.e. the cooking).
'Daddy pour the tea out.'

(One might include here the 'exception' noted earlier: 'the Mummy and the Daddy are in bed', where they are pictured as being in a large double bed. In Ceri's home, each child has their own bed to sleep in; only the adults share a bed.) This contrasts with the coding of joint activities engaged upon by both parties, in which the child and adult subjects are subsumed grammatically as a joint subject ('they'), as in: 'There they are, having breakfast.' Here the activity is in reality allowable to both parties and is coded according to a different set of lexico-syntactic rules.

Second, and here we rejoin Winnicott, it is significant also that the 14 per cent of sole references to adults includes a bias towards pictures including an adult male figure, while comparable ones which include the mother are omitted. Emphasis on 'Daddy' in the coding may be seen by comparing descriptions of two high interest pages (pages which, at each reading session, consistently generate a large amount of adult speech relative to other pages), where 'mother', and 'father', in the illustrations, feature equally frequently and in broadly equivalent activities (e.g. where children are getting dressed, Daddy has a pair of toddler's trousers in his hand, while Mummy holds out a child's dress). The linguistic coding, however, includes a total of fourteen mentions of Daddy (twelve lexical and two pronominal), while Mummy receives just three mentions. The bias here, it seems, is towards a disproportionate emphasis on 'Daddy'.

Summary

In reading a picturebook to Ceri aged between one and one-and-a-half years, this presenter may be observed to be putting forward to her child a certain view of the world and of a child's position within it;

- Some activities are entered upon jointly by both adults and children. Here the grammatical subject is pronominal or deleted, as in: 'Going to the park'; 'Going to have dancing'; 'There they are, having breakfast'.
- Others are carried out by the adult alone (and, implicitly, forbidden to the child). Examples are pouring juice from a bottle or ironing. Here the adult subject is singular and, most usually, lexicalised, as in: 'Daddy pour the tea out.' Among adult mentions, moreover, a disproportionate emphasis on 'Daddy' is to be noted.
- In a third group of activities, the child is given independent status. This may be because adults are not depicted as being engaged in the activity, as in: 'There they are in the garden' or 'watching TV'. But the attribution of autonomous status may also occur when, in the illustration, an adult is engaged

with the child upon an activity (dressing, having a bath). In these cases, the adult is, linguistically at least, totally excluded and the child is presented as agent of the activity.

There are two aspects of this mother's method of coding these pictures to which particular attention must be paid. The first observation is linguistic. With respect to a specific activity or book, parent–infant exchanges seemingly have their own, specific set of lexical and grammatical rules. It was noted in Chapter 6, for example, in connection with the 'Piggy' story, that animate referents occupied both subject and complement positions: 'Here's a wife, who has a pig.' In this picturebook however, only rarely does an animate referent take up a complement slot; animate referents are confined mainly to subject position. If indeed different selection restrictions are applied when reading different materials, it would follow that child-directed speech in the reading setting is governed by not one but a variety of book-specific and linguistically specifiable, grammatical sub-systems. It would be an argument, perhaps, for varying reading material with young infants as widely as possible.

The second observation concerns the structure of what might be termed this child reader's moral universe. In the tripartite division of prohibited adult activity versus allowable child activity (with areas of overlap), the child's place, in relation to others around, is clearly marked; the child, in other words, is positioned. Further, it is in the grammar of the adult language that these messages are encoded. Less subject to conscious control on the part of the speaker, syntactic choices, in association with lexical choice, are significant. They are, perhaps, the means via which this mother communicates messages to her infant of which she herself (and perhaps the infant too) is not fully aware.

4 DISCUSSION: MATERNAL SPEECH AND THE INFANT PSYCHE

This section discusses possible formative roles played by language-as-environment; specifically it reviews the claims for language as a determinant of how Ceri perceives the world and how, by implication, she experiences herself (consciously or unconsciously).

However, a note of caution must again be sounded. Adult speech, I earlier argued, is often polyvalent. This mother will undoubtedly be mindful of a number of aspects of infant growth, apart from that of the psyche; language, of course, is one. In this picturebook description, the grammatical subject slot is frequently filled, for instance, by a (human) agent, not recipient, of an activity, as in: 'Little girl riding her bike', and never 'The bike is ridden by the little girl'. It is a form of coding which is arguably of help to Ceri; in Standard English, grammatical categories often bear some relation to meaning (Palmer 1976:121). With these remarks in mind, consider now other possible roles of maternal speech.

MATERNAL SPEECH AND INFANT PSYCHIC DEVELOPMENT

4.1 Language as mediator between the child and the external world

In this chapter it has been shown that maternal speech does not faithfully 'report' reality. Through choice of subject matter and the manner in which this material is encoded by the speaker, language attends selectively to the extra-linguistic world, aspects of which are afforded thereby a greater or lesser degree of salience. In so far as infant attention and mother's description are jointly focused, this infant's perception of the illustrations must be influenced to a major extent by the construction which her mother places upon them. In providing Ceri with a view of what each page is about, this mother exemplifies, perhaps, the Whorfian conception of language as modulator between the individual infant and the external (two-dimensional) world.

4.2 Language as a mirror of infant social and psychic identity

However, this mother's linguistic behaviour as documented here, is further prompted by, and is in part a response to, her own child's current state of social and psychic development. Her description partly reflects processes on-going in her own child at the time these reading sessions take place. Ceri for example, inhabits a tripartite world in which some activities are allowed, others forbidden, and a third set entered upon jointly with adults. But the toddler age is also an age when independence and autonomy, disengagement from the mother and imaginative identification with the father assume critical importance. These, too, feature implicitly in this mother's linguistic presentation. That is, in her (apparent) description of the two-dimensional world, this mother is in effect holding up a mirror to her child reader's emerging sense of self.

But does this child reader sense that her mother is, in fact, talking about her? In view of this mother's many attempts to bring together Ceri's real-life experience and the world of the book, it might reasonably be concluded that such is indeed the case. Explicit parallels, readily discernible to an outside observer, are drawn between infant reader and the book characters: 'Boiled egg – like Wezzy has'. Here maternal speech merges the book with this child reader's real-world experiences quite explicitly.

However, parallels with Ceri's ongoing 'real-life' interests may be implicit. Selectivity – what mother chooses to talk about is one aspect of this. From among the myriad possible referents offered by the illustrations, this mother focuses on the telephone (Ceri likes to phone on her own toy phone) and the toy parrot (she, too, has a toy one), while disregarding in the same picture items of equal visual prominence, but of lesser emotional significance to the infant (xylophone, paper handkerchiefs, bricks, radio, bed, cupboard). Hats and shoes, swings and roundabouts are all aspects singled out for discussion by this mother and particularly enjoyed by Ceri in her real-life experience at this time.

Implicit links are also established through careful choice of lexis: not only what this mother chooses to talk about, but how she does so. As earlier noted, the adults in the book are almost invariably coded as 'Mummy' or 'Daddy' – the two most significant adults in this infant's life. There are other telling examples. What the book character drinks from a beaker is coded by this presenter as 'juice': 'Teddy got juice.' Nothing in the illustration itself determines this; the beaker could well contain liquid of any kind. Ceri herself at this age knows the words for juice, milk and water. Why then does this mother code teddy's drink as juice? I believe precisely because Ceri herself drinks juice (and not milk or water) from just such a beaker. In short, this mother's attempts to create a bridge between the two-dimensional world and the world of the child reader are diverse and manifold. Through such uses of language, infant reader and book character are often as one.

Once again, then, adult speech in the reading situation may be observed to be polyvalent. Identification between infant reader and book character lies at the heart of a literary response. But here the process has moral import too. This mother mediates, through language, a sense of her individual child's social, and by implication, moral and psychic world. Two points are of note. First, this child reader's moral universe is peopled by humans, objects and events which are linguistically familiar and significant to her, not by strangers derived from some externally imposed and uncontrolled experience. That is to say, the constitution of this infant's inner world is gradual, long-term, linguistic and non-traumatic. Second, what is dynamically appropriate for Ceri at a specific stage of development is not explicitly stated; this adult reader never asserts that: 'infants of eleven months are not allowed to do the ironing'. Such messages are instead implicit, part of a lexico-grammatical subtext. In the internal world statements of this kind are perhaps not so much understood, as assimilated; they become part, possibly, of an unconscious dynamic.

4.3 Language as the architect of infant psychic growth

The final and strongest claim of all is that this adult presenter, through her use of language, is 'the' or 'a main' architect of her child's psychic development. In her linguistic presentation, this mother portrays as autonomous a child that, in real life, as in the pictures, is not so. Neither the 'book' child nor the child reader as yet feeds, dresses or bathes unaided. Mother's description is one jump ahead: a statement of things as they are to become, not as they are.

Intrapsychically, the father is of especial importance not only in the infant's move towards separation from the mother but also as the personification of infant conscience and/or as the precursor, through imaginative identification on the part of the infant female, of a future relationship with a chosen man. The father, both psychically, and linguistically, is now playing a 'big part': it is towards him that this mother orients her presentation. These uses of language by the mother have, I believe, suggestive power. Rather than (or in addition to) lending support to psychic processes ongoing in the child, this mother actually structures their very content through her (unconscious) use of language.

Supporting evidence for the view that this mother is directing Ceri's present with an eye to the future comes from a consideration of the findings presented in Chapter 5. There too, the thoughts, feelings and experiences of book characters were couched in terms derived from this infant reader's own experience. There, as here, the adult presenter (apparently) describes the world inhabited by another in a manner which projects forward in time the actual day-to-day experiences of the observing child reader: Maisie gets dressed by herself. In talking to this infant reader about another, this mother seems to be actually drawing together the different strands of that infant's life into a coherent narrative.

Such evidence leads to the tentative conclusion that Ceri, in preparation possibly for a presumed (wished for?) future role, is the recipient, even preverbally, of a subtle form of verbal tutoring from her own mother. As already stated (section 1.2), psychosexual development is of course governed by instinctual biological tendencies and also by example – what adults in the environment are themselves perceived (by the infant) to be. But verbal influence, albeit of indirect and subtle form, seemingly has a part to play. Ceri does not develop in a vacuum; the unconscious wishes and dreams of her mother with regard to her present, and future, are contained, unwittingly, in this adult's speech.[2]

5 THE CONSTRUCTION OF THE SELF: WIDER IMPLICATIONS

5.1 Linguistic origins of the self

Considered in Chapter 7 is but one example of coding practices of pictorial information from a single picturebook, by one mother, with just one infant over a period of just seven months. It is not suggested, of course, that psychic development is always central in picturebook reading. Nor even that a mother is the only person of significance in a young child's life capable of influencing him or her. Nor has any evidence been presented for this father, or for Rhys. These data have suggestive power only, therefore, and must not be overinterpreted. Bearing in mind these reservations, let us now return to the issue posed at the start of Part IV. How do the findings of Chapter 7 contribute to a theoretical understanding of the construction of the infant self?

Just as the adult reader poses questions relating to the physical world: 'Where's the bee?' and then goes on to answer, on the child's behalf: 'There it is', so here this mother anticipates questions more ontological in kind: 'Who am I? Where do I stand in the scheme of things? Or in relation to significant events, and people in the world?' What has been observed is that answers to these questions are supplied to Ceri via a (personalised) grammar of interpersonal relationships implicitly inscribed within adult speech. It may be noted in addition that this mother includes in her discourse not simply a view of the child as she is, but also as she might become. The term psyche is apt: it is the shaper of the self which brings together in one body, not only past and present experiences, but the expectation of future ones as well. It would appear, then, that children have a need to know not only what is actually happening around them or to them, but also what is going to happen.

This very small example suggests that selective biases do exist in the speech of a parent; in this case these have been concerned with the moral and psychosexual development of the infant. The self, then, is a construct which is in part given and unfolds in the eyes of the beholder (cf. Chapter 2). But other aspects of the (infant) self are at the same time (unconsciously) shaped by that self-same beholder in a series of verbally mediated statements. The psyche, in other words, is in part linguistically constituted. This is a quite different argument from the instinctual/biological model proposed by Freud (for example), for whom moral and psychosexual development is very much a matter of libidinal impulse, non-verbally mediated – a 'wordless interplay of pressures and intensities' (Bowie 1991:10), though discourse, of course, is paramount in the therapeutic setting. There are a number of implications for infant growth which follow from this; two – the use which a child makes of adult speech, and potential areas of conflict are now briefly addressed.

5.2 Infant use of adult speech

For language to function as an agent of psychic growth, covert subtexts of the kind described here must somehow enter the mind of the child (Frosh 1989:175). Or, as Winnicott puts it (1988:99): 'whatever the degree of importance we may assign to environment, the individual remains, and makes sense of environment'. What evidence do we have that Ceri might, consciously or unconsciously, make something of what this mother says?

Evidence that an infant internalises a parent's use of language is speculative. The first kind of evidence is circumstantial. Close parallels apparently exist between this mother's use of language on the one hand and, on the other (non-linguistic) processes described by Winnicott to be ongoing intra-psychically: separation, individuation, autonomy, identification with the father, the child as a unit, included within, or excluded from, the adult world. One might speculate that the one and the other are at times syntonic and, at the very least, mutually determined. But it might also be that language, in some instances, is primary and urges the child towards the very processes that Winnicott describes as pre-existing within the infant.

Analogy provides the second kind of evidence. From areas of linguistic analysis more readily available to empirical verification (lexical acquisition or grammatical structures, for example), it is known that maternal speech is a critical determinant of children's cognitive and linguistic development. It might be hypothesised then that the messages encoded unconsciously by a mother in her ritualistic and repeated use of language might be taken over and 'used', to an extent at least, by the infant interlocutor, equally unconsciously, in the construction of her own internal world.

5.3 Matters of synchrony

The infant self, then, is nothing, if not a composite structure, predicated (in part) on the notion of the infant being susceptible to and internalising external linguistic influences. One might ask the question (in an empirical investigation, for instance): what view of the world does a given adult, through their use of language, create for a child, either by referring to the child directly (you ... child, boy, girl) or indirectly, by their own selective perceptions of the world, linguistically transmitted. In other words, the ideology of adult speech addressed to children in non-book situations can and may be the object of empirical research.

If the speech of adults does indeed contain subtexts of the kind described, further questions of theoretical interest arise. What is the effect upon a growing infant of different, possibly conflicting, messages at different stages of development, mediated by different caregivers? How are they experienced subjectively? How are they integrated? What influence do they have upon the construction of an infant's sense of self (or self-worth)? Sadly, it is beyond the scope of this enquiry to suggest answers to these questions.

6 CONCLUSION

This chapter has been concerned with the role of language in structuring Ceri's external world (available to visual perception) and, indirectly, her own internal world. In this example, a favourite picturebook has been shown to be more than a vehicle for teaching words and meanings. It also provides a forum in which Ceri's relationships with significant others and the different parts of the self, past, present and future, may be structured through adult use of language. Similar functions were attributed by Winnicott to the psyche; in this sense, maternal language may be seen as an agent of infant psychic development and picturebook reading as providing a setting for such processes to occur.

8

EMERGENT LITERACY
A Winnicottian view

1 READING DEVELOPMENT IN THE LONGER TERM

One of the objectives of this enquiry has been the identification of possible links between reading in infancy (before child age 2 years), and reading in later childhood (age 5–7 years). This chapter looks again at this theme, but from a perspective which is both linguistic and psychoanalytic. The intention is to revisit Rhys' and Ceri's first systematic contacts with books in the first year, follow them in detail until age 2 years and look forward to patterns of behaviour as they emerge at age 5–7 years. The aim is to demonstrate the extent to which these two infants 'go on being' in their reading. That is to say, there are characteristic patterns in their active responses as individuals which suggest continuity of development over several years. The nature of these characteristics and how they evolve over time constitute the linguistic argument to this chapter.

At the same time, however, these data will be discussed with reference to Winnicott's theory of transitional objects and phenomena, whose specific aim was to explain cultural activity in later years in terms of a child's earliest interchanges with the environment. The psychoanalytic/literary perspective is the second strand to the argument of this chapter. What is Winnicott's theory and what is its relevance to this discussion?

2 WINNICOTT'S THEORY OF TRANSITIONAL OBJECTS AND PHENOMENA

Throughout his life, Winnicott returned again and again to expand upon and redefine what has since become one of his best known theories: that creative living and the pursuit of cultural activity (the arts, music and, for the purposes of this enquiry, reading) have their roots very early on in an infant's life, and specifically in the infant's first relationship with the mother. A transitional object is that stuffed animal, rag doll, or piece of blanket which a child treasures, often carries about, and upon which he or she calls when falling asleep or when away from home, as a defence against anxiety. The transitional object is assigned a special status in Winnicott's thinking in that it belongs neither entirely to the 'outer world', as perceived by all persons in common, nor exclusively to the 'inner world' of dreams or hallucinations. Winnicott writes:

> From waking to sleeping the child jumps from a perceived world to a self-created world. In between there is a need for all kinds of transitional phenomena – neutral territory. I would describe this precious object by saying that there is a tacit understanding that no one will claim that this real thing is a part of the world, or that it is created by the infant. It is understood that both these things are true: the infant created it and the world supplied it.
>
> (Winnicott 1950 [1989:143])

Between the infant's inner world on the one hand, the outer shared world on the other, is a third area – 'neutral territory', a 'resting-place' between living in the external world, and dreaming (Winnicott 1964:171). It is to this intermediate area that transitional objects and phenomena belong. What, however, is the connection with cultural activity – art, or religion, for example? Man's cultural life – the experience of communication in art and religion, is described as the 'adult equivalent of the transitional phenomena of infancy and early childhood' (Winnicott 1963 [1990:184]). The infant's transitional object, the 'ancestor' of cultural experience, holds the key to the development of imaginative life and creative thinking. Winnicott makes the connection absolutely explicit:

> Transitional objects and transitional phenomena belong to the realm of illusion which is at the basis of initiation of experience.... This intermediate area of experience, unchallenged in respect of its belonging to inner or external (shared) reality, constitutes the greater part of the infant's experience, and throughout life is retained in the intense experiencing that belongs to the arts and to religion and to imaginative living, and to creative scientific work.
>
> (Winnicott 1953 [1974:16])

From the earliest moment, then, transitional objects are connected with psychic developments ongoing within the infant. Their purpose is to assist the infant in a process of psychic growth, to help him or her negotiate a relationship with the external world. Separation from the mother is inevitably part of this. Winnicott writes (1953 [1974:17]): 'It is not the object, of course, that is transitional. The object represents the infant's transition from a state of being merged with the mother to a state of being in relation to the mother as something outside and separate.'

Thus Winnicott distinguishes between the nature of an object, (i.e. what it is, rag doll, stuffed animal) and its use (i.e. its purpose, how it functions for the baby). 'Use', rather than the 'nature' of the object, is what Winnicott considers primary (Winnicott 1974:xii). It should be noted, too, that transitional objects are fundamentally under the control of the infant, not the adult. However much a parent may attempt to replace that old teddy bear with a brand new panda, it is the baby who, in the end, endows the object with special significance. In other words, transitional objects are freely selected; they cannot be imposed from without.

Transitional objects are to be found early on in an infant's life – between 4 and 12 months (1953 [1974:5]). They must be consistently available; they assume a particular form; they are chosen by the infant and are used for a specific purpose. They assist the baby in a state of transition, synchronically, between inner and outer, and diachronically, between an earlier and later stage of development. With regard to the quality of the experience associated with such objects, Winnicott writes:

> 1. The infant assumes rights over the object, and we agree to this assumption. Nevertheless, some abrogation of omnipotence is a feature from the start.
> 2. The object is affectionately cuddled as well as excitedly loved and mutilated.
> 3. It must never change, unless changed by the infant.
> 4. It must survive instinctual loving, and also hating and, if it be a feature, pure aggression.
> 5. Yet it must seem to the infant to give warmth, or to move, or to have texture, or to do something that seems to show it has vitality or reality of its own.
> 6. It comes from without from our point of view, but not so from the point of view of the baby. Neither does it come from within; it is not a hallucination.
> 7. Its fate is to be gradually allowed to be decathected, so that in the course of years it becomes not so much forgotten as relegated to limbo. . . . It is not forgotten and it is not mourned. It loses meaning, and this is because the transitional phenomena have become diffused, have become spread out over the whole intermediate territory between 'inner psychic reality' and 'the external world as perceived by two persons in common', that is to say, over the whole cultural field.
>
> (Winnicott 1953 [1974:5–6])

What of the differences between the sexes with regard to these objects? Both boys and girls alike are said to adopt this facility, although with regard to content, there is a gradual tendency to differentiation, boys preferring hard toys, while girls select soft ones (a doll or a teddy). It is hinted that transitional objects have a significant function with regard to the young child's psychosexual development, since girls may 'proceed right ahead to the acquisition of a family' (1953 [1974:5]). Ultimately, transitional objects become extended in range, diffused over the whole cultural field: 'there is a continuity between the child's use of this first object and the adult's later use of the cultural tradition as it becomes meaningful to him' (Phillips 1988:115).

The aspect of Winnicott's argument which has remained perhaps most obscure is the progression from 'object' to the 'wider cultural field'. Winnicott himself 'never makes clear' just how the child progresses from the relationship with a transitional object, for example, a teddy bear, to a broader interest in culture (Phillips 1988:115). Part of the purpose of this chapter is therefore to elucidate the progression in that area of cultural activity which has been of concern in this book, literacy.[1] The hypothesis is as follows:

- Observations of these children's first responses to certain images of picturebooks suggest that, early on, such images function for child readers very much as three-dimensional transitional objects.
- The patterns of spontaneous response manifested in the second year resemble those manifested by that same child when beginning to read written words at age 5 years plus.
- Close links are thus suggested between the infant's earliest and subsequent behaviours with regard to illustrated/written material.
- A key factor in this development is the use which the child (in conjunction with the adult) makes of the transitional object in two-dimensional form.

Three criteria are retained for analysis of the data. The first is spontaneity of choice: the object is freely chosen. Singled out for the purposes of discussion are those images to which Rhys and Ceri attend, as far as it is possible to tell, entirely of their own volition (distinguishing them from those which, in any given session, they identify because they have just been asked a question). The second criterion is the nature or content of the spontaneously chosen object: hedgehog or rabbit, lorry or motor car, or whatever it may be. What kind of objects, of all those available, do these children elect to attend to? The third criterion is the use made of the object: the nature of the construction placed upon it, or the purpose for which it seems to be used, by child, and parent alike. These criteria are utilised with reference to infant behaviour at different stages, namely: at an age when each infant first comes into systematic contact with books; at the period of transition from pre-speech to speech; and at the onset of literacy proper between 5 and 7 years, at which point both children begin to read written text and exercise their own choice with regard to reading materials.

3 TRANSITIONAL OBJECTS AND THE VERY YOUNG INFANT

At first glance it might appear farfetched, even preposterous, to equate, in the life of an infant, an image or images contained within a picturebook with a three-dimensional transitional object, teddy bear or piece of cloth. Yet according to the hypothesis, the link between early and later reading responses hinges upon just this notion. A first task is thus to identify those features which give cause to believe that Rhys and Ceri indeed respond to certain illustrations in books 'as if' they were transitional objects. What either baby is experiencing can, of course, never be known directly; it is only possible to observe

Selectivity and dominance

Transitional objects have, as a qualifying attribute, a severe restriction as to their number. But the quality of the experience associated with them is intense, and forms the 'greater part of infant experience'. The analysis of Chapter 1 revealed the degree of repetition of much noun phrase usage in the very early sessions. Thirty-three and sixty-two different nouns were cited in each of the 9-month sessions, yet three substantives by themselves accounted, for each child respectively, for one-third of the total noun mentions within adult speech at this age: 'teddy', 'baba', 'ickly prickly' (i.e. hedgehog) for Rhys, and 'teddy', 'pussy cat', 'bunny' for Ceri. In quantitative terms, then, it may be noted just how dominant each respective trio of nouns was.

Qualitatively too, this group of nouns evokes a particular and peculiar response from child and adult alike. We may observe, in the following examples, the enthusiastic response spontaneously produced by each infant and observe also these parents' attempts to structure that response.

Mother	Ceri (9 months)	Father	Rhys (9 months)
(*Turning page*)		(*Turning over pages*)	
Who's over the page?		Who coming over the page Rhysie?	
Who's there?		Who coming over page?	
Who's there Kezwez?			
	Squeals.	Who over page euh?	
	[e]	Look!	
	Draws in breath.	Ickly prickly.	
Teddy! (*high fall*)		Ickly prickly.	
There's teddy.			Smiles.
Yes darling.			Looks at book.
	Pats the book.	(*places child's hand on picture of hedgehog*)	
Oh!		Ooh! (*i.e. it prickles!*)	
Giving teddy big smack.			
Teddy having smack.		Ickly prickly.	
	Leans forward to book.		Laughs.
You like teddy!			
Oh teddy! Yes.		Rhysie ickly prickly!	
You're going to give him little kiss!			

As the constituents of this privileged group of nouns recur, they form the basis of renewed attention and enthusiasm, on the part of both adult and child:

Mother	Ceri (9 months)	Father	Rhys (9 months)
	Sees picture of teddy.		Sees picture of hedgehog.
	[e]	Oh look!	
	Pats book.		Puts hand on page.
Oh!		Ickly pricklys.	
Teddy again.		There the ickly pricklys.	
Getting another smack.			
Aaah! Teddy.			
Good old teddy.			
You like teddy Kezwez.			
	(*excitedly*)		
	[he he]		
Yes (*high fall*)			
Kezzy likes teddy.			

By contrast, other nouns, not qualified as transitional, elicit an attentive response on the part of the infant, but little further reaction. A rapid turning of the page by these infants indicates diminishing interest, for example, and leaves the adult with barely enough time to label the item even once. At a very basic level, then, these parents have no means of imposing their own view as to which pictures might evoke an intense reaction in the infant; to this extent, the object (image) is 'spontaneously chosen'. From the point of view of adult behaviour, a most important feature of a response to a transitional image is its quality: both these parents mirror their child's excitement, both anticipating and reinforcing it.

What other parallels are there with Winnicott's description of the transitional experiences of a baby? It is suggested that the 'strain' (for the baby) inherent in objective perception is offset by the allowable transitional experiences afforded to the infant by the mother (Winnicott 1953 [1974:16]). A parent lets the baby enjoy the object; this enjoyment forms the 'greater part' of the infant's experience. So too, it seems, with the transitional images to which these parents and their infants jointly attend in the first stages of picturebook reading.

Ambivalence

The foregoing characteristics of themselves do not confer upon an object the quality of being transitional. Objects in the intermediate area have other attributes: they engender an ambivalent response.

Certain systematic attitudes of the infants associated with the use of

FURTHER ASPECTS OF THE SELF

particular kinds of verbs in adult speech, together signal this ambivalence. Verbs in adult speech at the early sessions are principally of three types. The dominant category is that of encouraging the infant to 'seek', 'find' or 'look for' a referent as in: 'Rhysie find teddy'. Here the child is (grammatical) subject and the image (grammatical) complement. A second minority group has an iconic referent as subject. 'Baba crying', or 'woof woof, doggy say' are just two examples. But there is a third group, hitherto undiscussed, which relates child and image in a different way, and which is associated with an attitude of ambivalence.

In these instances, the child again becomes the subject of the verb, but the image of the book is the recipient of the action. (Excluded here are verbs of 'seeking' and 'looking'.) In such cases the infant will, for example, bang the palm of the hand hard down on top of a picture of a teddy bear, at which point the adult intervenes systematically: 'Oh! Giving teddy big smack' or, in its transform: 'Teddy having smack'. Yet immediately and with the same image, the infant leans toward the book, an action which is interpreted by the adult as 'You're going to give him little kiss'. Straightaway afterwards, on a new page, in two successive utterances, the infant's relationship with teddy is coded again in these terms: 'Kezzy like teddy! Oh! teddy having smack' and then, for yet a third time: 'Oh! Teddy again! Getting another smack. Aaah! (voicing 'concern' as child leans towards teddy) Teddy, good old teddy, you like teddy Kezwez!'

Not only is there no contradiction for either the infant or the adult in the variation of attitude displayed, alternating between love and hate (the transitional object, let us recall, must 'survive instinctual loving and hating'). There is a further important point. In Chapter 1 it was noted that spontaneous behaviours on the part of the infant which these parents wish to discourage often pass with little or no comment. This was the case, for example, when Rhys and Ceri turned the pages of a book backwards. But here 'smacking' and 'loving' teddy, far from being behaviours which pass unnoticed, are coded repeatedly. This leads to the (albeit indirect) conclusion that such attitudes are in fact being actively fostered by these adults. Ultimately, in some sense, consciously or unconsciously, for adult and child, these responses are significant and are to be encouraged.

It cannot be known of course whether the adult is articulating behaviours which are somehow already contained within the child (in which case the adult's comments constitute a simple act of representation on the child's behalf), whether the parent is interpreting what the child does 'as if' (in which case the adult's intervention is an act of meaningful interpretation – actually the child is simply banging down on the page in an attitude of non-specific excitement, but the adult renders this act as purposefully oriented towards teddy) or whether the parent's intervention is suggestive (i.e. the parent encourages an ambivalent response in the baby where it did not exist before). What is certain however is that infant attitudes and behaviours are structured meaningfully through language along lines similar to those which are characteristic of a response to actual transitional objects.

The alive quality of the object

Recalling Winnicott's criterial features, transitional objects have about them a certain aliveness. Some of this alive quality is present in the ambivalent attitude just described. But there are further aspects of infant behaviour and adult response which lead me to believe that images may function for these children not as 'lifeless' but as being somehow 'real'. What allows me to say this?

Evidence drawn from other studies (e.g. Snow and Ninio 1986:126) suggests, and observations of these infants interacting with their books confirm, that picturebook objects (i.e. images) are endowed with a vitality of their own. Infants will feed a (picture of a) baby in a book with their own actual spoon, offer a toddler a drink (from their own plastic cup), bring to them a teddy as a gesture of comfort. Like real-life transitional objects, image:objects are kissed and cuddled, fed and cared for. Or, to adopt Winnicott's formulation, the outer world supplies the object, but the infant creates it. The essence of this response has been documented in these terms:

> To begin with, the child does not react to the picture as an image at all (first phase): treating it merely as a multi-colored piece of paper, he grabs it and tears it. After a while, however, comes the second phase: ... the child begins to perceive the shapes and colours on the paper as an image, and begins to relate to the things depicted on it as if they were real. He tries to seize them, and talk to them – in other words, he fails to distinguish at all between real things and their images. Not until much later does the child reach the third phase, when he begins to distinguish between real things and their images, and his attitude to both becomes sharply differentiated.
>
> (Luria and Vygotsky 1930 [1992:94–5])

Parents here are once more in something of a dilemma. On the one hand they must encourage the idea that the image:object in a book cannot be grasped and manipulated (the drum cannot be banged, for example). Such images must on the contrary be contemplated, looked at, discussed, but not experimented with, turned over and upside down. They are not real. Yet on the other hand parents must somehow create, or rather leave undestroyed, the illusion that, nonetheless, these images are, in some sense, real. These parents describe images as if they are endowed with life: bunny 'runs away', teddy 'sleeps', and so on.

But, even more pertinently, the adult seems, at times, deliberately to encourage a direct interpersonal relationship between infant and image by speaking 'as if' the latter were in fact alive and living, 'as if' the object:image can actually sense and respond to the 9-month-old's behaviour towards it. 'Baba sleepies (whispers this father, putting finger to lips and talking about the picture in low tones) Sshh. Mustn't wake him up, very quietly!' Conversely, the image can, in its turn, affect the infant as a living creature might. Thus (father): 'Look! Ickly prickly! (putting child's hand on picture of hedgehog) Ooh! (i.e. it prickles)!', or 'Grr, Mr lion say'.

Images in books, just as characters in narrative fiction, are thus at one and the same time real and not real. But how can it be that an infant takes images to be real? Our adult rational selves interject immediately that 'of course' they are but pictures in books. Perhaps this is not the only way to 'think'. Rycroft's discussion of dream work in the pre-Cartesian age makes the point that images in dreams were, at that time, not thought to represent (i.e. stand in place of) a deity or the devil, but that 'actually' God or Satan (as the case may be) appeared to people in dreams (Rycroft 1979 [1991(a):143]). A somewhat analogous process might be at work in an infant's perception of their books. In which case, it is but one step further to argue that for the infant two-dimensional objects may be equated with, or are somehow equivalent to, three-dimensional ones. When the iconic becomes linguistic, similar responses are evoked, recaptured perhaps. As adults, we are moved or frightened by what we read; we shed tears over what we 'know', at another level, to be 'only' a story.

Objectively perceived, subjectively created

Intensity of infant response, its ambivalent nature, and the alive quality of the image are indications that pictures may function as do transitional objects for a reading infant. A further attribute of transitional image:objects, discernible at the outset (at age 9 months) and increasingly as the infant grows and develops (especially in Ceri), is their status of being both inner and outer. In the case of the picture of 'teddy' for example, he is outer in so far as he can be recognised (objectively) as a teddy by the infant, a parent, or anybody else who comes along. He is really out there, perceptible; his existence is an objective fact and can be corroborated by a third party. In another sense, however, teddy is inner, a creation of the infant, a source of joy and pleasure, whose presence is subjectively significant and also, at another level, partly hallucinated. That is to say, the infant sees in teddy things which perhaps have more to do with the infant than with the teddy. It is not the case (objectively) that teddy 'needs a rub', is a 'naughty boy needing a smack', or 'wants a cuddle'. These are aspects of teddy which the reader creates or 'reads into' teddy. In other words, the response to teddy is not a passive one, of absorption; to teddy, the infant brings something from within.

These more subjective responses to images are initiated by Rhys and Ceri. Their creation and nature is personal and outside, observers may not see at all what the infant sees in teddy. These responses, however, if not of the adult's making, are nonetheless never rejected by these adults. On the contrary, they are fostered and articulated on the infant's behalf. This could be the beginning of a literary response whereby what is perceived is in part outside of oneself, objective, and in part subjective, internally created. A reader of a work of fiction, it is said, will create that work very much as a function of himself (Tucker 1981).

Object and psychic process

The inner and outer quality is to become of increasing importance in the pre-speech period. Equally important, both with a very young infant and in the pre-speech period, is the connection of the image:object with psychic process, defined here as the process of separation from the adult. Separation can be of two kinds: physical (withstanding the physical absence of a beloved significant other) and psychological (growing up and away from a significant adult to become an independently functioning autonomous unit, for example).

Physical separation involves the infant, in the course of development, coming to terms with the disappearance and reappearance of a loved person. Separation anxiety in infants is independently known to be at its most acute at around age 12 months; moreover, the phenomenon is a universal one (Super and Harkness 1982). Freud, for his part, documents how a young child, using any object he could find, plays at throwing it out of sight (during which time the object is 'gone': 'fort'), and then finding it again, at which moment the object is there for him (and has 'come back': 'da'). Noting the pleasure experienced by the infant especially on the return of the object, Freud interprets the 'fort' and 'da' game as part of a process via which infants, through play and within themselves, come to terms with the fact that their mother cannot be permanently there for them. Play enables them to overcome a sense of anxiety at her disappearance by reassuring themselves as to her consistent reappearance. Most importantly, in the game it is the infant and not the parent who is in control (Freud 1920 [1955:15]).

Somewhat similarly, Winnicott, too, notes that an infant resorts to the use of a (three-dimensional) object to help overcome the (potentially traumatic) experience of the absence of the mother. A cuddly toy, symbolic of an imago of mother in the child's mind, helps the infant withstand the loss of mother when her absence threatens: 'The use of an object symbolizes the union of two now separate things, baby and mother, *at the point in time and space of the initiation of their state of separateness.*' (Winnicott 1967(a) [1974:114]). For both Freud and Winnicott then, the presence and absence, disappearance and return of a loved person are developmental aspects of an infant's emotional life which must be negotiated. For both, infants may rely upon an actual (three-dimensional) object to facilitate this process.

As observers, we cannot know to what extent images in books function developmentally or in the mind of the child, in a similar way to three-dimensional transitional objects, in so far as these latter facilitate the process of physical separation from the mother. What is certain, however, is that loss from sight and reappearance into view is an absolutely key feature of the use of certain book images, dominating the early sessions of both these infants.

Constantly Rhys and Ceri return to recover the same lost object – on no less than thirteen different occasions in the case of 'teddy' for Ceri at age 9 months. These image:objects are precisely those which engender an intense response in the infant, which survive loving and hating, and so on.

As already indicated in Chapter 1, this facet of loss and recovery, qualified as cyclical return, is taken up (i.e. 'used') by the adult for purposes both literary and linguistic. Just as the alive quality of images is transformed for adult literary purposes (fostering a belief that images are real), so here is the connection with loss and recovery similarly exploited. The return of the object from one page to the next is an early form of the hero who, in a children's story, forms the link from one page to the next, while locating, and relocating an absent referent is a key feature in the introduction of discourse routines.

From the point of view of Rhys and Ceri, however, one may speculate as to whether this ritual of lost objects subsequently regained may not function in a way similar to real-life objects. That is to say, reading may act as a forum within which psychic processes may be both expressed and facilitated. This is known in the psychoanalytic jargon as a process of 'working through'. Certainly the period during which separation anxiety in the toddler intensifies is the age when the phenomenon of cyclical return (in reading) is at its most predominant. What seems likely is that transitional image:objects may function simultaneously in different ways and at different levels, for adult and child respectively.

Summary

This section has been devoted to justifying the description of certain images in books as transitional. Situated in an intermediate area between subjective creativity (the realm of magical illusion and under the omnipotent control of the baby) and external reality, as objectively perceived, images in books and transitional objects share a number of different features. Certainly, other iconic referents are associated with at least some of the characteristics described, but it is the five criteria described above taken together which lead me to hypothesise that certain images in books function for infants as two-dimensional transitional objects. Their use, moreover is multifunctional, providing an opportunity for the child to work through different developmental stages, or for the adult to foster appropriate linguistic or literary attitudes. Around transitional image:objects, infant and adult needs apparently converge.

4 THE OBJECT IN THE PERIOD FROM PRE-SPEECH TO SPEECH

Consider now the use of the image:object in the period 11–27 months, during which time speech evolves. A presentation of further features common to two- and three-dimensional objects will be followed, in section 4.1, by an analysis

EMERGENT LITERACY

of the literary fate of these objects, while section 4.2 addresses the issue of how image:objects continue to facilitate psychic processes within the reading infant.

Empirical evidence is taken from the eight-month period during which Rhys and Ceri are first beginning to speak. Favourite books recorded at various intervals during this time were: *It's Fun Finding Out About People and Places* for Rhys and *My Day* for Ceri. Each of these books contained a range of referents, both animate (non-human and human: adult or child) and inanimate (buildings, equipment, furniture, etc). The analysis centres again upon the nature of the objects spontaneously chosen and their use, 'use' again being construed in both literary and psychic terms. The actual image:objects to which these infants attend in the relevant period (11–18 months for Ceri; 18–27 months for Rhys), and the frequency with which they do so, are given in Tables 8.1 and 8.2.

Analysis of these data reveals that each of these infants' spontaneous choice

Table 8.1 Iconic referents generating spontaneous contributions by Ceri

Session	1	2	3	4
Ceri's age in months	11	13	14	18
References to book				
Animate:human				
Adult				
Male		Daddy		Daddy*
Female				Mummy*
Child			Baby	Baby
				Little boy**
				Little girl*
Animate:non-human	Cat*	Cat*		Cat*
Inanimate				
Soft toys	Teddy			Teddy**
				Dolly**
				Dog*
Mechanical	Swing	Seesaw	Seesaw	Swing
	Car (pedal)		Car (pedal)*	Horse (wooden)
				Car (pedal)
				Bike
Parts of body				Neck
Others		Ball	Juice	Drink
				Spoon

* Denotes item returned to on a second (*) or subsequent (**) occasion in the same session
Base: All spontaneous contributions (gesture, vocalisation, word) produced by Ceri. One picturebook, *My Day*, presented at four age sessions

FURTHER ASPECTS OF THE SELF

Table 8.2 Iconic referents generating spontaneous contributions by Rhys

Session	1	2	3	4
Rhys' age in months	18	19	20	27

References to book
Animate:human
Adult

Male	Red Indian***	Indian	Indian	Indian
	Lumberjack	Driver (train)	Lumberjack	Driver
	Windsurfer		Policeman	(ambulance)
	Sailor		Soldier	Assistant
	Chef		Pilot	(ambulance)
			Doctor	Storeman
			Workers	Patient on
			Rubbertapper	crutches
				Patient in bed
Female		Doctor		
Child	—	—	—	—

Animate:non-human

	Horse*	Seal		
	Dogs*	Bees		
	Ducks			
	Cows			

Inanimate

Mechanical	Rocket	Rocket		Rocket
	Lorry**	Lorry	Lorry	
	Helicopter*	Helicopter	Helicopter	
	Cars (dinky)*	Caravan*	Cars (dinky)	
	Boats*	Tractor*		
	Train	Train		
	Aeroplane	Air balloon		
	Ambulance	Glider		
	Crane	Rollerskates		
	Big wheel	Skateboard		
Parts of body		Skeleton		
Others	Totem pole*		Saw (chain)	
	Church			

References to real-world experience

Parts of body	Arm/chest	Arm/leg	Leg	Arm/leg
	Finger	Finger	Chest	Finger/chest*
Locations	Grapes *in the kitchen*			
	Football *in the garden*			
	Totem pole *in the park*			

* Denotes item returned to on a second (*) or subsequent (**) occasion in the same session
Base: All spontaneous contributions (gesture, vocalisation, word) produced by Rhys. One picturebook, *It's Fun Finding Out About People and Places*, presented at four age sessions

of image:objects in this period is consistent with Winnicott's specification for the evolution of three-dimensional objects, in two respects: diffusion and sex variation. Consider the phenomenon of diffusion. The fate of the transitional object is described in these terms: 'Its fate is to be gradually allowed to be decathected. . . . It loses meaning, and this is because the transitional phenomena have become diffused' (Winnicott 1953 [1974:6]). That is to say, the transitional experience becomes spread over a wider area. The data for reading confirm a marked change in this regard: from a very few objects spontaneously identified at 9 months, a threefold, even fourfold increase is to be observed at 18 months, in both children.

The second phenomenon is variation in the choice of object on grounds of sex. 'Gradually in the life of an infant teddies and dolls and hard toys are acquired. Boys to some extent tend to go over to use hard objects, whereas girls tend to proceed right ahead to the acquisition of a family' (Winnicott 1953 [1974:5]). Ceri's preoccupation when reading is entirely as specified for three-dimensional objects: soft toys (e.g. teddy and dolly) and increasingly the human category, incorporating the whole family group (father, mother and children). No diminution in the intensity of the experience associated with such objects is implied, however. The pleasure and enthusiasm manifested at the sight of such images are patent still, even at 18 months. Rhys, for his part, divides his interest between representations of referents within the hard mechanical category (aeroplane, lorry) and, again, human figures. But for him, and ever increasingly, the orientation is not towards the family unit (as a whole) but almost exclusively towards adult male figures. Examples are lumberjack, pilot, rubbertapper. At a formal level, then, diffusion and differentiation along sexual lines accord with Winnicott's description of the fate of real-life transitional objects.

The phenomenon of diffusion of transitional image:objects (in the sense of their becoming numerically greater) is however a relative one, for both children. Even though the transitional nouns are more numerous than they were at age 9 months, expressed as a proportion of the total linguistically available in adult speech, they have declined, particularly for Rhys. In the 18-month session, for example, his father's speech contains 235 different substantives, of which those selected spontaneously by Rhys form just 11 per cent. Adult mentions of these same nouns account for 18 per cent of the total. Thus, by contrast with earlier sessions, transitional images no longer, as was the case at 9 months, constitute the 'greater part' of infant experience. Infants, as they mature, are better equipped to perceive the world objectively (i.e. to attend to the adult perspective on the complex set of illustrations before them). The 'allowable' aspect of transitional experiences is no longer dominant.

FURTHER ASPECTS OF THE SELF

4.1 Transitional objects and literary development

However, according to the argument, transitional objects underpin cultural activity, becoming transformed over time. Let us then take this facet of our argument one step further and examine the 'use' made of these objects from a literary point of view. What, in literary terms, is their eventual fate?

The phenomenon of diffusion extends beyond a simple quantitative statement relating to numbers of objects to which infants respond; the quality of the experience is also implicated. As these infants' interest broadens to a greater number of objects, a further significant development emerges. It seems that a state of excitement is generated in both children, not so much by a specific item, but rather by the very sight of a reading book. All but one of the eight book sessions here analysed (four sessions with the same book, for each child respectively) begins with an exchange of excited interest about the book as a whole and/or its contents. I shall illustrate with just two examples:

Mother	Ceri (18 months)	Father	Rhys (19 months)
	(*Agitated/excited*) [book]	(*Finishing previous book*) Which other one do you want?	
You want book darling?			[ahwa] (*Indian sound*)
Yes. Mummy going to give you book.	[book]	What? Is the Indian in here?	[ahwa]

Transitional objects perhaps play a significant part in early reading, in that they promote pleasure in literary experiences through the association of the 'part' with the 'whole'. Something of the quality of the experience originally associated with transitional objects is now spread out into the wider cultural field which is reading. By diffusion, then, may be understood both an extension of interest to a wider range of objects than hitherto and a qualitative response of enthusiastic pleasure in the reading experience as a whole.

But what of the adult's response? Again we touch upon the evolution of transitional objects in literary terms. In essence, those image:objects which engendered intense and affectionate responses from these infants at age 1–2 years become elevated from age 2–3 years onwards to the status of principal protagonist in a story. Consider two examples. The elephant, a picturebook favourite of Rhys, is retained as a hero of the story: *The Elephant and the Bad Baby* (by Raymond Briggs), much loved by him at age 2–3 years. The cat, on the other hand, so much the favourite in picturebooks read to Ceri, reappears at age 2 years in a different guise, as a main character in two stories: *Meg and Mog* (by Helen Nicoll and Jan Pienkowski) and *Mog and the Baby* (by Judith Kerr) (cf. Chapter 2, section 3.3). In literary terms, then, early objects become integrated within a number of stories, judiciously selected by an adult caregiver. They are now 'spread out over the whole territory between inner psychic reality and the external world as perceived by two persons in common', that is to say, private inclinations have entered a wider, more public domain. Through this process of transposition, the transitional experiences of infancy become part of the literary responses of early childhood.

4.2 Transitional objects and psychic growth

As Winnicott always observed, transitional objects have to do with the infant in a state of transition. Let us now view the role of these objects from the perspective of psychic growth. According to well-established tenets of psychoanalytic theory, psychosexual development entails the identification by the infant child with an adult member or members of the appropriate sex. The male infant assumes some of the perceived characteristics of significant male persons and the female infant does likewise. This is a developmental stage which children negotiate, whether readers or not. The purpose of this discussion is to examine whether, in the reading setting, image:objects might function as a vehicle of expression of inner psychic change.

If we consider the nature of the objects spontaneously identified by each infant in the pre-speech to speech period, differences between the sexes feature prominently. In accordance with Winnicott's thinking, a predominance of referents denoting members of a family group may be observed for Ceri, and adult males for Rhys (cf. Tables 8.1 and 8.2). These figures, emblems, perhaps, of a world which each infant contemplates through their parent's eyes (in this family, mother at the time raises children in the home, while father enjoys full professional status without), are a possible expression of a process of identification. It is a public manifestation of these infants' increasing sense of being female or male.

Just as early objects are retained for literary purposes, so too are psychic functions retained and offered new forms of expression. Separation, a psychic process dealt with at 9 months through a referent evolves, at age 2 years, into a theme. The risk of adventure and a safe return home are dominant in much of Ceri's early story reading, while Rhys' favourites: *Alfie Gets in First* and *Teddy Bears Go Shopping* are based entirely on the idea of separation and rediscovery of a lost 'object', in the sense of 'significant other'. Sexual identification and, particularly, possible professional roles of the adult male are also taken up as a theme in another favourite storybook: *Why Can't a Hippotamus be a ...?* (Chapter 2, section 3.3).

Reading, of course, is by no means indispensable to the process of psychic change. Separation (at 9–12 months), individuation (12–18 months) and sexual identification (around 18 months) occur independently anyway. What is argued here is that books, even very early on, might well have a role in allowing such growth processes to be worked through. Reading, an activity from which many of the practical considerations of life are debarred, constitutes a space in which very young children may explore and find themselves. And in reading language is central. This voyage of self-discovery is thus allied with that most potent means of individual self-expression, language (Sapir 1933 [1985:17]; Stern 1985:28).

Language use by the adult is well recognised in its capacity to scaffold the cognitive and linguistic development of a young infant. Researchers are accustomed to thinking about language in this way, and this is precisely what has been done in Parts II and III of this book. But what is less well recognised, perhaps, is the role of language as shaper of the infant's psyche. And it is not just the language of the parent which has this function. Reading offers the preverbal infant a unique opportunity for self-realisation and self-expression. A small infant cannot say in words: 'I do not enjoy loved persons going out of my sight; I need to come to terms with this by repeating the experience often, and in my own way, in a situation in which I feel in control.' S/he cannot say either: 'I am now establishing myself firmly as either male or female, and have a need to seek out and identify significant figures through whom I may communicate these changes.'

But in reading such sentiments may find their expression, indirectly at first through the adult's choice of lexis and grammatical constructions, or directly in gestured/vocal contributions on the part of both these infants, which the adult, albeit unwittingly, then puts into words on their behalf. If, as Winnicott believed, it is the articulation of experience which is the key to healthy integration, then reading, in so far as it permits the articulation, grammatically, lexically and thematically, of infant experience, may play a part in promoting infant psychic growth. Without such growth, the consequences for 'normal' language development are serious indeed (Préneron 1994).

Summary

In the second year of life, transitional objects have a literary purpose; they function to develop these toddlers' interest in the wider field of reading, either through a diffused experience of intense pleasure or through the retention, by the adult, of each child's favourite objects (as characters or themes) in stories. They also reflect a process of psychic growth in the infant, the infant in a state of transition, and afford expression to emerging states (separation and identification). The articulation of inner experiences is viewed here as a key aspect of reading below the age of two years, in both children.

But, similar as they may be in some respects, these children are nonetheless different. It is individual difference which is to help our understanding of the longer term link between infant and school age child. The connection is to be observed in the quality of the object chosen and the active construction which each of the children in this study places upon it. These features of behaviour are now explored in detail.

5 INDIVIDUAL RESPONSES TO READING

Winnicott writes (1953 [1974:5]) : 'there is no noticeable difference between boy and girl in their use of the original 'not-me' possession', and, to recapitulate the findings of Chapter 1, there was indeed little difference between Rhys and Ceri in the nature of the image:objects first selected. Both attended to mainly animate, non-human illustrations (hedgehog, bunny, and so on). But what becomes apparent over time is that the two subjects considered in this study do, in some respects, diverge: in their choice of object and in the relationship which each creates with it. Let us look again at these differences, first described in Chapter 2.

5.1 Reading attitudes at age 1–2 years

In accordance with Winnicott's observations, with regard to the images chosen, Rhys (at 18 months) shows a preference for the representational equivalent of real-world 'hard' objects: 'lorry' or 'helicopter', while Ceri looks more to dolls and soft toys (Tables 8.1 and 8.2). Other differences of active behaviour also emerge, from around 14 months. There are differences of interactional strategy. Rhys, for instance, reproduces very exact information in answer to adult prompts, learning labels for referents. Moreover, what he sees in his two-dimensional world can be checked for its truth value. The labels he remembers could, if necessary, be objectively verified with reference to an external source, such as a dictionary. There it is possible to check up that, indeed, a 'lumberjack' is different from a 'pilot'. Or a third party looking at the scene could confirm that an 'oil tanker' is not a 'yacht'. This is part of shared, external, perceptible reality (Chapter 2). Rhys would then very often 'use' the knowledge gleaned from picturebooks with which to interpret life in the real world as and when he encountered it (cf. Chapter 4, section 5.2).

Ceri, on the other hand, focuses on a domestic universe. She is more concerned with the internal world: the emotions, feelings, motives, the whys and wherefores of a character's actions. Readings to her are, moreover, frequently indeterminate; it would never be possible to ascertain, by referring to another source, for example, why a small child in the picture might be crying. Finally and most critically, the construction which Ceri makes of the image is often personal. She brings something of herself to her reading, offering an interpretation which is uniquely hers. Our reader may look back to the example cited in Chapter 2, in which the bath water is construed as hot; no one, given the evidence of the illustration, has any sure way of knowing whether it is or not.

The status of transitional objects as being neither inner nor outer, but situated between the two, is the cornerstone of Winnicott's belief that such objects are the source of creative living. Let us then review in further depth the empirical evidence in support of manifest differences of construction by these two infants of their picturebook world. Even pre-verbally, Rhys' spontaneous associations around a preferred topic were taxonomic in orientation; they had much to do with perceiving similarities and differences, with recognition and recall, but little to do with invention. The earliest associations ever made by him: the 'hat' and 'ladybird' extracts already quoted in Chapter 2, section 3.1, are a case in point; the following excerpt some four months later is a further illustration:

Father	**Rhys (17 months)**
Rabbit! Rabbit running away!	
	Points through window to neighbour's house.
Yes, we used to have a rabbit next door didn't we! In the garden.	

Rhys' propensity to categorise is again evident in this next extract:

Father	**Rhys (18 months)**
	Points to skeleton.
That's the skeleton. That gives all the bones in your body .. Rhysie got bones hasn't he?	
	Clasps own head.
Bones in his head, yes. A big bone in your head. Hmm.	
	Points to adult's head.
Bones in Daddy's head. Yes, there.	

The situation for Ceri upon speech acquisition in the reading setting is quite different. Ceri's use of the picturebook image is partly to discover, but also partly to create it, by endowing it with an interpretation of her own. Her perception of the bath water as hot is just one instance. Here is a further, comparable, example:

Mother	**Ceri (18 months)**
	Points to her book. [doggy]
Doggy, yes.	
	[ah]
Doggy barking, is he?	
	[ahahaha]
Panting! (*laughs*) [hahahaha]	
	[ahahaha]

Here we see the 'magical' quality (the term Winnicott used) of the transitional object. The dog exists (i.e. is real for both mother and Ceri), but it is Ceri who raises from the page a new creation; she, and she alone, perceives the dog as 'panting'.

To restate, Winnicott qualified the transitional experience as being at once inner and outer, on the borderline between reality as objectively perceived, shared by all others, and the inner world, subjectively created. From the first, Rhys is oriented largely towards the outer aspects of this equation; in psychoanalytic parlance, he takes 'from the outside in'. His interest is in the objectively verifiable, and in using information obtained in books with which to understand the real world around. Ceri's responses, by contrast, may be both outer and inner; she often uses the pictorial image to bring to it something from within herself. These attitudes, confined to a small subset of picturebook items in the second year of life, typify the early differences between these two children. But are they perpetuated?

5.2 The child's use of the 'written word' at age 2–7 years

This section looks forward in time to these children's development at preschool age, between the ages of 2 and 5 years, and at school age between 5 and 7 years. But it does so in the context of the hypothesis already mooted, namely that continuity between early and later behaviours might be found, not only at the level of semantic, discourse or narrative structures (as discussed in Parts II and III), but also at the level of a personal attitude with regard to reading. Personal attitude, which encompasses how each child, as an individual, spontaneously approaches, responds to or exploits the printed medium, has a direct bearing on later developments in literacy.

However, the definition of literacy initially advanced (see Introduction) must now be expanded – to cover both reading and writing. Literacy, furthermore, is not understood as a static capacity which a person 'has', but rather as a 'set of activities or operations that an individual performs' (Scribner and Cole 1981:18). Keeping accurate numerical accounts, writing a diary, following written instructions are examples of such activities. Scribner and Cole's understanding of literacy is that such practices are both recurrent and goal directed. They are repeated over and over in an individual's life and they serve a particular purpose. In addition, they depend of necessity upon the knowledge of a script (e.g. syllabic or alphabetic); the use of a particular technology (e.g. stylus and tablet; quill and parchment; pen and paper); on a certain knowlege of conventions of style and form (e.g. how to start and end a letter); and a prescribed means of transmission (e.g. messenger; fax machine). Literacy is therefore not so much the capacity to write and read a particular script, as the application of this knowledge 'for specific purposes in specific contexts of use' (Scribner and Cole 1981:236).

With these theoretical premises in mind, I shall now advance evidence of continuity of development between early and subsequent behaviours in the literacy careers of these two children. But I do so with two provisos. The first is that, in a study of this kind, associations between behaviours at different points in time can be demonstrated, but a casual connection between them never proven. The second concerns the nature of the evidence put forward, which, after the age of 2 years, was less rigorously documented than hitherto, not least because after that time, for these children, as for others, reading was no longer confined to book reading sessions (King 1989:11). Literacy events begin to take a variety of forms and occur in a whole variety of contexts: playing 'I Spy' when riding along in the car, deciphering signs, and so on (Goodman 1986). Despite this, certain behaviours appeared to be endowed with an indelible, even imperious quality, imposing themselves over time. However, whether or not the long-term connections to be described are justified is a matter for the reader to discern.

Writing

A first observation is that, ontogenetically, in the careers of both Rhys and Ceri, the production of the written code precedes the ability to read it. (Phylogenetically, too, of course, writing is logically prior to reading (Gelb 1952; Goody 1977)). Certainly, in real-life situations, some reading knowledge of a receptive kind was gained; individual alphabet letters were pointed out for them on road signs – P for parking, or H for hospital, for example, but on the whole, initial access to the printed code was not so much by reading as by writing. That written activities predated these children's receptive knowledge of the printed word may be due in part to the environmental circumstances of their upbringing. It was not the custom, when book reading within this particular family set-up, to show Rhys and Ceri that letters are the visual equivalent of sounds. They did not, as some do, follow the line along with their finger to establish a phoneme:grapheme correspondence between, for example, letter sound 'm' and the printed letter /m/ in initial position in a word. In common with many others, then, writing, and not reading, was much in evidence in the early years (cf. Goodman 1986).

The second observation is that Rhys and Ceri, already as toddlers, participate (albeit in rudimentary fashion) in what Scribner and Cole describe as cultural acts of literacy. From scribbling with a pencil on any piece of paper (15 months), they soon grasp the idea that writing is a purposeful activity: they 'pretend' to write. Appropriate materials are used and, even if they do not use alphabetic script, their 'writing' is goal oriented. In addition, such practices are recurrent; favourite activities are repeated day in day out, over months and months. Self-selection of topics and materials is, according to research, both to be expected and encouraged in young children (Dobson 1989:85); thus far, therefore, the behaviour of Rhys and Ceri is unexceptional. More remarkable, perhaps, is the particular route, from among the possible writing options available, which each child chooses, quite spontaneously, to demonstrate their respective understanding of the way in which writing is used.

Early uses of writing

To restate, the active behaviours discussed are those which are spontaneously manifested early on by each infant. By definition, this is what confers upon each their 'individual' personality. In Rhys' case, operations of a self-oriented, objective nature (pro-forma, diary or list), written as an *aide-memoire*, constitute the hallmarks of his early written production. His earliest preoccupation was to fill in words (in squiggles) on a printed form which he collected for this purpose from the bank, or (still in pretend writing) he made appointments in a diary which he carried about with him (age 2–3 years). Pretend maps were drawn; the first, quite unprompted, was at age 3.3 years.

When eventually he could form letters for himself, his greatest interest, again, was not in deciphering them but in writing them. Printing a single word (dad), or his own name (in upper case) was the start, but this grew eventually into lengthy shopping lists, dictated for him and written out conscientiously letter by letter (age 4 years). A preoccupation with supplying a unique answer in context (as a bank form requires), with objective information, and with recording taxonomies are here still, as they had been at 14 months, the main features of Rhys' first, entirely spontaneous relationship with the 'written' code at pre-school age.

The path which Ceri takes is notably different. For her, interpersonal and interpretative skllls continue to predominate. Her favourite pretend writing activity was correspondence (lines drawn on a piece of paper and folded and handed, in person, to Mummy to read, at age 2–3 years). Again content is significant; these notes were always of a personal kind, expressing thanks or enjoyment, rather than giving factual information or making requests of a practical nature. On being able to print lower case letters (at age 4 years) her dominant writing activity remained letter writing. (Rhys, in contrast, wrote just one letter a year, when motivation perhaps was at its highest, to Father Christmas!) First writing activities thus differ systematically for each child, and, for both, apparently bear traces of earlier times.[2]

Reading

Other aspects of these children's early literacy again correspond to the findings of other researchers: an awareness of the significance of print in context for example (Goodman 1986:7; King 1989). In this study, at age 4 years, Rhys 'reads' (aloud) the words: 'Thank you' printed on a bin in a McDonald's restaurant as: 'Bin.' Ceri, at an equivalent age, remarks on the print on the side of a school bus: 'That says: "School Bus"' when in fact the words were: 'Downsend

Lodge'. As earlier discussed, both children were eventually successful in deciphering and understanding print and in mastering the production of written script.

Early uses of reading

But what use did these two effectively make of their new-found skill to decipher print between the ages of 5 and 7 years, when able to get on independently at home? Again personal orientation comes into play, both at the level of material selection and the purpose for which the materials are exploited. Rhys elected, always, to read for himself material of a non-fictional kind. Typically, he checked sports results in a newspaper, read up the football scores or obtained information about times of television programmes. Alternatively, he sought out facts about football from books. Again, as before, there was a search in books and print for factual information of help in understanding external events in the real world. Or to paraphrase Bruner's vision of non-fictional reading material, the message is read in the form in which it is transmitted.

Ceri's newly found capacity to read, on the other hand, led her to choose fiction exclusively as her reading material. Fiction, as already observed in Chapter 5, has the following qualities: indeterminacy with regard to the text's meaning; an inherent reliance on the psychological reality of the protagonists; and a degree of dependency on the reader to raise from the text a personal creation. Ambiguity in the discussions surrounding pictures, a precocious interest in people, their motives and feelings and the personally creative nature of responses to pictures were features identified in the very earliest book-based interactions with Ceri (cf. Table 2.6). To restate Phillips: there is continuity between the child's use of a first object and the later use of the cultural tradition as it becomes meaningful to him or to her.

6 DISCUSSION: EMERGING PATTERNS OF LITERACY

6.1 A long-term view of literacy

The initial question for this chapter was: what links may be observed between the earliest reading behaviours of the infant and reading attitudes in later childhood? The argument here has been twofold. The linguistic argument has been that early attitudes to book reading, the active construction which individual children place upon their books, and the nature of the material spontaneously selected, form a continuum, in the reading setting, from infancy through to childhood.

The psychoanalytic argument goes further, to embrace both literary and psychic development. It has been suggested that certain images behave for the infant, formally and functionally, as three-dimensional transitional objects might. The central thesis has been that these children are passionately involved with a few image:objects which occupy them intensely in the first months and which have been called, following Winnicott, transitional. Early transitional responses are transformed into a specifically literary response, facilitated, in part, by the retention, in kind, by the parent of the initial picturebook object as it evolves from an iconic to a purely linguistic mode of representation.

As the very early objects become gradually decathected, the psychic function fufilled by early image:objects in reading is also perpetuated. Certain illustrations within books, initially, and later whole books allow infants scope for self-exploration, and for expressing their awareness, albeit subconscious, of who they are becoming. It is a journey mediated through the spontaneous use of pointing gestures and vocalisations. These exploratory overtures are retained, contained and articulated in language by the reading adult, the importance of which was underlined by Winnicott. The creative aspects of a child's life are integrated into that child's personality if, and only if, they are in some way reflected back to him or her (Winnicott 1974:75).

Over time, the children in this study develop differentiated responses to reading. In the longer term, the imperious quality of these early differences is such that they are apparently retained and perpetuated. They characterise the initial production of speech in the reading setting, they seemingly underpin the spontaneous use of the written medium in the early stages and they orient the spontaneous selection of reading materials and the use made of them by each child individually, as he or she first becomes able to read extended written text. In other words, individual attitudes towards early objects seemingly spread out over the whole field of literary activity spontaneously chosen: scribbling, written production, choice of reading materials. Such is the consistency of the progression from early transitional experiences to the wider cultural field.

This is not to suggest, however, that children stay with these early options; as Rhys and Ceri come into sustained contact with the wider culture, so their initial uses of the written (and spoken) medium broaden out. Finally, the part played by adults must not be overlooked – as a source of identification and in their capacity to scaffold an infant's spontaneous responses for literary and linguistic 'ends'. At the very least we might concur with Winnicott (1974:83): the history of an individual baby cannot be written in terms of the baby alone.

6.2 A transitional space

Matters of individual difference will now be discussed from a slightly different perspective. But a note of caution must again be sounded. The data presented in parts of this chapter are derived from just one picturebook read with each child respectively by only one parent, the configuration being: Rhys reading with his father and Ceri with her mother. Although many of the individual differences reported in this enquiry were readily apparent to both parents – Rhys, for instance, would typically home in on the Red Indian or answer direct questions, regardless of which parent read to him – psychic process did not at the time form part of these parents' conscious awareness. Thus it is not possible to confirm whether, had Rhys been reading with a female adult or Ceri with a male adult, each would have expressed aspects of, for instance, emerging sexual identity in the same way. This said, the data as they stand do apparently point to reading as a forum for the working through of psychic processes for each child respectively.

Consider now 'differences' between Rhys and Ceri in Winnicottian terms. Winnicott's view of the transitional area was that it is at one and the same time both inner and outer. Ceri's response to the book world may be thought of as transitional in the sense that reading for her is often an act of creation as well as discovery – hence the choice of fiction. But what of Rhys? His precocious encounter with the reality principle, the fact of the objective existence of the world whether the baby creates it or not, leads us to enquire whether and to what extent the response of this male child to reading may in the long term be qualified as truly transitional – on the borderline between inner and outer – as Winnicott understands it.

Let us recall that transitional objects function from the outset as an aid in the process of self-discovery. Considered in this light, they have everything to do with the inner world. This little boy may not raise from his reading material a new creation, linguistically mediated. There may exist, for him, no outward (linguistic) expression of the imaginative construction he places upon his books. But what, one might wonder, do the objective 'facts' of non-fiction signify within the inner phantasy world of this boy reader? Just as, at age 2, images depicting adult male figures had been a source of identification for him, so too perhaps do the real-life football heroes he reads about at age 7 become icons to which he aspires, significant 'objects' within his internal world. Non-fictional works may afford access to an imaginative life for many young readers of both sexes, whether the topic is sport, music or history. From a Winnicottian standpoint, the reading of non-fiction poses still the dialectic of the relationship between inner and outer.

7 CONCLUSION

Reading, in Part IV, has been discussed in terms of its contribution to infant moral, psychic and aesthetic development. These facets of development, before the age of 2 years, find their expression in linguistic behaviour, both in the lexical–syntactic patterns of adult speech and the spontaneous contributions, non-verbal and verbal, of these infants.

It has been suggested that certain image:objects, qualified as transitional, fulfil a dual role. Image:objects spontaneously chosen are the mediators of psychic change, in both children, while the origins of an aesthetic (literary) response may be located in the quality of the active construction volunteered by each of these two infants respectively. What begins as a non-verbal response to illustrated books, continues at the level of early speech production and then evolves into a specifically literary response, observed first in productive writing and culminating, finally, in preferred choices of material as each child becomes able to read text. It was Winnicott's theoretical belief that the origins of aesthetic development are to be found in early transitional experiences; it is a belief for which this longitudinal account offers substantial empirical support.

CONCLUDING REMARKS

Many children enter mainstream education with a history of having been read to while at home. Although many suppositions have been made as to what book-based interactions in the family might involve and what their significance might be, exactly what a given individual child's very early reading history actually consists of has rarely been documented. Thus, while the development of oral language has been observed longitudinally from its first beginnings, this account pioneers a situation-specific approach to the analysis of emerging patterns of literacy. This has been achieved by a series of video-recordings made in the home environment of one British family, comprising mother, father, son and daughter, where both parents have been educated to university level. The recordings are of parent–infant exchanges between the ages of 9 and 27 months based around a joint book-reading experience, the book being either a children's picturebook or illustrated story. The aim of this work has been to understand, taking linguistic behaviour as the starting-point and using appropriately developed analytical tools, something of what book-based interactions involve. Evolutionary processes and the developmental significance of early reading have been of major concern. However, as the number of subjects of this study are small, its terms of reference restricted and the empirical evidence limited to what happens in just one family, the discussion which follows must be read for what it is – evolving out of single case study example.

The initial theoretical premise was that illustrated books constitute a static, non-ephemeral stimulus, tangible, hugely varied in the range of pictorial data which may be made available for discussion and whose manner and pace of exploitation remain firmly under the joint control of the reading participants. Books, moreover, have the capacity to bring within the sphere of the reading infant aspects of life of which he or she may never have had first-hand experience. Taken together, they represent, potentially, an opportunity for a unique form of linguistic exchange in the life of a young infant.

From a linguistic standpoint, book-based interactions have been shown by these recordings to be both densely lexicalised and, to an extent, context-independent, in the sense defined by Lyons. Nonetheless, this language, while in the public domain, is at the same time embedded in the private unuttered

CONCLUDING REMARKS

context of the child's world where it vibrates with significance, and from which it draws much of its power and strength.

A variety of analytical perspectives has demonstrated the ways in which book-based exchanges 'work' at a number of different levels. It was revealed by analysis of picturebook exchanges that, at a discourse level, infants may become familiar with matters of selectivity, salience and ordering or, at a semantic level, with reference, denotation and contextual relations and, not least, knowledge of real-world events. All these are of intrinsic value to the infant; they contribute to an understanding not only of discourse, be it spoken or written, but also of life's events and experiences.

Through their storybooks, these children become acquainted with the structural conventions of narrative. They are familiarised with the notion of multiple perspectives and with the expression of a range of value judgements which narrative fiction in particular offers. They seemingly grow to adopt a critical stance to what they read, yet with their literary imagination fuelled by the sometimes carefully adapted linguistic interpretations of an adult reader.

Reading as the embodiment of moral conscience, as a forum for the working through of psychic processes and as a setting where creation and discovery both play a part – these are possible further aspects of literacy which have been observed to occur very early in these two infants' lives.

These observations have also led me to remark on the preponderance, in book reading (as well as, possibly, in other areas of life), of the articulation and construction of the infant self. Whether through the linguistic exploration of books by the infant (which is itself contingent upon the child learning the appropriate conversational rules) or whether via narrative accounts of present, past and expected future variously mediated, the integration in language of the infant self appears a constant and ongoing preoccupation in the exchanges studied here. It raises the question as to whether cognitive and linguistic developments are not themselves predicated upon the successful negotiation of the constitution of that self.

At all these different levels, then, conversational exchanges based around books may be seen to be 'working'. Three further salient features of these exchanges have repeatedly been referred to: the part played by each child's acceptance of and response to the material placed before them, the affective response to that material as a trigger to further development, and a systematically available adult who responds to these infants' initiating cues and contextualises for them in some meaningful sense the books which are to hand.

The question which needs to be addressed is: what, in the last resort, is the significance of early book-based exchanges such as those observed here? The issue is, first of all, of long-term relevance.

The answer is necesssarily tentative. Early reading experiences of the type described may well be helpful to reading in the longer term, but it cannot be argued that they constitute either a sufficient or even a necessary part of learning to read. Many other factors are involved, in the language system itself, in the child, in the home, at school (cf. Ellis 1984; Thomson 1984). The issue of how these two infants were introduced to written text at school, for instance, has not even been touched upon. As pointed out in the Introduction, schoolchildren with no previous experience of books can become successful readers. Indeed, national literacy campaigns in some countries, Algeria for example, are specifically designed for 6-year-olds whose parents are not literate, who have no books in the home, and who have never been read to in early childhood (Pouder 1994). These children learn to read. In other words, reading, unlike oral language acquisition, is not age critical. Failure to meet books early does not necessarily entail a failure to read. Literate parents are not even a prerequisite. Nor are books an indispensable medium for imparting the linguistic foundations of literacy. Not only might illustrated books be used for a variety of non-linguistic purposes: teaching the Bible, or keeping alive the memory of absent relatives; nursery rhymes, songs, discussions, stories, the recounting of an event can be rehearsed without recourse to books (Bryant and Bradley 1985). Certainly, the acquisition of word meanings or the ordering, in discourse, of real-world events, is not specific to books alone.

Nonetheless, set against these arguments is the growing conviction, manifest in a number of educational policy statements, in much theoretical discussion and supported to an extent by empirical research, that, in literate societies, early contact with books is somehow related to later success in literacy. In what ways might this be true?

There is, first of all, the developmental view. Our theoretical understanding of how children accede to the written word has undergone a sea change in the last four decades. No longer (purely) a question of maturation, of 'reading readiness' or of 'just' reading (productive writing is now included), early childhood in literate homes is now viewed as a seed bed for all kinds of incipient acts of literacy (Teale and Sulzby 1986a). Such acts vary greatly, take many different forms and are apparent very early. By the time such children reach school, they already have a grounding in literacy. The question for researchers is to ascertain how and in what ways these precocious and extremely diverse forms of literacy are effectively fostered and to study the longer term effects.

Second, there is the contribution of specialists in literary theory. The reading of novels and stories, it is now recognised, is not merely a question of decoding the spoken word, but in a different mode. Such an event has its own particular rules, a basic knowledge of which the reader must possess; the rules are not explicated within the text (Rabinowitz 1987). The argument of Chapters 3 to 6 was that the experience of reading illustrated books, especially with very young children, prepares the ground, at a discourse level, for later interpretations of written narrative.

Third, there are further arguments derived from research in linguistics. Despite the restrictions imposed by the cultural context in which this enquiry has been conducted, it remains the case that, in many countries of the world, picturebooks and stories have been shown to develop linguistic understanding,

CONCLUDING REMARKS

both in younger and older children. While not impossible to meet in other types of exchanges, book-based interactions constitute, perhaps, a privileged forum for fostering the kind of semantic knowledge and active responses to printed text which have been identified in Chapters 3 and 8 as an inherent part of subsequent engagement in the experience of literacy.

Fourth, there is the cross-cultural perspective. As with oral language (Lieven 1994), research is rendering it increasingly apparent that the development of literacy, too, is culturally (and linguistically) specific. It is not the 'same thing' to be literate in the USA, or China, or Korea (Dubin and Kuhlman 1992). Different peoples value different literary genres, the initiation into which has a long history extending way back into early childhood (Lee and Scarcela 1992). This study has been limited to a consideration of the early presentation of books in just one British family and findings should be seen in that context. However, it seems that the provision of a static visual stimulus, the experience of which is not 'hands on', during which children cannot 'move off' and which is mediated purely via language, replicates a type of exchange which occurs subsequently in many a school setting (Chapter 1). It may be, too, that interrogating the adult and/or the written text prefigures an attitude which is enshrined in much academic teaching in the UK (cf. Kuhlman 1992).

In addition, possibly, illustrated stories and picturebooks may be viewed as the pictorial precursors of two practices found almost universally in British mainstream education, that is the use, first, of storybooks as the main vehicle for the introduction of the written word, which is then followed by creative story writing and the use, second, of non-fictional texts as 'documentation', from which a written project on a specified topic must be composed.

This brings me to the final argument for the long-term significance of literary activities in the home: the institutional argument. The educational benefit of a history of literacy accrues, possibly, from the fact that such activity confers an advantage in relation to other children. Children in literate societies in the Western world do not begin school, as in Algeria, with a clean slate, nor are they received as such (Heath 1983). A culture of literacy does not impose itself uniformly; it can be easily avoided (Goody and Watt 1972). Yet, a grasp of the rudiments of literacy upon entry to school at age 5 years is the surest predictor of subsequent scholastic achievement (Wells 1986:144). Indeed, those who enter mainstream schooling with little or no previous literary experience are perceived as being 'at academic risk' (McCormick and Mason 1986:95). The school is an institutional setting which differentiates, as no other, between the various individuals who reside there (Edwards and Garcia 1994). The basis for the differentiation is very often the type of knowledge which children bring with them to school from their home backgrounds (Jones 1981).

The linguistic and literary foundations of early reading, as discussed in this book, are therefore plausibly connected with later achievements in learning to read and write at school. But a naturalistic study of this kind cannot prove that this is so. Indeed, it may be that learning to write, read or even speak hinges upon factors quite different from those reviewed here. The paths to literacy are likely to be diverse in the extreme. The question, then, as to the importance of early reading exchanges requires, perhaps, a different answer. That answer is a short-term one and concerns the intrinsic value to young infants of early reading dialogues.

This description represents a start, but only a start, to understanding the significance, linguistic, literary, and moral, of book-reading activities in early infancy. Along with others, it has documented the densely lexicalised and context-independent quality of much of the language which the reading of books characteristically generates. If, with Bakhtin, one believes that meanings are socially distributed, or with Vygotsky that achievements are socially mediated — existing first at an interpersonal level before becoming intrapersonal — if one conceives of language as a tool which modifies, not simply people's perceptions of that to which it refers (the real world), but also the mind of the speaking subject, then perhaps it might be concluded that not only is children's understanding of the world transformed as that world is brought in to language; those children, through language and in a variety of ways, are themselves transformed.

APPENDIX

The incidence of word class usage in adult speech by child, and by child age session

		Nouns N=	Verbs N=	Adjectives N=	Total
Rhys Age in months					
9	different lexemes	33	24	4	61
	lexical mentions	124	70	9	203
14	different lexemes	33	13	2	48
	lexical mentions	121	54	2	177
18	different lexemes	235	72	17	324
	lexical mentions	688	190	38	916
Ceri Age in months					
9	different lexemes	62	23	11	96
	lexical mentions	293	124	28	445
14	different lexemes	132	52	7	191
	lexical mentions	338	163	19	520
18	different lexemes	145	61	17	223
	lexical mentions	329	201	60	590

Base: Total nouns, verbs and adjectives contained in adult speech addressed to Rhys and to Ceri respectively at three age sessions: 9 months, 14 months, and 18 months

NOTES

INTRODUCTION

1 With the exception of one book presented in the very first sessions, 'pictures' are drawings, not photographs.
2 The International Phonetic Alphabet has therefore not been used in the data transcriptions.

1 READING AND THE VERY YOUNG INFANT

1 Only very rarely, in the first two years of life, did either child share a reading session with a sibling. At age 1, Rhys' sister was only just born, and when he was 2 years old, and listening to *Goldilocks*, she was barely able to point out one or two items in her book. It was only when Ceri had reached 2 years of age, and had caught up her elder brother, that it became feasible to read to both children together.

2 A SENSE OF SELF

1 Structurally, the 'child contribution–adult feedback' frameworks of early reading are similar to those identified by Sinclair and Coulthard (1975) in certain classroom settings. Just as with the listening skills discussed in Chapter 1, this form of discourse routine in early reading may be construed as useful preparation for subsequent classroom activity (cf. Heath 1982; Wells 1985).
2 Videorecorded data cited in this chapter of Rhys reading with both parents confirm this child's interactional and conversational preferences with each adult respectively. Self-report data of Ceri reading with her father confirm her recurring interest in 'teddy' or 'cat', her reluctance to answer direct questions and so on, irrespective of adult interlocutor.
3 Object-orientedness is defined by Abrams and Neubauer (1978) in a wider sense than the definition proposed in the Introduction. 'Objects' here would include soft toys, for example.

3 PICTUREBOOK READING AND WORD MEANING

1 The 'stories' utilised are 'read' as 'picturebooks' (cf. Introduction, section 3.2).
2 Three factors at least contribute to a parent's 'reading' of a complex pictorial scene, namely a written title; the integration of a number of elements of the scene: the tunnel, swing and roundabout, when taken together, suggest a playground; chronological order: a mealtime scene at the start of a book is coded as 'breakfast', while one at the end is 'supper'. This is not to suggest, of course, that the infant also 'reads' scenes in this way (see Chapter 4).
3 The examples quoted here are of substantives, though the approach applies equally to other

word classes. 'Crawling' for instance is used of a baby at the seaside; ants over apple cores; and a child through a tunnel.

4 PICTUREBOOK READING AS EVENT INTERPRETATION

1 Referred to here are those instances where actions which lie 'beyond' pictures are explicated by language alone. Chapter 6 discusses sequences of pictures where, in picture (a), the protagonist is in a state of undress, and in picture (b), dressed. What 'must have happened' between the pictures can be 'proved' by pointing to the second picture in the series. Discussions of this latter type, as will be seen, take place much earlier than 18 months.
2 The difference between home and classroom, of course, is that in a classroom it is a very skilful operation indeed simultaneously to adopt the perspective of a large number of interlocutors.

5 THE WORLD OF THE STORY

1 In Chapter 1 it was observed that the emergence of turntaking mechanisms in the infant is rooted in gaze (as one of the precursors of speech). The supposition here is that the mirroring function of speech, too, has its origins in gaze, but this time in the gaze of the mother.
2 Bollas' (1979) suggestion of the rediscovery of the first relationship in aesthetic experience does not specifically include the reading experience. This study thus extends the scope of the aesthetic experience to include reading, and offers empirical support to Bollas' more speculative insight regarding the origins of that experience. In the case of reading, there seems to be a moment during the early months when a transforming image of the infant is literally reflected back, in language, by the mother.

6 STORY GRAMMAR AND TEXT

1 A diary note at child age 19 months reads that, on a day-to-day basis, more than 50 per cent of the interchanges between Rhys and his mother include references to book reading. Even if exaggerated, this figure is suggestive of the extent to which books form part of the fabric of Rhys' daily life, and are a constant 'talking' point, even when they are not actually being 'read'.

7 MATERNAL SPEECH AND INFANT PSYCHIC DEVELOPMENT

1 Exceptionally, 'verbal' here denotes pertaining to 'verbs', not 'words'. As indicated in the Introduction, this mother's speech is unusual: verb inflections, auxiliaries and pronouns, for instance, are sometimes omitted, as in: 'Little boy running away.'
2 One wonders: would such 'tutoring' occur at the hands of a caregiver who is not herself a mother? Naturally on this point this study does not permit of any firm conclusion.

8 EMERGENT LITERACY

1 Winnicott did not mean, of course, that infants had to be exposed to actual music or art or reading, as babies, in order for these experiences to take hold in adulthood. Rather it is the nature of the early transitional experience which is later rediscovered. But, for the purposes of this enquiry, the progression is investigated by following Rhys and Ceri throughout the period during which they are, initially, in contact with books.
2 The capacity to write complete words was not matched, in either child, by a concomitant

NOTES

ability to read them back. Writing the code seemed initially independent of the ability to read it, and production was what interested these children most. In the home, writing preceded reading, though this is not what generally occurs in a school setting (cf. M. Clark 1976).

REFERENCES

Abrams, S. and Neubauer, P. (1978) 'Transitional objects: animate and inanimate', in S. A. Grolnick, L. Barkin, and W. Muensterberger (eds) *Between Reality and Fantasy*, New York: Jason Aronson.
Adams, A. K. and Bullock, D. (1986) 'Apprenticeship in word use: social convergence processes in learning categorically related nouns', in S. A. Kuczaj and M. D. Barrett (eds) *The Development of Word Meaning*, New York: Springer Verlag.
Anglin, J. M. (1986) 'Semantic and conceptual knowledge underlying the child's words', in S. A. Kuczaj and M. D. Barrett (eds) *The Development of Word Meaning*, New York: Springer Verlag.
Austin, J. L. (1962) *How To Do Things With Words*, Oxford: Clarendon Press.
Barrett, M. D. (1986) 'Early semantic representations and early word-usage', in S. A. Kuczaj and M. D. Barrett (eds) *The Development of Word Meaning*, New York: Springer Verlag.
Barrett, M. D., Harris, M. and Chasin, J. (1991) 'Early lexical development and maternal speech: a comparison of children's initial and subsequent uses of words', *Journal of Child Language* 18: 21–40.
Barton, M. E. and Tomasello, M. (1994) 'The rest of the family: the role of fathers and siblings in early language development', in C. Gallaway and B. J. Richards (eds) *Input and Interaction in Language Acquisition*, Cambridge: Cambridge University Press.
Bates, E., Marchman, V., Thal, D., Fenson, L., Dale, P., Reznick, J. S., Reilly, J. and Hartung, J. (1994) 'Developmental and stylistic variation in the composition of early vocabulary', *Journal of Child Language* 21: 85–123.
Berlin, B. and Kay, P. (1969) *Basic Color Terms*, Berkeley and Los Angeles: University of California Press.
Bettelheim, B. and Zelan, K. (1982) *On Learning to Read*, London: Thames and Hudson.
Blurton-Jones, N. G. and Leach, G. M. (1972) 'Behaviour of children and their mothers at separation and greeting', in N. G. Blurton-Jones (ed.) *Ethological Studies of Child Behaviour*, Cambridge: Cambridge University Press.
Bollas, C. (1979) 'The transformational object', *International Journal of Psycho-analysis* 60: 97–107.
Bowie, M. (1991) *Lacan*, London: Fontana.
Britton, J. (1977) 'Response to literature', in M. Meek, A. Warlow and G. Barton (eds) *The Cool Web: the pattern of children's reading*, London: Bodley Head.
Brown, G. and Yule, G. (1983) *Discourse Analysis*, Cambridge: Cambridge University Press.
Brown, R. W., Copi, I. M., Dulaney, D. E., Frankena, W. F., Henle, P. and Stevenson, C. L. (1958) *Language, Thought, and Culture*, Ann Arbor: University of Michigan Press.
Bruner, J. (1983) *Child's Talk: learning to use language*, Oxford: Oxford University Press.
—— (1986) 'Two modes of thought', in J. Bruner, *Actual Minds, Possible Worlds*, Cambridge, Mass.: Harvard University Press.

REFERENCES

—— (1990) *Acts of Meaning*, Cambridge, Mass.: Harvard University Press.
Bruner, J. and Haste, H. (eds) (1987) *Making Sense: the child's construction of the world*, London: Methuen.
Bryant, P. and Bradley, L. (1985) *Children's Reading Problems*, Oxford: Basil Blackwell.
Bus, A. G. and IJzendoorn, M. H. van (1988) 'Mother–child interactions, attachment, and emergent literacy: a cross-sectional study', *Child Development* 59: 1262–1272.
Butler, D. (1979) *Cushla and Her Books*, London: Hodder and Stoughton.
—— (1980) *Babies Need Books*, London: Bodley Head.
Butterworth, G. and Jarrett, N. (1991) 'What minds have in common is space: spatial mechanisms serving joint visual attention in infancy', *British Journal of Developmental Psychology* 9: 55–72.
Chomsky, N. (1965) *Aspects of the Theory of Syntax*, Cambridge, Mass.: M. I. T. Press.
Clark, M. M. (1976) *Young Fluent Readers*, Oxford: Heinemann Educational.
Clark, R. A. (1978) 'The transition from action to gesture', in A. Lock (ed.) *Action, Gesture and Symbol: the emergence of language*, London: Academic Press.
Cochran-Smith, M. (1983) 'Reading stories to children: a review-critique', in B. A. Hutson (ed.) *Advances in Reading/Language Research*, vol. 2, London: JAI Press.
Cox, M. V. (1986) *The Child's Point of View*, Hemel Hempstead: Harvester Wheatsheaf.
Crain-Thoreson, C. and Dale, P. S. (1992) 'Do early talkers become early readers? Linguistic precocity, preschool language and emergent literacy', *Developmental Psychology* 28: 421–429.
Cruse, D. (1986) *Lexical semantics*, Cambridge: Cambridge University Press.
Deleau, M. (1990) *Les origines sociales du développement mental*, Paris: Armand Colin.
Deloache, J. S. and DeMendoza, O. A. P. (1987) 'Joint picturebook interactions of mothers and 1-year-old children', *British Journal of Developmental Psychology* 5: 111–123.
Dobson, L. (1989) 'Connections in learning to write and read', in J. Mason (ed.) *Reading and Writing Connections*, Boston: Allyn and Bacon.
Dockrell, J. and Campbell, R. (1986) 'Lexical acquisition strategies in the preschool child', in S. A. Kuczaj and M. D. Barrett (eds) *The Development of Word Meaning*, New York: Springer Verlag.
Dolan, B. (1993) 'The Marie Clay reading programme', unpublished paper presented to South West Thames Group in developmental speech and language impairment.
Donaldson, M. (1978) *Children's Minds*, London: Fontana.
Dubin, F. and Kuhlman, N. A. (eds) (1992) *Cross-cultural Literacy: global perspectives on reading and writing*, New Jersey: Regents/Prentice Hall.
Dunn, J., Bretherton, I. and Munn, P. (1987) 'Conversations about feeling states between mothers and their young children', *Developmental Psychology* 23: 132–139.
Dunn. J. and Shatz, M. (1989) 'Becoming a conversationalist despite (or because of) having an older sibling', *Child Development* 60: 399–410.
Edwards, D. (1978) 'Social relations and early language', in A. Lock (ed.) *Action, Gesture and Symbol: the emergence of language*, London: Academic Press.
Edwards, P. A. and Garcia, G. E. (1994) 'The implications of Vygotskian theory for the development of home–school programs: a focus on storybook reading', in V. John-Steiner, C. P. Panofsky, and L. W. Smith (eds) *Sociocultural Approaches to Language and Literacy*, Cambridge: Cambridge University Press.
Ellis, A. W. (1984) *Reading, Writing and Dyslexia: a cognitive analysis*, London: Lawrence Erlbaum Associates.
Emde, R. (1992) 'Individual meaning and increasing complexity: contributions of Sigmund Freud and René Spitz to developmental psychology', *Developmental Psychology* 28: 347–359.
—— (1994) 'The early self: dynamics of evaluation, culture, and consciousness', paper presented to the 'Ninth International Conference on Infant Studies', Paris, France, 2–5 June.
Firth, J. R. (1957) *Papers in Linguistics 1934–1951*, London: Oxford University Press.
Fivush, R. (1987) 'Scripts and categories: interrelationships in development', in U. Neisser (ed.) *Concepts and Conceptual Development*, Cambridge: Cambridge University Press.

REFERENCES

Freud, S. (1920) 'Beyond the pleasure principle', in J. Strachey (ed.) *The Standard Edition of the Complete Psychological Works of Sigmund Freud*, vol. 18, London: Hogarth Press, 1955.
Frosh, S. (1989) *Psychoanalysis and Psychology: minding the gap*, London: Macmillan.
Furrow, D. and Nelson, K. (1984) 'Environmental correlates of individual differences in language acquisition', *Journal of Child Language* 11: 523–534.
Garman, M. (1990) *Psycholinguistics*, Cambridge: Cambridge University Press.
Garton, A. and Pratt, C. (1989) *Learning to be Literate; the development of spoken and written language*, Oxford: Basil Blackwell.
Gelb, I. J. (1952) *A Study of Writing*, Chicago: University of Chicago Press.
Gibson, E. J. and Levin, H. (1975) *The Psychology of Reading*, Cambridge, Mass.: M. I. T. Press.
Gleason, J. B. (1993) *The Development of Language*, New York: Macmillan.
Goldfield, B. A. (1993) 'Noun bias in maternal speech to one-year-olds', *Journal of Child Language* 20: 85–99.
Golinkoff, R. M. (1986) '"I beg your pardon?": the preverbal negotiation of failed messages', *Journal of Child Language* 13: 455–476.
Golinkoff, R. M., Mervis, C. B., and Hirsh-Pasek, K. (1994) 'Early object labels: the case for a developmental lexical principles framework', *Journal of Child Language* 21: 125–155.
Golombok, S. and Fivush, R. (1994) *Gender Development*, Cambridge: Cambridge University Press.
Gombrich, E. H. (1960) *Art and Illusion*, London: Phaidon Press.
—— (1972) 'Action and expression in Western art', in R. A. Hinde (ed.) *Non-verbal Communication*, Cambridge: Cambridge University Press.
Goodman, Y. M. (1986) 'Children coming to know literacy', in W. H. Teale and E. Sulzby (eds) *Emergent Literacy*, Norwood, NJ: Ablex.
Goody, J. (1977) *The Domestication of the Savage Mind*, Cambridge: Cambridge University Press.
Goody, J. and Watt, I. (1972) 'The consequences of literacy', in P. P. Giglioli (ed.) *Language and Social Context*, London: Penguin.
Greenfield, P. M. (1984) *Mind and Media*, London: Fontana.
Harris, M. and Coltheart, M. (1986) *Language Processing in Children and Adults*, London: Routledge and Kegan Paul.
Harris, M., Barrett, M. D., Jones, D. and Brookes, S. (1988) 'Linguistic input and early word meaning', *Journal of Child Language* 15: 77–94.
Heath, S. B. (1982) 'What no bedtime story means: narrative skills at home and school', *Language and Society* 11: 49–76.
—— (1983) *Ways with Words*, Cambridge: Cambridge University Press.
Hinde, R. A. (1992) 'Developmental psychology in the context of other behavioral sciences', *Developmental Psychology* 28: 1018–1029.
Hudson, L. and Jacot, B. (1991) *The Way Men Think*, New Haven and London: Yale University Press.
Ingram, D. (1989) *First Language Acquisition*, Cambridge: Cambridge University Press.
Izard, C. E., Huebner, R. R., Risser, D., McGinnes, G. C. and Dougherty, L. M. (1980) 'The young infant's ability to produce discrete emotion expressions', *Developmental Psychology* 16: 132–140.
Jones, R. (1981) 'Le langage en milieu scolaire: aspects de l'échange maître–élèves', unpublished doctoral thesis, University of Paris-Sorbonne.
King, M. L. (1989) 'Speech to writing: children's growth in writing potential', in J. M. Mason (ed.) *Reading and Writing Connections*, Boston: Allyn and Bacon.
Klauber, J. and others (1987) *Illusion and Spontaneity in Psychoanalysis*, London: Free Association Books.
Kuhlman, N. A. (1992) 'Literacy in Poland', in F. Dubin and N. A. Kuhlman (eds) *Cross-cultural Literacy: global perspectives on reading and writing*, New Jersey: Regents/Prentice Hall.
Lakoff, G. (1987) *Women, Fire, and Dangerous Things*, Chicago: University of Chicago Press.

REFERENCES

Langsdorf, P., Izard, C. E., Rayias, M. and Hembree, E. A. (1983) 'Interest expression, visual fixation, and heart rate changes in 2–8-month-old infants' *Developmental Psychology* 19: 375–386.

Lee, C. and Scarcella, R. (1992) 'Building upon Korean writing practices: genres, values and beliefs', in F. Dubin and N. A. Kuhlman (eds) *Cross-cultural Literacy: global perspectives on reading and writing*, New Jersey: Regents/Prentice Hall.

Lemish, D. and Rice, M. L. (1986) 'Television as a talking picture book: a prop for language acquisition', *Journal of Child Language* 13: 251–274.

Lieberman, P. (1991) *Uniquely Human*, Cambridge, Mass.: Harvard University Press.

Lieven, E. V. M. (1978) 'Conversations between mothers and young children: individual differences and their possible implications for the study of language learning', in N. Waterson and C. Snow (eds) *The Development of Communication: social and pragmatic factors in language acquisition*, New York: Wiley.

—— (1994) 'Crosslinguistic and crosscultural aspects of language addressed to children', in C. Gallaway and B. J. Richards (eds) *Input and Interaction in Language Acquisition*, Cambridge: Cambridge University Press.

Linell, P. and Jönsson, L. (1991) 'Suspect stories: perspective-setting in an asymmetrical situation', in I. Marková and K. Foppa (eds) *Asymmetries in Dialogue*, Hemel Hempstead: Harvester Wheatsheaf.

Luria, A. R. and Vygotsky, L. S. (1930) *Ape, Primitive Man and Child: essays in the history of behaviour*, trans. E. Rossiter, Hemel Hempstead: Harvester Wheatsheaf, 1992.

Luria, A. R. and Yudovich, F. Ia (1956) *Speech and the Development of Mental Processes in the Child*, reprinted by Penguin Books, 1971.

Lyons, J. (1968) *Introduction to Theoretical Linguistics,* Cambridge: Cambridge University Press.

—— (1972) 'Human language', in R. A. Hinde (ed.) *Non-verbal Communication*, Cambridge: Cambridge University Press.

—— (1977) *Semantics: I*, Cambridge: Cambridge University Press.

McCormick, C. E. and Mason, J. M. (1986) 'Intervention procedures for increasing preschool children's interest in and knowledge about reading', in W. H. Teale and E. Sulzby (eds) *Emergent Literacy*, Norwood, NJ: Ablex.

McGinn, C. (1984) *Wittgenstein on Meaning*, Oxford: Basil Blackwell.

Marcelli, D. (1983) 'La position autistique: hypothèses psychopathologiques et ontogénétiques', *Psychiatrie de l'enfant* XXVI: 17–55.

Marková, I. and Foppa, K. (eds) (1990) *The Dynamics of Dialogue*, Hemel Hempstead: Harvester Wheatsheaf.

—— (1991) *Asymmetries in Dialogue*, Hemel Hempstead: Harvester Wheatsheaf.

Mead, G. H. (1936) 'The problem of society: how we become selves', in Merritt H. Moore (ed.) *Movements of Thought in the Nineteenth Century*, Berkeley and Los Angeles: University of California Press.

Meek, M. (1991) *On Being Literate*, London: Bodley Head.

Meek, M., Warlow, A. and Barton, G. (eds) (1977) *The Cool Web: the pattern of children's reading*, London: Bodley Head.

Murphy, C. (1978) 'Pointing in the context of a shared activity', *Child Development* 49: 371–380.

Nelson, K. (1973) *Structure and Strategy in Learning to Talk*, Monographs of the Society for Research in Child Development, 38 (149).

—— (1981) 'Individual differences in language development: implications for development and language', *Developmental Psychology* 17: 170–187.

Ninio, A. (1980) 'Picture-book reading in mother–infant dyads belonging to two subgroups in Israel', *Child Development* 51: 587–590.

—— (1983) 'Joint book-reading as a multiple vocabulary acquisition device', *Developmental Psychology* 19: 445–451.

REFERENCES

Ninio, A. and Bruner, J. (1978) 'The achievement and antecedents of labelling', *Journal of Child Language* 5: 1–15.
Nonnon, E. (1992) 'Fonctions de l'aide et du questionnement de l'enseignant dans la lecture et la compréhension de textes', *Recherches* 17: 97–132.
Oakhill, J. and Garnham, A. (1988) *Becoming a Skilled Reader*, Oxford: Basil Blackwell.
Olson, D. R. (1988) 'Some oral language antecedents of literacy', in N. Mercer (ed.) *Language and Literacy from an Educational Perspective*, vol. 1, Buckingham: Open University Press.
Palmer, F. R. (1976) *Semantics*, Cambridge: Cambridge University Press.
Panofsky, C. P. (1994) 'Developing the representational functions of language: the role of parent–child book-reading activity', in V. John-Steiner, C. P. Panofsky and L. W. Smith (eds) *Sociocultural Approaches to Language and Literacy*, Cambridge: Cambridge University Press.
Phillips, A. (1988) *Winnicott*, London: Fontana.
Pine, J. M. (1995) 'Variation in vocabulary development as a function of birth order', *Child Development* 66: 272–281.
Pouder, M. C. (1994) Personal communication.
Préneron, C. (1994) 'Referential elaboration and construction of meaning: reflections from language impairment – the example of picture stories', *International Journal of Psycholinguistics* X(2): 147–166.
Rabin-Jamain, J. and Sabeau-Jouannet, E. (1991) 'Conduites de soutien et gestion du dialogue entre mères et enfants africains et français à Paris', unpublished paper presented at 'L'analyse des interactions', International Conference, La Baume-les Aix, France.
Rabinowitz, P. J. (1987) *Before Reading: narrative conventions and the politics of interpretation*, New York: Cornell University Press.
Roberts, C. and Horowitz, F. D. (1986) 'Basic level categorization in seven-and nine-month-old infants', *Journal of Child Language* 13: 191–208.
Rycroft, C. (1979) [1991a] *The Innocence of Dreams*, London: Hogarth Press
—— (1991b) *Viewpoints*, London: Hogarth Press.
Sapir, E. (1933) 'Language', *Encyclopaedia of the Social Sciences 9*, New York: Macmillan, reprinted in D. G. Mandelbaum (ed.) (1949) *Selected Writings in Language, Culture, and Personality*, Berkeley and Los Angeles: University of California Press (references are to the 1985 edition).
Saussure, F. de (1916) *Cours de linguistique générale*, Paris: Payot (references are to the 1972 edition).
Schaffer, H. R., Hepburn, A. and Collis, G. M. (1983) 'Verbal and nonverbal aspects of mothers' directives', *Journal of Child Language* 10: 337–355.
Scollon, R. (1985) 'Language, literacy, and learning: an annotated bibliography', in D. R. Olson, N. Torrance and A. Hildyard (eds) *Literacy, Language, and Learning*, Cambridge: Cambridge University Press.
Scribner, S. and Cole, M. (1981) *The Psychology of Literacy*, Cambridge, Mass.: Harvard University Press.
Sheridan, M. D. (1960) *The Developmental Progress of Infants and Young Children*, Reports on Public Health and Medical Subjects no. 102, London: Her Majesty's Stationery Office.
Sinclair, J. McH. and Coulthard, R. M. (1975) *Towards an Analysis of Discourse*, London: Oxford University Press.
Singly, F. de (1994) 'A quoi sert la famille?', *Sciences Humaines* 7: 28–31.
Snow, C. E. (1976) 'The language of the mother–child relationship', in S. Rogers (ed.) *They Don't Speak Our Language: essays on the language world of children and adolescents*, London: Edward Arnold.
Snow, C. E. and Goldfield, B. A. (1983) 'Turn the page please: situation-specific language acquisition', *Journal of Child Language* 10: 551–569.
Snow, C. E. and Ninio, A. (1986) 'The contracts of literacy: what children learn from learning to read books', in W. H. Teale and E. Sulzby (eds) *Emergent Literacy*, Norwood, NJ: Ablex.
Stern, D. N. (1985) *The Interpersonal World of the Infant*, New York: Basic Books.

REFERENCES

Straten A. van der (1991) *Premiers gestes, premiers mots*, Paris: Centurion.

Super, C. M. and Harkness, S. (1982) 'The development of affect in infancy and early childhood', in D. Wagner and H. Stevenson (eds) *Cultural Perspectives on Child Development*, New York: W. H. Freeman.

Taylor, C. (1989) *Sources of the Self*, Cambridge: Cambridge University Press.

Teale, W. H. and Sulzby, E. (1986a) 'Emergent literacy as a perspective for examining how young children become writers and readers', in W. H. Teale and E. Sulzby (eds) *Emergent Literacy*, Norwood, NJ: Ablex.

—— (1986b) (eds) *Emergent Literacy*, Norwood, NJ: Ablex.

Thomson, M. E. (1984) *Developmental Dyslexia*, London: Edward Arnold.

Thorpe, W. H. (1972) 'The comparison of vocal communication in animals and man', in R. A. Hinde (ed.) *Non-verbal Communication*, Cambridge: Cambridge University Press.

Todorov, T. (1981) *Mikhaïl Bakhtine: le principe dialogique*, Paris: Seuil.

Tolkien, J. R. R. (1964) *Tree and Leaf*, London: Allen and Unwin.

Tomasello, M. (1992) *First Verbs*, Cambridge: Cambridge University Press.

—— (1994) 'Understanding the self as social agent', paper presented to the 'Ninth International Conference on Infant Studies', Paris, France, 2–5 June.

Trân Duc Thao (1973) *Recherches sur l'origine du langage et de la conscience*, Paris: Editions Sociales.

Trease, G. (1977) 'Old writers and young readers', in M. Meek, A. Warlow and G. Barton (eds) *The Cool Web: the pattern of children's reading*, London: Bodley Head.

Trevarthen, C. (1982) 'The primary motives for cooperative understanding', in G. Butterworth and P. Light (eds) *Social Cognition: studies of the development of understanding*, Brighton: Harvester Press.

—— (1992) 'Playing into reality', unpublished paper presented to the Squiggle Foundation, London.

Tucker, N. (1981) *The Child and the Book*, Cambridge: Cambridge University Press.

Urwin, C. (1978) 'The development of communication between blind infants and their parents', in A. Lock (ed.) *Action, Gesture and Symbol: the emergence of language*, London: Academic Press.

Valdez-Menchaca, M. C. and Whitehurst, G. J. (1992) 'Accelerating language development through picture book reading: a systematic extension to Mexican day care', *Developmental Psychology* 28: 1106–1114.

Voloshinov, V. (1926) 'Discourse in life and discourse in poetry: questions of sociological poetics', in A. Shukman (ed.) (1988) *Bakhtin School Papers*, Oxford: RPT Publications.

Vygotsky, L. S. (1934) *Thought and Language*, trans. E. Hanfmann and G. Vakar, Cambridge, Mass.: M. I. T. Press, 1962.

—— (1987) *The Collected Works of L. S. Vygotsky*, vol. 1., R. W. Rieber and A. S. Carton (eds), New York: Plenum Press.

Warlow, A. (1977) 'What the reader has to do', in M. Meek, A. Warlow and G. Barton (eds) *The Cool Web: the pattern of children's reading*, London: Bodley Head.

Wells, G. (1985) 'Preschool literacy-related activities and success in school', in D. R. Olson, N. Torrance and A. Hildyard (eds) *Literacy, Language and Learning*, Cambridge: Cambridge University Press.

——(1986) *The Meaning Makers*, London: Hodder and Stoughton.

Wertsch, J. V. (1990) 'Dialogue and dialogism in a socio-cultural approach to mind', in I. Marková and K. Foppa (eds) *The Dynamics of Dialogue*, Hemel Hempstead: Harvester Wheatsheaf.

Wheeler, M. P. (1983) 'Context-related age changes in mothers' speech: joint book reading', *Journal of Child Language* 10: 259–263.

Whitehead, M. R. (1990) *Language and Literacy in the Early Years*, London: Paul Chapman.

Whitehurst, G. J., Falco, F. L., Lonigan, C. J., Fischel, J. E., DeBaryshe, B. D., Valdez-

REFERENCES

Menchaca, M. C. and Caulfield, M. (1988) 'Accelerating language development through picture-book reading', *Developmental Psychology* 24: 552–559.

Whorf, B. L. (1927) 'On psychology', previously unpublished manuscript in B. L. Whorf (1956).

—— (1936) 'A linguistic consideration of thinking in primitive communities', reprinted in B. L. Whorf (1956).

—— (1940) 'Science and linguistics', *Technological Review* 42(6): 229–231, 247–248, reprinted in B. L. Whorf (1956).

—— (1945) 'Grammatical categories', *Language* 21: 1–11, reprinted in B. L. Whorf (1956).

—— (1956) *Language, Thought, and Reality: selected writings of Benjamin Lee Whorf*, J. B. Carroll (ed.), Cambridge, Mass.: M. I. T. Press.

Winnicott, D. W. (1950) 'The deprived child and how he can be compensated for loss of family life', reprinted in D. W. Winnicott (1989) *The Family and Individual Development*, London: Routledge.

—— (1952) 'Anxiety associated with insecurity', paper presented to the British Psychoanalytical Society, reprinted in D. W. Winnicott (1958) *Through Paediatrics to Psychoanalysis*, London: Hogarth Press.

—— (1953) 'Transitional objects and transitional phenomena', *International Journal of Psychoanalysis* 34(2), reprinted in D. W. Winnicott (1974) *Playing and Reality*, London: Pelican Books.

—— (1954) 'The depressive position in normal emotional development', paper presented to the British Psychological Society, reprinted in D. W. Winnicott (1958) *Through Paediatrics to Psychoanalysis*, London: Hogarth Press.

—— (1963) 'Communicating and not communicating leading to a study of certain opposites', reprinted in D. W. Winnicott (1990) *The Maturational Processes and the Facilitating Environment*, London: Karnac Books.

—— (1964) *The Child, the Family and the Outside World*, London: Pelican Books.

—— (1967a) 'The location of cultural experience', *International Journal of Psycho-analysis* 48, reprinted in D. W. Winnicott (1974) *Playing and Reality*, London: Pelican Books.

—— (1967b) 'Mirror role of mother and family in child development', in P. Lomas (ed.) *The Predicament of the Family: a psychoanalytical symposium*, London: Hogarth Press and the Institute of Psycho-analysis, reprinted in D. W. Winnicott (1974) *Playing and Reality*, London: Pelican Books.

—— (1969) 'The use of an object in the context of Moses and Monotheism', in C. Winnicott, R. Shepherd and M. Davis (eds) (1989) *Psycho-analytic Explorations – D. W. Winnicott*, London: Karnac Books.

—— (1970) 'Cure', talk given at St Luke's Church, Hatfield, reprinted in D. W. Winnicott (1986) *Home is Where We Start From*, London: Pelican Books.

—— (1974) *Playing and Reality*, London: Pelican Books.

—— (1988) *Human Nature*, London: Free Association Books.

AUTHOR INDEX

Abrams, S. and Neubauer, P. 13, 87, 240
Adams, A. K. and Bullock, D. 9, 13, 52, 102, 126
Anglin, J. M. 120
Austen, J. 146
Austin, J. L. 55

Bakhtin, M. 238
Balzac, H. de 146
Barrett, M. D. 96–97, 103, 111–112
Barrett, M. D. *et al.* 96
Barton, M. E. and Tomasello, M. 87, 88
Bates, E. *et al.* 78, 87
Bettelheim, B. and Zelan, K. 12, 13
Berlin, B. and Kay, P. 192
Blurton-Jones, N. G. and Leach, G. M. 54
Bollas, C. 162, 163, 241
Bowie, M. 209
Brecht, B. 144
Britton, J. 147
Brown, G. and Yule, G. 115
Brown, R. W. *et al.* 138, 192
Bruner, J. 12, 15, 40, 83, 102, 143–144, 145, 150, 165, 180, 230
Bruner, J. and Haste, H. 12
Bryant, P. and Bradley, L. 236
Bus, A. G. and IJzendoorn, M. H. van 135
Butler, D. 8
Butterworth, G. and Jarrett, N. 38

Chomsky, N. 2, 180
Clark, M. M. 8, 242
Clark, R. A. 55, 59
Cochran-Smith, M. 8
Coleridge, S. T. 161
Cox, M. V. 54

Crain-Thoreson, C. and Dale, P. S. 115, 186
Cruse, D. 94–95, 106, 109

Deleau, M. 161
DeLoache, J. S. and DeMendoza, O. A. P. 9, 126, 127
Descartes, R. 162
Dickens, C. 146
Dobson, L. 228
Dockrell, J. and Campbell, R. 126
Dolan, B. 114
Donaldson, M. 12
Dubin, F. and Kuhlman, N. A. 237
Dunn, J. *et al.* 12, 86
Dunn, J. and Shatz, M. 88

Edwards, D. 28
Edwards, P. A. and Garcia, G. E. 7, 237
Ellis, A. W. 236
Emde, R. 52, 84, 161

Firth, J. R. 14
Fivush, R. 97, 106
Freud, S. 206, 217
Frosh, S. 11, 12, 206
Furrow, D. and Nelson, K. 85

Garman, M. 93, 103, 114
Garton, A. and Pratt, C. 9
Gelb, I. J. 6, 228
Gibson, E. J. and Levin, H. 12
Gleason, J. B. 7
Goldfield, B. A. 84
Golinkoff, R. M. 55
Golinkoff, R. M. *et al.* 93, 102
Golombok, S. and Fivush, R. 86

AUTHOR INDEX

Gombrich, E. H. 137, 168
Goodman, Y. M. 228, 229
Goody, J. 5–6, 12, 187, 228
Goody, J. and Watt, I. 158, 159, 237
Greenfield, P. M. 58

Harris, M. and Coltheart, M. 59, 60, 180
Harris, M. et al. 96
Heath, S. B. 7, 29, 139, 237, 240
Hinde, R. A. 52
Hudson, L. and Jacot, B. 86

Ingram, D. 7
Izard, C. E. et al. 12

Jones, R. 237

King, M. L. 228, 229
Klauber, J. 141
Kuhlman, N. A. 60, 237

Lakoff, G. 102, 111, 117, 192
Langsdorf, P. et al. 39
Lee, C. and Scarcella, R. 237
Lemish, D. and Rice, M. L. 89
Lieberman, P. 32
Lieven, E. V. M. 85, 237
Linell, P. and Jönsson, L. 136
Luria, A. R. and Vygotsky, L. S. 215
Luria, A. R. and Yudovich, F. Ia 7
Lyons, J. 6, 45, 84, 94, 96, 173, 192, 234

McCormick, C. E. and Mason, J. M. 7, 237
McGinn, C. 117
Marcelli, D. 88
Marková, I. and Foppa, K. 11, 14
Mead, G. H. 52
Meek, M. 8, 23
Meek, M. et al. 141, 146
Murphy, C. 9, 13, 54

Nelson, K. 32, 85, 86, 87
Ninio, A. 9, 37
Ninio, A. and Bruner, J. 8, 9, 13, 23, 39, 85, 100, 102
Nonnon, E. 115, 185

Oakhill, J. and Garnham, A. 12
Olson, D. R. 8

Palmer, F. R. 14, 96, 114, 192, 202
Panofsky, C. P. 29, 58

Pepys, S. 159
Phillips, A. 210–211, 230
Pine, J. M. 88
Pouder, M. C. 236
Préneron, C. 139, 224

Rabin-Jamain, J. and Sabeau-Jouannet, E. 7
Rabinowitz, P. J. 28, 115, 164, 168, 236
Roberts, K. and Horowitz, F. D. 27
Rousseau, J.-J. 159
Rycroft, C. 53, 69, 84, 161, 189, 216

St Augustine of Hippo 159
Sapir, E. 52, 224
Saussure, F. de 38
Schaffer, H. R. et al. 26
Scollon, R. 7
Scribner, S. and Cole, M. 227, 228
Sheridan, M. D. 54
Sinclair, J. McH. and Coulthard, M. 240
Singly, F. de 52
Snow, C. E. 5, 89
Snow, C. E. and Goldfield, B. A. 9, 13, 85
Snow, C. E. and Ninio, A. 9, 39, 126, 134, 215
Stern, D. N. 52, 141, 161, 224
Straten, A. van der 39
Super, C. M. and Harkness, S. 20, 52, 217

Taylor, C. 52, 189
Teale, W. H. and Sulzby, E. 7, 236
Thomson, M. E. 236
Thorpe, W. H. 84
Todorov, T. 128
Tolkien, J. R. R. 144
Tomasello, M. 12, 113
Tràn Duc Thao 95
Trease, G. 146
Trevarthen, C. 12, 132
Tucker, N. 217

Urwin, C. 102

Valdez-Menchaca, M. C. and Whitehurst, G. J. 7
Voloshinov, V. 11, 144, 151, 152
Vygotsky, L. S. 1, 12, 15, 37, 50, 182, 238

Warlow, A. 145, 147, 158, 164
Wells, G. 8, 9, 237, 240
Wertsch, J. V. 15
Wheeler, M. P. 9

Whitehead, M. R. 7, 141, 142
Whitehurst, G. J. *et al.* 7
Whorf, B. L. 12, 99, 180, 192
Winnicott, D. W. 14–15, 19, 21, 136, 146–147, 153, 162, 170, 189, 191, 193–194, 206, 207, 208–210, 213, 217, 221, 223, 225–227, 231–232
Woolf, V. 144, 154

Zola, E. 146

SUBJECT INDEX

affect: and child's response to book 12, 27, 40–42, 50, 107, 117, 124, 136, 181, 210, 212–213, 214, 235; and enhancement of skills 2, 36, 45, 48, 49–50, 75–76, 86, 119, 126–128, 133, 135, 140, 151–152, 160–161, 178, 187, 215–217, 222–223; and mirror role of mother 160–163; and shared bond with parent 42, 135; theories of 12, 40–42, 146, 147, 161–162, 210; in relation to word meaning *see* mood; *see also* empathy
ambivalence 210, 213–214
atmosphere *see* mood
autonomy 76, 156, 194–195, 200, 201, 203, 204, 206, 217–218

biography 19, 141, 159, 161, 163, 205
bridging 47–48, 126, 148, 151, 155, 156–157, 187, 203–204

classroom *see* education
context-independent language 6, 102, 173, 234
contextual relations *see* lexical relations
critical judgement 5, 144–145, 147, 155, 157, 158–159, 160, 186
cultural attitude 3, 7, 17, 21, 29–30, 32, 58, 60, 117, 136, 192, 237; *see also* norms
cyclical return 43, 44–45, 57, 67, 69, 71, 110, 118, 123, 212–213, 218; *see also* loss and recovery

data 15–19, 25, 28, 41, 45, 60, 66, 72, 74–78, 84, 98, 104, 110, 149, 155, 164, 168, 178, 195–196, 219–220, 222–223, 228–230; *see also* tables
denotation 45, 96, 103, 235

dialogue 2, 8, 10, 11, 19, 31, 49, 50, 53–54, 77, 89–90, 118, 125, 133–136, 148, 153, 196, 200, 238; impact of child behaviour upon 11, 40–43, 45, 55–58, 60, 61–64, 66–69, 71–75, 85–86, 118, 148; principles of 10, 85, 125–126, 133–134, 136, 140; proto-dialogue 32–38, 53; *see also* direct speech; discourse
direct speech 70, 167, 173–174, 183, 184
disappearance *see* loss and recovery
discourse 2, 7, 10, 18, 26, 32–38, 55, 64, 70, 71, 73, 79, 81–82, 115–116, 133, 135, 136, 153–154, 157–158, 171, 186, 206, 218, 235, 236; topic priority within 100–101, 105–106, 112, 115, 119–120, 123-124, 127, 128–130, 133, 154, 197–202; *see also* dialogue; written text
education 7–8, 16, 17, 33, 49, 60, 93, 136, 186, 234–237, 240, 241, 242
empathy 125, 135–136
environment 5, 15, 21, 54, 64, 67, 88, 113, 203, 205, 228; linguistic *see* lexical relations; mother as 15, 146–147, 161, 173, 193, 206, 208–209; *see also* material truth
event archetype 104–109, 111, 112–113, 117–120, 122, 126–130, 132–133, 140

father 16–19, 20, 86, 193–195, 199–201, 203, 204, 221, 223
fiction 75, 141, 143–148, 155, 159–161, 216–217, 230, 232, 235, 237; *see also* narrative; stories

gaze 17, 26, 30–37, 39, 41, 53, 54–55, 57, 58, 87, 162, 241

253

SUBJECT INDEX

grammar 2, 10, 18, 21, 50, 61, 67, 107, 115, 119, 135, 166–167, 169, 170, 172, 173–174, 176, 184, 202, 205–206, 224, 232; and Whorfian hypothesis 192, 202, 203; *see also* utterance typology

hyponomy 96, 102–103, 104, 105–106, 109–113, 114, 119–120, 175

identification 19, 86, 102, 160–161, 163, 194, 204, 223–224, 231, 232; imaginative 194–195, 203, 204, 206
imagination 19, 161, 163, 209, 232, 235
independence *see* autonomy
individual difference 1–2, 11, 13, 15, 19, 20, 40–41, 46, 50–53, 60–70, 77, 78–84, 85–89, 110, 128, 133, 135, 139, 146, 178, 186–187, 189, 193, 225–227, 229–232; impact upon parent of 62–64, 67, 69, 71–75, 85–88, 90; in long term 1, 6, 22, 53, 208, 211, 229–232, 234, 236–237; *see also* self
individuation 193–194, 206, 223, 224
intra-linguistic relations *see* lexical relations

labelling 7–9, 11, 21, 30, 35, 38–48, 55, 64, 69, 81, 83, 88, 95, 109, 110, 119, 121, 137–138, 196, 213, 225; *see also* lexis; paradigm; topic
lexical relations 75, 85, 91, 93–96, 98, 109–110, 112–113, 114, 117, 131, 174, 235, 236; *see also* hyponyms; superordinates; traits
lexis 2, 6, 9, 10–11, 18, 19, 43–45, 55, 71–72, 85, 86, 89, 91, 98, 114, 119, 135, 136, 169, 172–173, 176, 183, 187, 191–192, 202–204, 206, 224, 234; in relation to syntax *see* utterance typology; systematic use of 99, 100, 104, 105, 109, 110, 134, 178–180, 187; unfamiliar lexis 9, 11, 18, 46, 69, 73, 78–79, 88–89, 96, 119–122, 167, 174–176, 179–180, 185, 187; *see also* labelling; lexical relations; vocabulary
listening 8, 10, 19, 23, 26, 33, 38, 45, 48–50, 56, 73, 76–77, 86, 101, 125, 144, 148, 150, 164, 170, 180–181, 184, 185, 188
literacy 1, 3, 6–9, 17, 21–22, 91, 93–94, 113–116, 158, 185–188, 211, 227–233, 235–237; definition of 3, 227–228; *see also* reading; perception; writing; written text
looking 3, 6, 12, 25–27, 30–32, 38–42, 48, 55, 59, 96–97, 117, 124, 130, 162, 215; *see also* gaze; perception

loss and recovery 36, 39–40, 42–43, 76, 217–218, 223–224; *see also* cyclical return

material truth 146–147, 148, 150–152, 155, 156–157, 159–160, 163; *see also* environment
materials used *see* data
mirroring 129, 156, 160–163, 203–204, 213, 231, 241
moments of time out 176–181
mood 42, 49, 107, 121–122, 147, 152, 215
moral development 19, 132, 191, 202, 203–204, 206, 232, 235, 238
multisensorial approaches 25, 113–114, 121–122, 147

narrative 1, 19, 205; key characteristics of 115, 141–142, 143–147, 155, 158, 159–161, 163, 164, 180, 204, 216; structure of *see* story grammar; *see also* biography; stories
non-fiction 79, 143–144, 230, 232, 237
non-verbal communication 10, 11, 13–15, 19, 21, 33, 53–70, 79, 82–84, 87, 162–163, 193, 206, 232–233; *see also* gaze; pointing
norms 2, 16, 52–53, 54, 90, 104, 128, 132, 158
novel 3, 88, 141, 143, 145, 159, 163, 168, 236

onomatopoeia 47, 64, 100–103, 119, 122, 178
orthography 16, 93, 114, 228–229
ostensive definition 9, 33, 48, 74, 96, 131–132, 146, 148, 182

paradigm 94, 96, 98–103, 104–106, 109–112, 119, 126–127, 138, 143
patterns 2, 50, 52, 62, 71, 77, 90, 115, 116, 142, 148, 181, 189; of adult behaviour 43, 71, 85, 128, 134, 147, 179, 188, 232; of child behaviour 46, 53, 60, 65, 66, 82, 84, 208, 211, 212, 230, 234
perception (visual) 13, 33–37, 41, 45, 49, 55, 56, 58, 94, 102, 117, 120, 130, 133, 137, 145, 153, 162, 177, 209, 210, 213, 218, 221, 223, 225–227; as central to reading 4–6, 103–104, 113–114, 116, 215–217; language as structuring 31, 99–101, 104, 128–130, 135, 137–139, 191–192, 196, 202–203, 207, 238; *see also* perspective
perspective 117–118, 136; adopting another's perspective 15, 86, 122–125,

254

133–136, 145, 221, 241; as analytical tool 7, 9, 13–15, 19, 20–21, 48, 77, 91, 98, 115, 160, 189–190, 208, 222, 223, 230–232, 235–237; transformation of 125–130; unity of 133, 143, 154, 170, 182, 186, 188; variety of 133–136, 143–144, 145, 165–166, 183, 185, 186, 235

phonology 10, 18, 32, 42, 73, 93, 114, 115, 122, 129, 135, 136, 196

picturebooks 1, 3, 7–9, 18, 19, 91, 202, 235; and infant perception *see* perception; as lexical resource 7–9, 38–39, 43–46, 49, 58–59, 62, 66–68, 71–75, 78–79, 84, 88–89, 93, 96, 97–98, 100–103, 104, 109–110, 112, 113–117, 119–122, 131–132 (*see also* labelling; lexis); and scholastic achievement *see* education; and stories interrelated 13, 28, 42, 43, 45–47, 49, 75–77, 115, 129, 132, 145–146, 167, 168–169, 170, 174, 178–180, 187–188, 202, 204, 205, 216–217, 222–223, 236–237

pointing 6, 9, 10, 17, 19, 23, 26, 34, 37–38, 50, 53–70, 78, 82–85, 89, 100, 125, 134, 137, 154, 157, 178, 231; adult use of 6, 18, 30, 33, 34, 38, 73–74, 95, 113–114, 119, 122, 153, 170, 172; *see also* non-verbal communication

prototypes 96–97, 111–112

psyche 189–191, 193–195, 202–207, 209, 217–218, 223–224, 231

psychology (of book characters) 64, 65, 70, 71, 79, 80–83, 86, 89, 132, 138, 143–144, 145–146, 148, 152, 155, 159–161, 167, 205, 225, 230

psychosexual development 1, 191, 194, 205, 206, 210, 223–224; *see also* identification

questions 10, 19, 23, 26, 32–37, 55, 60, 65, 85, 118, 134; adult use of 8–9, 27, 39, 58–60, 61–64, 67, 68–69, 71–72, 100–101, 103–104, 110, 137, 153–154, 157, 170, 171, 182, 205, 240; child response to 23, 26, 32–37, 43, 50, 55, 58–64, 66, 69, 71–73, 74, 78–79, 82, 83, 85, 100–101, 118, 153, 158, 225, 229, 232

reading 1–2, 19, 21–22, 23, 26, 91, 188; difficulties with 114–115, 138–139, 171, 185; initial achievements of 27–30, 49–51, 168–169; long-term perspectives on 16, 53, 162–163, 189, 208, 216, 227–233; responses *see* response; specific contributions of 3–6, 32, 54, 55, 59, 73, 79, 88–89, 97–98, 103–104, 110, 122, 134–135, 137–139, 157–158, 162–163, 195, 224, 238; *see also* literacy; narrative; perception; written code

reference 45, 84, 96, 110, 114, 116

response: of adult 27–42, 50, 55, 57, 66, 86, 87, 100, 128–129, 135–136, 155, 157, 203, 212–216, 222, 231; of child 1, 6, 8, 19, 31, 38, 45, 46, 48, 52–53, 58, 143–148, 186–187, 204, 208, 211–218, 222–223, 225–227, 230–233; *see also* affect; questions

scripts 97–98, 114

Secondary World 144–145, 155, 159

self 2, 52–53, 54, 84, 141, 161, 189–191, 193, 203, 205–207, 224, 235; *see also* biography; individual difference; psyche

semantic convention: illustrations as 4, 117, 122, 168, 172–173

sense relations *see* lexical relations

separation 76–77, 193, 194, 204, 206, 209, 217–218, 223–224

sequences *see* topic extension

sex differences 46, 86–87, 194, 210, 221, 223, 232

socialisation: processes of 27–30

stories 3–4, 7–8, 17, 18, 86, 141–142, 149, 155, 160–164, 184–185, 216–217, 222–224, 234, 236–238; length of 149–150, 153, 164, 168, 169, 181–182, 183; and picturebooks interrelated *see* picturebooks; rudiments of 28, 45, 46, 47, 49, 168–169; *see also* data; fiction; narrative; story grammar; storyline

story grammar 143, 164–166, 169–171, 182–183

storyline 56, 145, 149–151, 152–155, 156–157, 159, 168, 178, 180–181,184, 196

superordinates 13, 96, 102–103, 104, 106, 107, 109–112, 119–120, 129, 131, 174–175

syntax *see* grammar

tables 37, 44, 63, 68, 71, 72, 80–81, 83, 101, 108, 109, 111, 123, 130, 169, 174, 198, 219–220

television 2, 5, 6, 32, 86, 89, 122, 139, 230

title 11, 28, 115, 165, 166, 170

topic 9, 43, 60, 85, 117, 232; continuity of 75–76, 129, 222–223; extension of 42, 47–48, 57–58, 64–65, 67, 69–71, 83, 226–227; *see also* discourse

255

SUBJECT INDEX

traits 95–98, 100–103, 104, 107–112, 119–122, 131
transitional objects 19, 21; and early reading 211–218; long-term perspectives on 225–233; in pre-speech period 218–225; theory of 208–210
turntaking 10, 19, 23, 32–38, 49, 50, 55, 60, 118

utterance typology 8–9, 10, 19, 31, 35–37, 38, 42, 47, 71, 73–74, 78, 79, 80, 82, 89, 99, 100, 114, 119, 154, 157, 176, 184, 196–202, 213–214, 224; *see also* grammar

viewpoint *see* perspective

vocabulary: of adult *see* lexis; of child 7–9, 11, 13, 18, 27, 38, 69, 73, 75, 76, 78–82, 84, 88–89, 96–98, 114–115, 131, 135, 152, 159, 196, 204, 206, 235–238

writing (productive) 6, 16, 227–229, 231, 236–237, 242
written text 3–6, 16, 49, 60, 93, 103–104, 114–115, 143–144, 145, 149–150, 153, 156–159, 164, 166–169, 171–176, 182–186, 196, 202, 211, 227–231, 235–237; cited extracts of 102, 149, 166–167, 173–177, 179, 183; in relation to illustrations 150–153, 155, 169–173, 185–186, 188